From Beakers to Billions

Turning Chemistry into Marketable Gold

Stephen Watathi

ISBN: 9798859643684

Table of Contents

1. The Chemistry Classroom Spark

*Introducing the journey from classroom learning to real-world application.
Highlighting the potential of chemistry knowledge in various industries.*

1.1. Introduction

Imagine sitting in a chemistry classroom, the air filled with the acrid scent of chemicals, surrounded by equations, formulas, and the mysterious dance of molecules. It's a scene that's familiar to many, where we grapple with the intricacies of chemical reactions—those moments of revelation when the pieces of the molecular puzzle click into place. As we wrestle with the enigma of balancing equations and strive to wrap our minds around the seemingly complex patterns of the periodic table, we are, in essence, unlocking the secrets of matter itself.

But in the midst of this intellectual struggle, there exists a profound realization—one that often escapes us as we strive to decipher the language of atoms. Little do we know that this very classroom, with its rows of beakers and Bunsen burners, is the birthplace of a transformative journey—a journey that has the potential to turn these seemingly abstract concepts into something far more tangible and valuable than we could ever have imagined.

This journey, a narrative that bridges the gap between the laboratory bench and the world of commerce, unfolds before us as we embark on the first chapter of *From Beakers to Billions: Turning Chemistry into Marketable Gold*. In this chapter, aptly titled "The Chemistry Classroom Spark," we will venture beyond the boundaries of traditional education and delve into the uncharted territory where chemical knowledge and entrepreneurial spirit intersect. Our exploration will reveal how the seemingly arcane and bewildering knowledge gained in the classroom can blossom into innovation, create industries, and shape economies.

Welcome to a chapter that will illuminate the path from educational enlightenment to practical enterprise—a path that, when followed with determination and vision, can turn the sparks of classroom experimentation into the blazing success of marketable products. With insights drawn from scientific research and real-world success stories, this chapter will guide you through the maze of possibilities that lie beyond the classroom doors.

As we traverse this captivating landscape, you'll encounter the tales of audacious pioneers who, armed with chemical knowledge and unwavering conviction, transformed their ideas into products that now grace our daily lives. Their narratives are interwoven with the expert voices of those who have navigated the complex terrain of industry, offering advice and insights that can pave the way for your own ventures.

So, fasten your seatbelt and prepare to embark on a journey that will reshape your perception of the chemistry classroom. The beakers and burners that populate this realm are not just vessels for experimentation; they are the crucibles of innovation, the catalysts of discovery, and the birthplace of marketable gold. Let us dive into the tales, strategies, and intricacies that connect classroom learning to real-world application, and let the journey begin.

1.2.   From The Lab to the World: A Journey of Discovery

Our journey starts in the chemistry classroom, a sanctuary of knowledge where the foundations of understanding the molecular world are meticulously laid. Here, as we don our metaphorical lab coats and peer through the lenses of curiosity, we enter a realm where atoms and molecules come alive in a symphony of reactivity. The equations on the chalkboard and the intricate models in our textbooks are the building blocks of something far grander—a bridge that spans from the lab to the world beyond.

In a pivotal study by Hardy et al. (2021), we gain a deeper appreciation for the classroom's role in shaping the chemists of tomorrow. The potential of chemistry in teaching activities is illuminated, with insights that extend far beyond the confines of academia. What may initially seem like a daunting labyrinth of chemical concepts soon reveals itself to be a playground of endless possibilities.

As we navigate the complexities of chemical reactions and immerse ourselves in the patterns of the periodic table, we're not merely absorbing theoretical knowledge; we're embarking on an extraordinary journey—a journey that possesses the power to catalyze innovation and reshape entire industries.

The classroom becomes a crucible where the sparks of curiosity are nurtured, where the flames of discovery are kindled. The theoretical concepts that we grapple with are not stagnant facts but dynamic blueprints, waiting to be harnessed for real-world applications. Through our experiments, we learn to wield the power of molecular transformations, uncovering the alchemy that turns raw materials into the products that define our modern lives.

But it's not just about the experiments themselves; it's about cultivating a mindset of inquiry, of challenging conventions, and of seeing beyond the immediate. This is a journey of transformation—a metamorphosis from students of chemistry to architects of innovation. We learn to ask the right questions, to identify the gaps in existing knowledge, and to envision the unexplored possibilities that lie on the horizon.

As we thread the path from the classroom to the realm of practical application, we weave a tapestry of innovation and impact. The molecular insights gained within the four walls of the laboratory become the blueprints for revolutionary products, sustainable practices, and groundbreaking technologies. The chemistry classroom, often regarded as a microcosm of the scientific world, is in fact a launchpad for creativity that knows no bounds.

In the subsequent chapters of this book, we will traverse the landscapes of various industries, where chemistry's potential is harnessed to craft solutions that resonate with society's needs. From green chemistry's commitment to sustainability (Silvestri et al., 2021) to the frontiers of flow chemistry and entrepreneurship (Hartman, 2020), we will explore how the classroom's sparks can ignite the flames of success.

So, as we move forward in our exploration, let us remember that the chemistry classroom is not merely a starting point—it's a catalyst for change, a crucible of inspiration, and a forge where ideas are shaped into realities.

1.3. Chemistry Unleashed: A Glimpse into Multidisciplinary Magic

Chemistry doesn't exist in isolation—it's a dynamic force that intertwines with various disciplines, crafting a multidisciplinary symphony that resonates across industries. As we step beyond the classroom and venture into the vast expanse of practical application, we encounter a realm where chemistry's impact reverberates far beyond its traditional boundaries. Silvestri et al. (2021) serve as our guides, shedding light on a profound truth: chemistry's contributions extend to equitable global sustainability and the creation of a circular economy.

In this dance of atoms and molecules, chemistry wields its power to transform the very fabric of our society. It's not just about deciphering reactions; it's about orchestrating a harmonious balance between human progress and environmental preservation. The classroom's lessons in molecular interactions lay the groundwork for cleaner production processes—methods that minimize waste and reduce the ecological footprint of industries. This is the essence of green chemistry—an approach that champions both scientific advancement and ecological responsibility.

The chemistry classroom, where we once marveled at chemical equations, now becomes the nexus of innovation that drives sustainable practices. Innovative materials emerge from the crucible of discovery, materials that are as gentle on the planet as they are revolutionary in their applications. These materials, born from the fusion of chemistry and engineering, redefine product design, inspire technological breakthroughs, and lay the groundwork for industries built on a circular economy.

The notion of a circular economy, as Silvestri et al. (2021) elucidate, is not just a theoretical concept—it's a paradigm shift that reshapes the way we produce, consume, and discard. It's a departure from the linear model of extraction, production, and disposal. Instead, it's a holistic approach where products are designed for durability, repairability, and recyclability. Chemistry's role is pivotal in this transformation, as it guides us towards materials that can be repurposed and regenerated without compromising quality.

Yet, the magic doesn't stop at sustainability. The convergence of chemistry with engineering, economics, and other disciplines ignites a cascade of innovation that reverberates across industries. It's the chemistry of collaboration that catalyzes the birth of new technologies, from advanced materials to renewable energy sources. Chemistry becomes the common language that bridges disparate fields, fostering a collective drive towards progress and sustainable growth.

As we journey deeper into this multidisciplinary tapestry, we'll witness firsthand how chemistry, when interwoven with other disciplines, becomes a powerhouse of innovation. The chemistry classroom's teachings now extend to the realization of visionary ideas that transcend boundaries and propel society forward. We'll explore real-life examples of how chemistry's collaboration with engineering, economics, and more has yielded remarkable solutions to complex challenges.

So, buckle up for an expedition into the heart of multidisciplinary magic, where the chemistry classroom's sparks are fanned into the flames of groundbreaking transformation.

1.4. Flowing Beyond Boundaries: From Lab Coats to Entrepreneurial Dreams

In the world of chemistry, the concept of flow extends beyond the reactions that occur in beakers and flasks. It's a modern paradigm, as Hartman (2020) eloquently explains, that transcends the boundaries of traditional chemical processes. Flow chemistry isn't solely about the mechanics of reactions; it's a symphony of ideas, innovation, and entrepreneurship that transforms the chemistry classroom's sparks into entrepreneurial flames.

As we step out of the classroom and onto the stage of real-world application, we are greeted by a cast of remarkable individuals—the entrepreneurs who dared to see beyond the confines of laboratory walls. These visionaries, armed with a deep understanding of chemical principles, embarked on a journey that led them to transform their theoretical knowledge into tangible, marketable products. Their stories, filled with audacity and determination, narrate the journey from calculated risks to triumphant rewards—a journey that is the embodiment of chemistry's untapped potential.

Flow chemistry, with its emphasis on continuous processes and streamlined reactions, serves as a metaphor for the entrepreneurial journey. Just as chemicals flow through interconnected reactors, so do ideas traverse the neural pathways of creative minds. The chemistry classroom's teachings become the catalysts that initiate a cascade of innovative thoughts, birthing concepts that have the power to revolutionize industries.

In the realm of entrepreneurship, chemistry isn't confined to the laboratory bench; it's a driving force that propels startups, shapes business strategies, and fuels technological breakthroughs. Entrepreneurs leverage their chemical insights to solve real-world problems, crafting solutions that resonate with the needs of society. It's the marriage of scientific knowledge and business acumen that transforms laboratory experiments into marketable innovations.

The stories of these entrepreneurs are woven with threads of risk and reward, challenges and triumphs. They are tales of persistence in the face of adversity, of believing in one's vision even when the odds seem insurmountable. The chemistry classroom's sparks are not extinguished after the experiment ends; they fuel the fires of ambition, guiding entrepreneurs through uncharted territories.

The journey from lab coats to entrepreneurial dreams is not just about building successful businesses—it's about embodying the essence of chemistry's potential. It's about viewing the world through the lens of possibility, recognizing that every challenge is an opportunity waiting to be seized. These entrepreneurs, who defied convention and transformed their chemistry knowledge into impactful products, inspire us to embrace innovation, embrace risk, and embrace the entrepreneurial spirit that resides within us all.

As we journey through their stories and learn from their experiences, we gain insights into the strategies, decisions, and innovations that propelled their ventures forward. Their lessons serve as beacons of inspiration, guiding us as we embark on our own paths to turn chemistry concepts into marketable gold.

1.5.   Navigating the Maze: Wisdom from Industry Pioneers

In the grand tapestry of innovation, turning the threads of classroom chemistry into marketable gold requires a deft hand—one that balances scientific acumen with a keen understanding of industry dynamics. As Moeen and Agarwal (2017) aptly point out, the journey from the laboratory to the marketplace is a multifaceted endeavor that extends beyond the realm of chemical equations. It's a journey that demands the ability to navigate a complex maze—one that encompasses market trends, regulations, and the nuances of value capture.

The classroom's role in this intricate journey is undeniable. It equips us with the foundational knowledge needed to comprehend the molecular intricacies that underscore product development. However, as we transition from academic settings to the corridors of industry, we encounter a landscape that is simultaneously exhilarating and daunting. It's here that the lessons from pioneers who have successfully traversed this terrain become invaluable.

The pioneers, often fueled by a passion for innovation and a deep-rooted understanding of chemistry, have ventured where few dare to tread. They understand that the journey doesn't end with understanding chemical reactions—it begins there. Armed with this knowledge, they chart their course through a maze of market demands, industry trends, and regulatory frameworks. They recognize that a successful product is not solely defined by its scientific ingenuity, but also by its alignment with the needs and desires of consumers.

Navigating this maze involves more than technical expertise; it requires the ability to build networks and forge partnerships that amplify impact. The chemistry classroom, once a place of solitary learning, now becomes a training ground for collaboration and communication. Pioneers teach us that the relationships we foster within and beyond our discipline are instrumental in transforming concepts into products. It's through these networks that ideas are refined, tested, and refined again—ultimately emerging as innovative solutions that find their place in the market.

Regulations, often perceived as barriers, are woven into the fabric of this maze. Pioneers remind us that regulations are not roadblocks; they are guideposts that ensure safety, efficacy, and ethical conduct. Navigating these regulatory landscapes requires an understanding of compliance, an appreciation for standards, and an unwavering commitment to delivering products that meet societal expectations.

In essence, turning classroom chemistry into marketable gold requires us to embrace the multifaceted nature of the journey. It's about merging the art of science with the science of commerce. It's about honing our ability to innovate not only within the confines of the laboratory but also within the broader context of industry needs.

As we delve further into this chapter, we'll explore case studies that illuminate the strategies, decisions, and insights that guided industry pioneers along their path. These narratives will inspire us to develop a holistic perspective—one that appreciates the intersection of chemistry with business, innovation, and societal impact. With the wisdom of pioneers as our guide, we're poised to tackle the maze and transform chemistry concepts into tangible products that resonate with the world.

1.6.   A World Beyond Textbooks: Chemistry in Industry

As we journey from the confines of the classroom to the expansive landscapes of industry, we're confronted with a realization that transcends the boundaries of disciplines. In a study by Martin et al. (2005), the spotlight turns to engineering graduates, and their perceptions provide us with a valuable lesson—one that echoes across all scientific fields. This lesson underscores the fact that the transition from academia to industry is not merely a passage from theory to practice; it's a bridge that must be solidly built to enable successful navigation of the professional world.

The chemistry classroom, once a realm where equations danced across chalkboards and formulas filled pages, takes on a new dimension when viewed through the lens of industry readiness. It's not solely about mastering reactions and memorizing molecular structures; it's about cultivating a mindset that flourishes in the realm of real-world challenges. The study's findings emphasize the importance of developing this mindset—one that thrives in the face of problem-solving, innovation, and adaptation.

Graduates stepping into the world of industry encounter scenarios that aren't scripted in textbooks. They encounter challenges that require creative problem-solving and the ability to adapt theories to the dynamic landscape of practical application. The chemistry classroom, with its controlled experiments and structured curricula, provides the foundation for this adaptation. It equips us not only with knowledge but with the cognitive tools to traverse uncharted territories.

The significance of bridging the academia-industry gap is paramount. The insights gained within the classroom's walls must be translated into the language of innovation, commercial viability, and societal impact. This is where the chemistry classroom's transformative power shines brightest. It's not merely about the solutions we discover—it's about the approach we cultivate. It's about fostering a way of thinking that transcends the formulas and equations, enabling us to craft innovative solutions that address real-world challenges.

The lessons learned from engineering graduates' experiences resonate far beyond their field. They speak to the heart of what education should provide—a holistic readiness for the world beyond textbooks. They remind us that the chemistry classroom isn't just a place for learning reactions; it's a haven for nurturing the skills that will allow us to be effective contributors to industries, communities, and economies.

As we journey deeper into this chapter, we'll uncover case studies that illuminate the practical application of chemistry principles in various industries. We'll gain insights into how graduates, armed with a mindset of innovation, have navigated the intricacies of their professional journeys. By infusing their stories with our own aspirations, we stand poised to bridge the gap and transform our chemistry education into a catalyst for industry success.

1.7.   Green Chemistry: Paving the Way to a Sustainable Future

Amidst the fervor of chemical exploration, a paradigm shift emerges—one that transcends the confines of laboratories and marketplaces. Jiménez-González et al. (2012) usher us into the world of green metrics, where the chemistry of innovation intertwines with the imperative of sustainability. It's a reminder that the impact of chemistry extends beyond mere products; it's about responsible innovation that ensures our strides in science are aligned with the well-being of our planet.

In the chemistry classroom, the seeds of green chemistry are sown. It's not just about mastering reactions; it's about fostering a mindset that places environmental responsibility at the forefront of innovation. The classroom becomes a crucible where the sparks of curiosity are ignited, but more importantly, where the flames of sustainability are kindled. Green chemistry, as introduced by Jiménez-González et al. (2012), becomes more than an approach—it's a movement, an ethos, and a call to action.

This approach challenges us to reexamine every facet of chemical production, from raw materials to disposal. It's about reimagining the very nature of products, processes, and materials. The chemistry classroom, as a hub of inquiry and exploration, propels us to think beyond traditional solutions and consider the broader consequences of our innovations. It encourages us to seek pathways that minimize waste, reduce environmental impact, and foster a harmonious coexistence between industry and ecology.

Green metrics, as a framework, prompts us to evaluate the "greenness" of chemical processes and products. It's not just about the end result; it's about the journey taken to achieve that result. This journey involves selecting greener alternatives, minimizing hazardous materials, and maximizing efficiency. The classroom, with its emphasis on critical thinking and problem-solving, becomes the incubator for creative solutions that align with these principles.

As we journey forward in this chapter, we'll witness the tangible results of green chemistry—products that are not only marketable but also environmentally sustainable. We'll delve into case studies that showcase the transformation of chemical concepts into innovations that have a positive impact on both industry and the planet. These stories serve as a testament to the power of green chemistry— an approach that proves that profitability and sustainability need not be mutually exclusive.

Ultimately, the chemistry classroom's role transcends theoretical education; it nurtures a mindset that shapes the future of industries. The sparks ignited within its walls burn brightly in the pursuit of solutions that address global challenges. Green chemistry exemplifies this pursuit, guiding us to create products that resonate with consumers, benefit society, and safeguard the planet—a legacy that extends far beyond any individual classroom.

1.8. Innovating with Intelligence: Chemistry and Artificial Neural Networks

In the ever-evolving landscape of scientific exploration, Pirdashti et al. (2013) beckon us into a realm where chemistry converges with the cutting-edge prowess of artificial neural networks. This fusion of computational might and chemical insight is heralding a new era—one where products are not only created but also refined, tested, and improved with unprecedented efficiency. The doors that swing open in this synthesis of disciplines reshape our understanding of innovation itself.

As we step into the chemistry classroom, we're greeted by a transformation—algorithms and equations sharing the same space, harmonizing in a symphony of data-driven discovery. The classroom, once a sanctuary for theory, is now a breeding ground for computational experimentation. The integration of artificial neural networks redefines the very nature of experimentation. It's no longer confined to the boundaries of physical laboratories; it extends into the virtual realm, where data flows like chemicals through a reaction vessel.

Artificial neural networks, inspired by the architecture of the human brain, mimic the interconnectedness of neurons to process vast amounts of data. This technological marvel, when married to the insights gleaned from chemical experimentation, generates a powerful synergy. It's not just about replacing traditional methods; it's about enhancing our understanding, accelerating our pace, and revolutionizing the way we approach innovation.

The chemistry classroom's transformation into a hub of data-driven discovery is a testament to the adaptability of science. It's about embracing technology as an ally rather than a competitor. The algorithms we encounter in this transformed classroom serve as guides that illuminate new pathways, unravel hidden correlations, and predict outcomes that would have remained elusive through traditional methods.

The applications of artificial neural networks in chemistry are as diverse as they are impactful. From predictive modeling of molecular properties to optimizing reaction conditions, these networks amplify our ability to design and refine products with precision. The classroom's role evolves from a space of passive learning to one of active experimentation, where algorithms become partners in discovery.

As we delve deeper into the chapters ahead, we'll witness firsthand how this convergence of chemistry and artificial intelligence translates into tangible products and solutions. We'll explore case studies that showcase the practical applications of this synergy—products that are not only innovative but also informed by data-driven insights. These stories will inspire us to embrace technology's potential as an enhancer of human creativity, enabling us to navigate the intricacies of the modern world with unprecedented intelligence.

1.9. From Conception to Reality: Biobased Chemicals

In the world of innovation, the journey from idea to industrial reality is a passage fraught with challenges and triumphs. Dapsens et al. (2012) invite us to explore this odyssey—a narrative that bridges the chasm between imagination and practical application. Within this narrative, the chemistry classroom emerges not as a mere repository of theories, but as a crucible where new possibilities are conceived and catalyzed.

The chemistry classroom, with its periodic table and molecular equations, ignites a spark—a spark that is not confined to the pages of textbooks. It's a spark that kindles the imagination and propels us to envision new frontiers. Biobased chemicals, a hallmark of this innovation journey, exemplify chemistry's transformative power. Derived from renewable resources, these chemicals stand as tangible evidence of chemistry's role in reshaping the materials that permeate our daily lives.

The journey from biobased chemical conception to industrial reality mirrors the essence of innovation—a dance between collaboration, experimentation, and the courage to innovate. It's a journey that spans disciplines, transcending the traditional boundaries of chemistry and converging with biology, engineering, and beyond. The classroom's role expands to encompass not only scientific insights but also the ability to collaborate effectively, communicate ideas, and drive collective progress.

Biobased chemicals, often born from the marriage of chemistry and biology, exemplify the symbiosis between scientific knowledge and environmental stewardship. The chemistry classroom becomes a place of inspiration—a hub where sustainable solutions are envisioned, tested, and nurtured. As we explore this journey, we'll witness the evolution of ideas as they transform from concepts to tangible products that bear a positive imprint on both industry and ecology.

The narrative we embark upon is one that celebrates innovation's tenacity. It's a story of pushing boundaries, challenging conventions, and refusing to succumb to obstacles. It's a testament to the pioneers who dared to translate their insights into tangible solutions, navigating uncharted territories and defying the odds. Their experiences remind us that innovation thrives on audacity—a willingness to traverse the unknown in pursuit of a better future.

As we delve deeper into the chapters that follow, we'll encounter stories of biobased chemical innovations that have carved their mark on industries and economies. These stories will serve as guides, offering insights into the strategies, partnerships, and methodologies that pave the way from conception to reality. The chemistry classroom, once a realm of equations, now becomes a launchpad for ideas that transcend theory and impact the world.

1.10. Fueling the Future: The Ammonia Revolution

As we gaze towards the horizon of energy innovation, Valera-Medina et al. (2021) extend an invitation—a journey into the potential of ammonia as a fuel. In this landscape of possibilities, chemistry's role isn't confined to products; it's about reshaping the very foundation of our energy landscape. The chemistry classroom, once a realm where equations danced on chalkboards, now emerges as a launchpad for sustainable energy solutions that hold the power to fuel the world of tomorrow.

The prospect of ammonia as a fuel isn't just an incremental development; it's a paradigm shift that redefines the way we think about energy sources. The chemistry classroom, as the incubator of scientific insight, now evolves into a hub of innovation that bridges the gap between theory and application. Ammonia, long known for its role in agriculture and industry, now takes center stage as a potential green energy carrier that can drive a transition towards a more sustainable future.

The significance of this transition is profound. Ammonia, when harnessed as a fuel, has the potential to address critical energy challenges—ranging from the reduction of greenhouse gas emissions to the diversification of energy sources. The classroom's teachings, grounded in the principles of chemical reactions, equip us with the foundation to understand the intricacies of ammonia's behavior as a fuel and its potential to power a wide range of applications.

This journey isn't without its challenges, but it's the kind of challenge that pioneers and innovators are drawn to. The transformation of ammonia into a viable fuel involves multidisciplinary collaboration, cutting-edge technology, and a deep understanding of chemical and engineering principles. It's a journey that demands us to leverage our classroom knowledge not just for academic pursuits but for the advancement of sustainable solutions that transcend generations.

As we dive into this chapter, we'll delve into the intricate details of the ammonia revolution. We'll explore case studies that highlight the progress made in harnessing ammonia's energy potential, from synthesis to applications. These stories will serve as a testament to the power of chemistry—chemistry that isn't confined to laboratory benches but resonates through power plants, vehicles, and industries that shape the modern world.

The chemistry classroom's role evolves yet again, this time as a springboard for innovation that powers a greener tomorrow. As we absorb the knowledge presented within these pages, we're inspired not just to understand ammonia's potential as a fuel but to become catalysts ourselves—agents of change who can drive the ammonia revolution forward, igniting a brighter and more sustainable energy future.

1.11. Smart Polymers and Coatings: Where Chemistry Meets Practicality

In the intricate web of material science, Hosseini and Makhlouf (2016) beckon us to explore the frontiers of intelligence—the realm of smart polymers and coatings. Here, the chemistry classroom's role transcends the traditional imagery of bubbling beakers and molecular equations; it transforms into a gateway to understanding materials that possess the remarkable ability to adapt and respond intelligently to their environment. These polymers and coatings, with their multifaceted properties, bear witness to chemistry's transformative power in enhancing everyday products and experiences.

The evolution of polymers from static materials to dynamic entities with responsiveness is a journey that showcases the multidisciplinary essence of chemistry. The classroom, with its emphasis on fundamental principles and reactions, sets the stage for the exploration of these intelligent materials. Smart polymers and coatings are a symphony of chemical engineering, material science, and design—a harmonious blend that empowers materials to sense, react, and adapt in ways that were once confined to the realm of science fiction.

What sets smart polymers and coatings apart is their ability to interact with their surroundings in a controlled and meaningful manner. The classroom, which once introduced us to chemical equilibrium and reaction kinetics, now reveals the inner workings of these adaptive materials. It's no longer just about understanding how reactions proceed; it's about crafting materials that, like living organisms, can sense changes and respond accordingly.

Imagine materials that can change their shape, color, or properties in response to external stimuli—such as temperature, pH, or light. This metamorphosis is not a flight of fancy; it's a reality that chemistry, in conjunction with material science and engineering, has brought to life. The chemistry classroom, now reimagined as a hub of innovation, nurtures the mindset necessary to conceive and engineer such marvels.

As we dive deeper into this chapter, we'll explore the intricate world of smart polymers and coatings through real-world examples and case studies. We'll witness how these materials have transformed industries ranging from healthcare to aerospace, enhancing products and processes along the way. These stories are a testament to chemistry's evolution—an evolution that transforms it from a study of reactions into an art of practicality, innovation, and transformative impact.

The chemistry classroom, with its vibrant history and evolving role, echoes in the creation of these intelligent materials. It embodies the transition from theoretical understanding to the application of science in shaping tangible solutions. The journey into smart polymers and coatings is a journey into the heart of chemistry's ability to not only explain the world but to change it—one responsive material at a time.

1.12. Reflection and Action: Your Journey Starts Here

As the final strokes of this chapter unfurl, it's a moment to pause—a juncture where personal contemplation merges with the grand narrative we've traversed. I extend an invitation—to you, the reader—to embark on a voyage of introspection, guided by the insights we've gleaned from entrepreneurs, pioneers, and the crossroads of chemistry and innovation. This journey, a culmination of narratives and discoveries, has illuminated the path from the chemistry classroom to the realm of marketable gold. Yet, beyond the absorption of knowledge, lies the call to action— to apply, to innovate, and to transform the mundane into the extraordinary.

The chemistry classroom is more than a place of equations and experiments; it's a sanctuary where sparks of inspiration are ignited. Reflect on that spark that first caught your attention—the moment when chemistry's potential flickered to life within you. This spark, whether born from the mesmerizing dance of molecules or the allure of innovation, serves as the North Star guiding your journey.

The tales of entrepreneurs who transformed ideas into marketable products remind us that the journey is not reserved for the extraordinary few. It's a path accessible to all who dare to embrace their potential. Reflect on your own aspirations, and envision the possibilities that await when your chemistry knowledge converges with your passions and ambitions.

The stories of industry pioneers resonate as compasses that guide us through the labyrinthine world of commerce and innovation. Consider the lessons they've imparted—the navigation of market demands, the cultivation of networks, and the embrace of change. These pioneers remind us that the journey is a process of continuous learning, adaptation, and growth.

As we stand at this juncture, we're not passive observers of a narrative; we're active participants in the unfolding story. The call to action echoes through the pages— an invitation to transform the theoretical into the practical, to innovate with purpose, and to craft solutions that resonate with the world. Think beyond the classroom's confines, and envision how your chemistry knowledge can intersect with diverse industries, revolutionizing products, processes, and paradigms.

The journey from the chemistry classroom to the world of marketable gold is a symphony of reflection and action. It's about channeling your knowledge into tangible initiatives that drive change. With each step forward, you contribute to the legacy of chemistry's transformative power. With every innovation, you paint strokes on the canvas of progress.

The journey, as illuminated by the chapters preceding, awaits your unique imprint. The chemistry classroom's role extends beyond the physical space; it's an enduring force that accompanies you in your quest to turn knowledge into impact. As you close this chapter and embark on your own journey, remember that the sparks of innovation are within your reach—the journey starts here.

Are you ready to take your first step? The chemistry classroom is just the beginning; the world of chemistry-driven products awaits your creativity and determination.

1.13. References

[1]   Dapsens, P. Y., Mondelli, C., & Pérez-Ramírez, J. (2012). Biobased chemicals from conception toward industrial reality: lessons learned and to be learned. *Acs Catalysis*, *2*(7), 1487-1499. https://doi.org/10.1021/cs300124m

[2]   Hardy, J. G., Sdepanian, S., Stowell, A. F., Aljohani, A. D., Allen, M. J., Anwar, A., ... & Wright, K. L. (2021). Potential for chemistry in multidisciplinary, interdisciplinary, and transdisciplinary teaching activities in higher education. *Journal of Chemical Education*, *98*(4), 1124-1145. https://doi.org/10.1021/acs.jchemed.0c01363

[3]   Hartman, R. L. (2020). Flow chemistry remains an opportunity for chemists and chemical engineers. *Current Opinion in Chemical Engineering*, *29*, 42-50. https://doi.org/10.1016/j.coche.2020.05.002

[4]   Hosseini, M., & Makhlouf, A. S. H. (Eds.). (2016). *Industrial applications for intelligent polymers and coatings* (Vol. 1, pp. 1-710). Berlin/Heidelberg, Germany: Springer. https://doi.org/10.1007/978-3-319-26893-4

[5]   Jiménez-González, C., Constable, D. J., & Ponder, C. S. (2012). Evaluating the "Greenness" of chemical processes and products in the pharmaceutical industry—a green metrics primer. *Chemical Society Reviews*, *41*(4), 1485-1498. https://doi.org/10.1039/C1CS15215G

[6]   Martin, R., Maytham, B., Case, J., & Fraser, D. (2005). Engineering graduates' perceptions of how well they were prepared for work in industry. *European journal of engineering education*, *30*(2), 167-180. https://doi.org/10.1080/03043790500087571

[7]   Moeen, M., & Agarwal, R. (2017). Incubation of an industry: Heterogeneous knowledge bases and modes of value capture. *Strategic Management Journal*, *38*(3), 566-587. https://doi.org/10.1002/smj.2511

[8]   Pirdashti, M., Curteanu, S., Kamangar, M. H., Hassim, M. H., & Khatami, M. A. (2013). Artificial neural networks: applications in chemical engineering. *Reviews in Chemical Engineering*, *29*(4), 205-239. https://doi.org/10.1515/revce-2013-0013

[9]   Silvestri, C., Silvestri, L., Forcina, A., Di Bona, G., & Falcone, D. (2021). Green chemistry contribution towards more equitable global sustainability and greater circular economy: A systematic literature review. *Journal of Cleaner Production*, *294*, 126137. https://doi.org/10.1016/j.jclepro.2021.126137

[10]   Valera-Medina, A., Amer-Hatem, F., Azad, A. K., Dedoussi, I. C., De Joannon, M., Fernandes, R. X., ... & Costa, M. (2021). Review on ammonia as a potential fuel: from synthesis to economics. *Energy & Fuels*, *35*(9), 6964-7029. https://doi.org/10.1021/acs.energyfuels.0c03685

2.   Unearthing Marketable Ideas

2.1.   Introduction

The world of chemistry isn't confined to the laboratory beakers and chemical equations we once memorized in school (Zahra, 2008; McNally et al., 2009). Rather, it's a dynamic landscape brimming with potential for turning innovative chemical concepts into real-world marketable gold. Just as Zahra (2008) elucidates, this transformation is akin to a virtuous cycle—a continuous interplay between discovery and creation of entrepreneurial opportunities. The chemistry of innovation thrives not only in academic settings but also in the heart of industries hungry for novel solutions (Kampers et al., 2022).

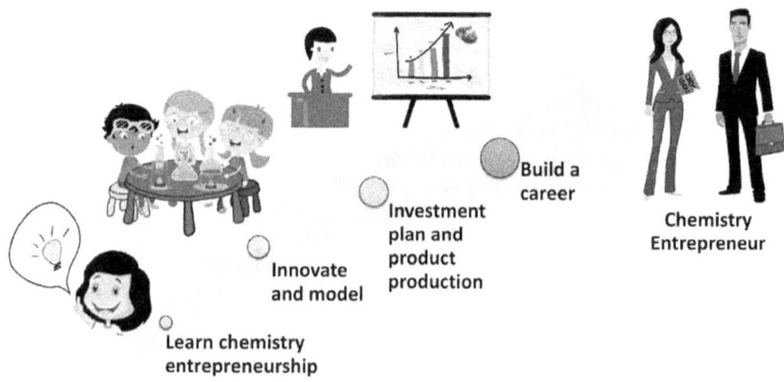

In this chapter, we'll embark on a journey through industries where chemistry innovation thrives. We'll venture into sectors such as nanotechnology and sustainable food processing, where the boundaries between laboratory experimentation and commercial viability blur (Ravichandran, 2010). Together, we'll explore the exhilarating process of identifying market gaps and opportunities—a critical step in the transformation of chemistry into marketable products. McNally et al. (2009) emphasize the pivotal role of managers' dispositional traits in shaping the direction of innovation, underscoring the human factor in this dynamic process.

As we navigate this transformative voyage, we won't simply present a dry collection of facts. Instead, we'll weave together captivating narratives that bridge the gap between chemistry theory and tangible impact (Sakellariou & Vecchiato, 2022). We'll unravel simplified chemical equations, demystifying complex reactions and showcasing how seemingly abstract concepts align with real-world applications (Ravichandran, 2010). But this journey is not one taken alone; we'll be joined by the voices of trailblazing entrepreneurs who've ventured beyond the confines of laboratories and classrooms to shape industries with their innovative ideas (Mahdad et al., 2022).

Moreover, insights from industry experts serve as beacons, guiding us through the labyrinthine pathways of turning chemistry into marketable gold (Zahra, 2008). Their practical wisdom—born from years of experience—provides invaluable signposts for aspiring chemistry-driven entrepreneurs. Our exploration won't be complete without addressing the challenges that arise in the quest for marketable ideas. We'll delve into the "Valley of Death," where innovation often falters and examine strategies for overcoming this formidable obstacle (Kampers et al., 2022).

So, fasten your seatbelt as we journey through the chemistry-driven realms of nanotechnology, sustainable practices, and collaborative business models (Ravichandran, 2010; Mahdad et al., 2022). Prepare to be captivated by stories of audacious innovators who dared to bridge the gap between laboratory concoctions and marketable realities (Sakellariou & Vecchiato, 2022). Equipped with the insights of industry experts, we'll traverse the landscape where chemistry evolves from concepts to creations, unearthing ideas that have the power to change industries and, ultimately, the world.

2.2. Navigating the Chemistry of Entrepreneurial Opportunities

2.2.1. Understanding the Virtuous Cycle of Discovery

Zahra (2008) introduces us to the virtuous cycle of discovery and creation of entrepreneurial opportunities, a concept deeply rooted in the dynamics of innovative chemistry. This cycle serves as a roadmap for turning abstract chemical ideas into tangible marketable products. As Zahra outlines, the cycle commences by identifying untapped market niches and unmet needs—areas where innovative chemistry can create transformative solutions. This identification phase is not a passive endeavor but an active exploration of gaps where chemistry can be harnessed to bring about substantial change (Zahra, 2008).

This initial spark, driven by the recognition of a market gap, sets off a chain reaction that propels chemistry concepts towards commercial viability. As Zahra (2008) aptly puts it, this is where the virtuous cycle takes flight, as the quest for solutions triggers a series of creative processes. Chemistry innovation becomes a dynamic interplay of ideation, experimentation, and strategic thinking. Ideas born from the laboratory's crucible evolve into prototypes, and those prototypes morph into marketable products. This iterative journey mirrors the very essence of chemistry itself—a process of continuous transformation and refinement (Zahra, 2008; Sakellariou & Vecchiato, 2022).

Furthermore, this virtuous cycle echoes the sentiments shared by other scholars in the field. Kampers et al. (2022) observe a similar rhythm of discovery in their analysis of perceptions from industry and academia. These perceptions underscore the importance of aligning research with market needs—a crucial step in breathing life into chemistry-driven innovations. The alignment of these perspectives reinforces the idea that successful chemistry entrepreneurship hinges on a nuanced understanding of market dynamics and the ability to identify and capitalize on opportunities (Kampers et al., 2022; Zahra, 2008).

As we delve deeper into the chapters that follow, keep in mind this virtuous cycle. This cycle isn't just theoretical jargon; it's a guiding principle that will illuminate the pathways of chemistry innovation. The journey from identifying market niches to creating marketable products is infused with creativity, strategic vision, and a touch of entrepreneurial spirit—a recipe for transforming chemistry concepts into true marketable gold.

2.2.2.	The Role of Dispositional Traits in Innovation

Intriguingly, McNally et al. (2009) delve into the dispositional traits of managers and how these traits impact their decisions in driving new product portfolio management. These traits encompass a range of characteristics, such as risk-taking propensity and proactiveness. The insights from this study resonate deeply with the world of chemistry innovation, as they shed light on the human dimensions that shape the trajectory of turning ideas into marketable realities.

McNally et al. (2009) emphasize that these dispositional traits are not merely idiosyncratic qualities but influential factors that guide strategic choices. When translated to the realm of chemistry entrepreneurship, these traits become vital tools for navigating the complex landscape between innovative concepts and marketable outcomes. A budding chemistry entrepreneur who possesses a higher risk-taking propensity might be more inclined to invest in experimental ideas with transformative potential, even if they carry an element of uncertainty. On the other hand, a proactively-oriented individual might be more adept at recognizing emerging market trends and adapting their chemistry concepts to align with evolving demands (McNally et al., 2009).

Understanding and harnessing these dispositional traits can become a pivotal aspect of an entrepreneur's toolkit. By recognizing one's own inclinations and aligning them with the demands of the market, chemistry entrepreneurs can tailor their approach to innovation. This alignment enhances the likelihood of transforming chemistry concepts into tangible products that not only fulfill market needs but also resonate with the individual strengths and inclinations of the entrepreneur.

This integration of personal traits with strategic decision-making bridges the gap between the theoretical and practical aspects of chemistry entrepreneurship. As you embark on your journey to transform chemistry into marketable gold, consider the wisdom offered by McNally et al. (2009). Embrace your innate strengths, cultivate your risk-taking propensity, and exhibit proactiveness in identifying opportunities—elements that, when combined, could set you on a path of innovation that resonates with both your personal journey and the dynamics of the market landscape.

2.3. Transforming Chemistry Concepts into Marketable Products

2.3.1. Harnessing Nanotechnology for Innovative Food Solutions

Ravichandran (2010) introduces us to the world of nanotechnology applications in food and food processing—a realm where chemistry innovation intersects with practical needs, sustainability concerns, and technological advancements. This innovative approach, as revealed by Ravichandran's study, represents a transformative leap forward in addressing complex challenges in the food industry.

In this context, nanotechnology serves as a bridge between the intricacies of chemistry and the tangible needs of consumers. Ravichandran's work showcases how this fusion not only caters to market demands but also addresses critical aspects such as sustainability and efficiency. By tapping into the potential of nanoscale materials and processes, chemistry-driven innovations have the capacity to revolutionize the way we produce, package, and consume food (Ravichandran, 2010; Liao & Wang, 2021).

As we journey through the nanoscale dimensions explored in Ravichandran's work, we witness the remarkable transformation of complex chemistry into simple yet impactful solutions. This transformation is not merely confined to laboratories; it reverberates through the entire food value chain, touching the lives of consumers, producers, and industries alike. The chemistry of innovation, which once seemed remote and abstract, now manifests as cutting-edge products that redefine what is possible in the realm of food (Misra & Mention, 2022).

Furthermore, this intersection of nanotechnology and food showcases how chemistry's potential is best realized when its complexities are distilled into practical solutions. The elegant simplicity of these solutions resonates with consumers, while the underlying chemistry underscores the innovation's potential for addressing global challenges such as resource scarcity and environmental impact (Ravichandran, 2010; Pace, Saritas, & Deidun, 2023).

As you continue to delve into the chapters ahead, remember the lessons from Ravichandran's work. Consider how chemistry's transformative power can reshape industries and drive sustainable practices, even in unexpected domains like food processing. Let the journey through the nanoscale world inspire you to bridge the gap between complex chemistry and the tangible impact it can have on everyday lives.

2.3.2.	The Lean Enterprise: A Case Study in Chemical Innovation

Liao and Wang (2021) present a compelling case study that offers a deep dive into the world of chemical innovation through the lens of enterprise architecture. This unique approach highlights how the marriage of lean manufacturing, digitalization, and sustainability principles can transform chemistry-driven ideas into marketable products. The case study not only underscores the potential for innovation within the chemical industry but also emphasizes the significance of a holistic approach that transcends traditional boundaries.

In this case study, Liao and Wang (2021) shed light on the practical integration of lean manufacturing methodologies with digital technologies, all while fostering sustainability. This integration serves as a prime example of how chemistry's potential can be harnessed to address contemporary challenges in production and environmental stewardship. The amalgamation of these elements generates a synergy that goes beyond incremental improvement, leading to the creation of novel, marketable solutions (Liao & Wang, 2021; Sakellariou & Vecchiato, 2022).

The case study's implications extend beyond the chemical industry, serving as a testament to the universality of holistic innovation. It illustrates how innovative ideas can flourish when disparate threads of technology, efficiency, and sustainability are woven together into a comprehensive tapestry. This holistic approach reflects a deep understanding of the intricate interplay between chemistry, operational strategies, and consumer demands—a perspective that resonates with both established professionals and budding entrepreneurs alike (Liao & Wang, 2021; Zahra, 2008).

As you navigate through the chapters that follow, consider the multifaceted lessons from Liao and Wang's study. Contemplate how the principles of lean manufacturing, digitalization, and sustainability can intersect with your own chemistry-driven ideas. Embrace the concept that innovation thrives not in isolation but through the harmonious integration of diverse elements. Through this lens, you'll uncover the transformative power of chemistry to reshape industries, transcend limitations, and bring marketable ideas to life.

2.4.   Crossing the Valley of Death: From Idea to Reality

2.4.1.   Industry-Academia Collaboration in Biotechnology

Kampers et al. (2022) embark on a journey through the challenging terrain known as the "Valley of Death," a term that resonates with innovators across industries, including those in chemistry-driven fields. This metaphor encapsulates the transitional phase where innovative ideas often falter, unable to traverse the treacherous gap between research-based concepts and marketable products. Drawing upon insights from both industry and academia, Kampers and colleagues offer an illuminating analysis that not only exposes the challenges but also uncovers strategies to navigate this perilous journey.

By delving into perceptions from both sides of the industry-academia spectrum, this study reveals the contrasting viewpoints that often characterize the transition from innovative chemistry concepts to tangible market offerings (Kampers et al., 2022; Sakellariou & Vecchiato, 2022). The chasm between research and commercialization is not merely one of knowledge but also of perspective. The researchers' findings highlight this discrepancy and expose the underlying factors that contribute to the languishing of promising ideas within the Valley of Death.

In addition to identifying the challenges, Kampers et al. (2022) present a wealth of strategies, insights, and collaborative models that can act as bridges across this divide. This synthesis of perspectives from academia and industry enriches our understanding of how chemistry-driven innovations can harness the momentum needed to emerge successfully. The mutual comprehension of challenges, needs, and expectations facilitates more effective collaboration and can ultimately catalyze the transformation of chemistry ideas into products that thrive in the market (Kampers et al., 2022; Zahra, 2008).

As you proceed through the chapters ahead, keep the notion of the "Valley of Death" in mind. Reflect on the strategies and collaborative approaches that Kampers and colleagues have unearthed, and consider how these insights might illuminate your own path. The challenges and opportunities revealed in this study underscore the significance of unity between academia and industry, offering you a blueprint for steering your chemistry-driven ideas through the Valley of Death and onto the path of success.

2.4.2. Open Innovation in the Food Value Chain

Misra and Mention (2022) contribute to our understanding of open innovation within the context of the food value chain—a framework that resonates strongly with the world of chemistry innovation. This comprehensive review illuminates the potential of cross-sector collaboration in catalyzing the transformation of chemistry concepts into tangible, marketable products.

The discussion put forth by Misra and Mention (2022) underscores the role of collective expertise in breaking down the traditional silos that can hinder the innovation process. The food value chain becomes a vivid canvas where chemistry-driven visions intersect with diverse domains, such as agriculture, processing, distribution, and consumption. By recognizing that innovation thrives at the crossroads of these sectors, chemistry entrepreneurs gain a broader perspective that extends beyond the confines of laboratory walls (Misra & Mention, 2022; Kampers et al., 2022).

Furthermore, this review highlights how open innovation redefines the relationship between academia, industry, and other stakeholders in the food value chain. The collaborative model encourages the exchange of knowledge, ideas, and resources, resulting in a more dynamic and resilient ecosystem. This ecosystem, in turn, serves as a nurturing ground for chemistry concepts to evolve into marketable realities that cater to evolving consumer demands (Misra & Mention, 2022; Zahra, 2008).

As you journey through the chapters that follow, consider the lessons from Misra and Mention's exploration of open innovation. Reflect on how your chemistry-driven ideas can be enriched by engaging with experts from various sectors. Embrace the concept that innovation flourishes when knowledge is shared, and expertise is leveraged collectively. By embracing open innovation principles, you can amplify the impact of your chemistry concepts and turn them into solutions that transcend individual disciplines, reshaping industries and shaping a more vibrant and collaborative future.

2.5.1. Exploring a Sustainable Blue Economy

Pace, Saritas, and Deidun (2023) propel us forward into a vision of the future—a future intertwined with the concept of a sustainable blue economy. This forward-looking exploration transcends traditional boundaries by delving into the intricate interplay of chemistry, innovation, and environmental stewardship. The study projects us into a realm where chemistry's potential is harnessed not only for economic gains but also for the betterment of our planet.

As revealed by Pace et al. (2023), the sustainable blue economy embodies a harmonious synergy between human activities and ocean ecosystems. This synergy underscores the need to align chemistry-driven products with global sustainability goals. The study draws a vivid connection between chemistry innovation and the preservation of our oceans, recognizing the imperative to develop products that not only generate economic value but also contribute to the broader goal of environmental preservation (Pace, Saritas, & Deidun, 2023; Zahra, 2008).

Glimpsing ahead into the sustainable blue economy offers profound insights into the potential impacts of chemistry innovation. The study reinforces the idea that chemistry isn't an isolated endeavor but a force that must be wielded responsibly to create positive change. By aligning chemistry-driven products with global sustainability objectives, chemistry entrepreneurs can contribute to a future that marries technological progress with ecological equilibrium—a perspective that resonates with individuals and industries alike (Pace, Saritas, & Deidun, 2023; Ravichandran, 2010).

As you navigate through the chapters ahead, consider the lessons embedded in the vision of the sustainable blue economy. Reflect on how your own chemistry-driven ideas can contribute to this greater mission of sustainability. Embrace the concept that chemistry innovation isn't just about creating products but about sculpting a better future. By aligning your chemistry concepts with global sustainability goals, you can pave the way for solutions that don't merely cater to consumer demands but also safeguard our planet's well-being, creating a legacy that extends far beyond market success.

Sakellariou and Vecchiato (2022) delve into the intricate relationship between foresight, sensemaking, and new product development—a relationship that resonates profoundly with the journey of chemistry innovation. This exploration illuminates how these cognitive processes can empower chemistry innovators to transcend the immediate confines of their ideas and venture into the uncharted territory of future applications.

Foresight, as articulated by Sakellariou and Vecchiato (2022), is the art of envisioning potential futures—a skill that holds remarkable significance for chemistry-driven entrepreneurs. By applying foresight, innovators can project their concepts into the horizon, anticipating the trajectories they might follow, the markets they might penetrate, and the value they might generate. This proactive stance transforms chemistry innovation from a reactive process into a strategic endeavor, steering ideas toward marketable outcomes (Sakellariou & Vecchiato, 2022; Liao & Wang, 2021).

Coupled with foresight is sensemaking—an equally potent cognitive process that involves interpreting and making sense of complex information. Sakellariou and Vecchiato (2022) emphasize that sensemaking isn't confined to the individual but extends to collaborative efforts. When applied to chemistry innovation, sensemaking fosters an environment where collective expertise converges to unravel the potential hidden within intricate chemical concepts. This process enables chemistry innovators to navigate the intricate web of uncertainties that often accompanies innovation, equipping them to make informed decisions that transcend the immediate context (Sakellariou & Vecchiato, 2022; Zahra, 2008).

As you navigate the upcoming chapters, absorb the lessons from Sakellariou and Vecchiato's study. Reflect on how you can integrate foresight and sensemaking into your own chemistry-driven journey. Embrace the transformative power of envisioning futures and making sense of complexities. By weaving these cognitive processes into your innovation strategies, you'll find yourself emboldened to face the uncertainties of chemistry innovation, empowered to steer your concepts toward a future where chemistry truly becomes marketable gold.

2.6.1. Enabling Collaboration through the Internet of Things (IoT)

Mahdad et al. (2022) present an insightful exploration of a smart web—an intricate tapestry interweaving firms, farms, and the Internet of Things (IoT) within the agri-food industry. This portrayal of an interconnected ecosystem resonates profoundly with the world of chemistry innovation, illustrating how chemistry-driven products can seamlessly fit into collaborative business models that extend far beyond traditional boundaries.

The depiction of a smart web as envisioned by Mahdad and colleagues captures the essence of collaboration within the agri-food industry. This interconnectedness not only highlights the potential for chemistry-driven innovations to become integral components of larger systems but also showcases how chemistry concepts can serve as pivotal points of synergy within these models. Chemistry-driven products are no longer stand-alone entities but pieces that contribute to the intricate puzzle of interconnectedness, amplifying their impact (Mahdad et al., 2022; Sakellariou & Vecchiato, 2022).

By embracing this collaborative approach, chemistry innovators can harness the power of collective efforts to transform their ideas into marketable ventures. The smart web presented by Mahdad et al. (2022) underscores the idea that innovation thrives when boundaries are blurred and sectors unite. This synergistic model transcends traditional notions of entrepreneurship, offering a path where chemistry-driven concepts are integrated into the fabric of industry ecosystems, elevating their potential for success (Mahdad et al., 2022; Kampers et al., 2022).

As you embark on your journey of chemistry innovation, consider the lessons from Mahdad and colleagues. Reflect on how your chemistry-driven ideas can fit into collaborative business models, enriching and being enriched by a broader ecosystem. Embrace the power of synergy and interconnectedness, and recognize the potential of your concepts to thrive within a larger web of collaboration. By weaving your chemistry ideas into the fabric of interconnected business models, you'll amplify their impact, transforming them from isolated innovations into marketable ventures that ripple through industries and transform the landscape of possibility.

In closing, this chapter has been a guide to a transformative journey through the multifaceted landscape of chemistry-driven innovation. From the initial spark of identifying market opportunities to the intricate interplay of cutting-edge technologies, we've ventured into the very heart of turning chemistry concepts into tangible marketable gold. The culmination of insights from various fields, case studies, and practical tips has provided you with a compass to navigate the dynamic terrain of entrepreneurship.

As you embark on your own entrepreneurial voyage, keep in mind the wisdom shared by experts like Zahra (2008) and McNally et al. (2009), who emphasized the significance of recognizing market gaps and the role of dispositional traits in shaping innovation decisions. The case studies explored, such as Ravichandran's (2010) exploration of nanotechnology in food processing and Mahdad et al.'s (2022) insights into collaboration through the Internet of Things, have illuminated the practicality and potential of chemistry-driven ideas.

The dynamic nature of the chemistry of innovation, as portrayed by Sakellariou and Vecchiato (2022), beckons you to embrace challenges as opportunities for growth. The collaborative spirit advocated by Kampers et al. (2022) and Misra and Mention (2022) urges you to recognize the power of collective knowledge and open innovation. The vision of a sustainable blue economy, as projected by Pace, Saritas, and Deidun (2023), serves as a reminder of the greater impact your chemistry-driven products can have on the environment.

As you embark on your journey, remember that the chemistry of innovation is a continuous evolution, much like the concepts and products it brings to life. Embrace the challenge, learn from the experts who have paved the way, and infuse your journey with the boundless spirit of discovery that courses through the veins of successful entrepreneurs. It's time to unearth your own marketable ideas, armed with the insights you've gained, and set forth on a voyage that has the potential to shape industries, transform lives, and impact the world in ways you've never imagined.

2.8.   Call to Action: Your Chemistry-Driven Odyssey

As you've navigated through the pages of this chapter, a rich tapestry of insights into the world of chemistry innovation has been woven before you. Now, the time has come for you to step into the spotlight and embrace your role as an agent of transformation. Draw upon the knowledge you've acquired, the case studies you've explored, and the wisdom of experts who have paved the way.

Reflect on the chemistry concepts that ignite your passion and imagination. Consider the untapped market gaps that lie before you, waiting to be discovered and filled. Align your chemistry-driven ideas with the broader trends illuminated by scholars like Zahra (2008), McNally et al. (2009), and Liao and Wang (2021). Ponder how your innovations could be harnessed to address the challenges of a sustainable future, as envisioned by Pace, Saritas, and Deidun (2023).

Allow the stories of entrepreneurial pioneers to infuse your journey with inspiration. Draw strength from the narratives of those who have transformed chemistry concepts into tangible marketable gold. The tales of innovators who have navigated the complexities of the industry-academia landscape (Kampers et al., 2022) and harnessed collaborative power (Mahdad et al., 2022) serve as beacons illuminating the path ahead.

As you embark on this odyssey, remember that the journey from beakers to billions is not just a metaphor—it's a reality that you have the potential to shape. With the insights gleaned from Sakellariou and Vecchiato's (2022) exploration of foresight and sensemaking, craft a strategic vision for your chemistry-driven ideas. Let the holistic approach advocated by Ravichandran (2010) guide your choices, ensuring that your innovations resonate with consumer needs and broader societal goals.

The time has come for action. Take that first step—the step that transforms your chemistry dreams into marketable gold. Your journey is unique, and the impact you can create through chemistry-driven innovation is boundless. Armed with the knowledge, strategies, and inspiration you've gained, set forth on this transformative path. The world of possibilities awaits, and the chemistry-driven odyssey is yours to shape, to nurture, and to turn into a reality that leaves an indelible mark on the world.

2.9.   References

[1]   Kampers, L. F., Asin-Garcia, E., Schaap, P. J., Wagemakers, A., & dos Santos, V. A. M. (2022). Navigating the Valley of Death: Perceptions of Industry and Academia on Production Platforms and Opportunities in Biotechnology. *EFB Bioeconomy Journal*, *2*, 100033. https://doi.org/10.1016/j.bioeco.2022.100033

[2]   Liao, M. H., & Wang, C. T. (2021). Using enterprise architecture to integrate lean manufacturing, digitalization, and sustainability: A lean enterprise case study in the chemical industry. *Sustainability*, *13*(9), 4851. https://doi.org/10.3390/su13094851

[3]   Mahdad, M., Hasanov, M., Isakhanyan, G., & Dolfsma, W. (2022). A smart web of firms, farms and internet of things (IOT): enabling collaboration-based

business models in the agri-food industry. *British Food Journal, 124*(6), 1857-1874. https://doi.org/10.1108/BFJ-07-2021-0756

[4]   McNally, R. C., Durmusoglu, S. S., Calantone, R. J., & Harmancioglu, N. (2009). Exploring new product portfolio management decisions: The role of managers' dispositional traits. *Industrial Marketing Management, 38*(1), 127-143. https://doi.org/10.1016/j.indmarman.2007.09.006

[5]   Misra, A., & Mention, A. L. (2022). Exploring the food value chain using open innovation: A bibliometric review of the literature. *British Food Journal, 124*(6), 1810-1837. https://doi.org/10.1108/BFJ-04-2021-0353

[6]   Pace, L. A., Saritas, O., & Deidun, A. (2023). Exploring future research and innovation directions for a sustainable blue economy. *Marine Policy, 148*, 105433. https://doi.org/10.1016/j.marpol.2022.105433

[7]   Ravichandran, R. (2010). Nanotechnology applications in food and food processing: innovative green approaches, opportunities and uncertainties for global market. *International Journal of Green Nanotechnology: Physics and Chemistry, 1*(2), P72-P96. https://doi.org/10.1080/19430871003684440

[8]   Sakellariou, E., & Vecchiato, R. (2022). Foresight, sensemaking, and new product development: Constructing meanings for the future. *Technological Forecasting and Social Change, 184*, 121945. https://doi.org/10.1016/j.techfore.2022.121945

[9]   Zahra, S. A. (2008). The virtuous cycle of discovery and creation of entrepreneurial opportunities. *Strategic Entrepreneurship Journal, 2*(3), 243-257. https://doi.org/10.1002/sej.47

3.   Elements of Success: Market Research

Turning Chemistry into Marketable Gold

3.1.   Introduction: Navigating the Chemistry-Commerce Nexus

As we embark on this transformative journey from abstract chemistry concepts to tangible marketable products, we find ourselves at the crossroads of scientific elegance and consumer dynamics. This chapter, titled "*Elements of Success: Market Research*," unveils the crucial role that comprehensive market research and analysis play in shaping this remarkable conversion. Our expedition navigates through the intricate interplay of chemical insights and market insights, revealing how understanding customer needs, sizing up competitors, and anticipating industry trends are the essential catalysts for turning chemistry into a sought-after commodity.

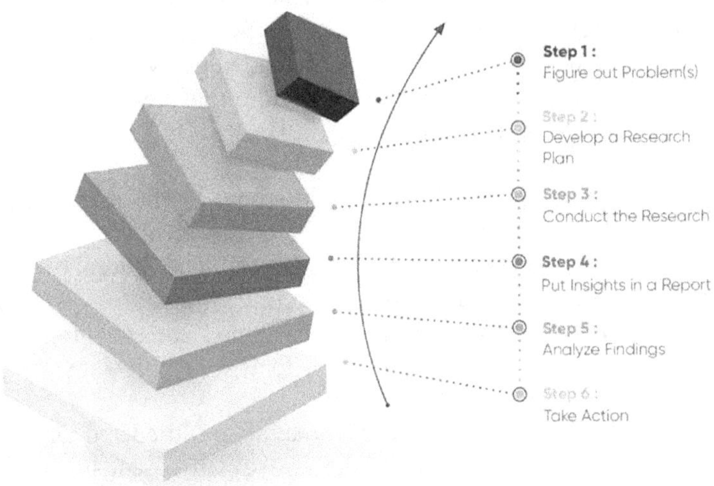

The graceful dance of the periodic table's elements finds resonance in the ever-changing symphony of consumer demands. Just as chemical compounds react to yield new substances, so does the fusion of chemistry and commerce yield innovative products that captivate the market. This chapter embarks on a quest to illuminate the nuances of this transformation, highlighting the invaluable role that market research plays as a guiding star in this journey.

At the core of this exploration lies the profound connection between chemistry and consumer behavior. This marriage of disciplines is underscored by Rosário and Raimundo (2021) in their investigation of consumer marketing strategy and its intersection with e-commerce. Their comprehensive literature review delves into the intricate dynamics of how consumer preferences, behaviors, and expectations shape the landscape of marketable products. Just as chemists study reactions to uncover hidden patterns, understanding consumer behavior unveils hidden opportunities.

Furthermore, as Moisander, Närvänen, and Valtonen (2020) suggest through their work on interpretive marketing research, ethnography becomes a potent tool for capturing the essence of consumer desires. By immersing ourselves in the world of our target audience, we move beyond mere data points and delve into the emotional and cultural factors that drive consumer choices. This ethnographic approach forms a bridge between the sterile laboratory environment and the vibrant world of consumer preferences.

Intricately intertwined with consumer insights is the profound impact of emerging trends on the trajectory of chemistry-driven innovations. The work of Qiu, Jie, Wang, and Zhao (2020) delves into the realm of green product innovation, a concept that marries environmental consciousness with the ingenuity of chemical transformations. Their research underscores the potent intersection of chemistry and sustainability, showing how businesses that align with the green dynamic capability can create a competitive advantage that resonates with modern consumers' eco-conscious sensibilities.

As we embark on this journey from the classroom to the marketplace, we are reminded by Varadarajan (2020) that a chempreneur must wield the dual swords of chemistry knowledge and market awareness. The interplay of customer information resources advantage and marketing strategy is akin to a well-orchestrated chemical reaction. Just as reactants lead to products, a deep understanding of competitors' strategies leads to a competitive advantage.

This chapter will be your guide as we traverse this multifaceted landscape. From the elegance of chemical reactions to the dynamism of consumer desires, the journey promises to be both enlightening and transformative. With insights from market research and wisdom gleaned from successful chempreneurs, you are poised to embark on an alchemical expedition where chemistry metamorphoses into marketable gold.

"Market research is not merely a passive activity; it's a dynamic process that breathes life into your chemistry-driven innovation."

In the fast-paced world of chemistry-driven products, operating in isolation is a recipe for missed opportunities. The importance of active engagement with market research becomes vividly apparent in light of Rosário and Raimundo's (2021) exploration of consumer marketing strategy. Their work serves as a guiding beacon, illuminating how this strategy steers the course of triumphant innovations. At the heart of this strategy lies market research—a beacon that guides chempreneurs through the labyrinth of consumer preferences, needs, and behaviors.

Market research is your compass, a steadfast guide that ensures your journey from concept to commodity remains on course. Just as skilled chemists navigate intricate reactions, chempreneurs navigate the vast ocean of consumer desires. Rosário and Raimundo's findings highlight that market research unveils the intricate map of this ocean, guiding you toward lucrative shores of innovation. Every decision, every transformation, is directed by insights garnered from meticulous analysis.

However, the magic of market research doesn't solely lie in numbers and charts. It's a dynamic, evolving process that taps into the very essence of consumer behavior. This sentiment resonates with Moisander, Närvänen, and Valtonen's (2020) exploration of interpretive marketing research. Ethnography, their instrument of choice, offers a rich, holistic perspective on consumer behavior— one that transcends mere data points.

By embracing ethnography, chempreneurs gain the power to immerse themselves in the world of their target audience. It's a transformative lens that allows you to step into their shoes, understand their challenges, and unearth the emotional drivers behind their choices. This goes beyond quantitative metrics; it's about seeing consumers as people, not just as data points. Ethnography, as Moisander et al. suggest, empowers you to connect on a human level, enabling insights that conventional data might overlook.

In essence, Section 1 elucidates that market research is no mere footnote in the journey from chemistry to commerce. It's an active, dynamic process that breathes life into your innovation, infusing it with the essence of consumer needs and desires. Just as chemical reactions thrive under controlled conditions, successful chemistry-driven products thrive under the guidance of insightful market research. With the lessons learned from Rosário and Raimundo, along with the immersive approach of ethnography detailed by Moisander, Närvänen, and Valtonen, you're equipped to unravel the mysteries of your target audience and navigate the seas of innovation with precision and purpose.

3.3.   The Dance of Innovation and Trends

"Every successful chemistry-driven product is a harmonious blend of innovation and an astute grasp of emerging trends."

In the realm of chemistry-driven products, success thrives at the intersection of innovation and trends. The synthesis of these two elements creates a powerful formula that catapults chempreneurs into the vanguard of marketable offerings. This section unveils how successful chempreneurs not only comprehend the intricacies of chemical reactions but also possess the foresight to navigate the molecular shifts of emerging trends.

The work of Qiu, Jie, Wang, and Zhao (2020) illuminates the transformative potential of green product innovation—a phenomenon where chemistry aligns with sustainable practices, creating a dynamic synergy. This fusion is more than a buzzword; it's a strategic path to gaining a competitive advantage. The symbiosis between green practices and chemistry expertise echoes the harmony that emerges when chemical compounds react in concert.

Qiu et al.'s research underscores that green innovation isn't just an ecological consideration—it's a market-driven imperative. By embracing green dynamic capability, chempreneurs tap into the current zeitgeist of environmental consciousness. A deep understanding of chemistry coupled with an awareness of sustainable practices amplifies the impact of your innovation, resonating with consumers who are increasingly inclined to support eco-friendly products.

From the laboratory beakers, the journey extends to market shelves. This journey, while paved with potential, is often fraught with challenges. However, the roadmap is clear: the marriage of chemistry with innovation and trends is your compass. It's a journey where understanding the intricate dance of chemical reactions finds resonance in anticipating and embracing emerging trends. The lessons drawn from Qiu et al.'s exploration of green product innovation offer a blueprint—an embodiment of how chemistry can play an instrumental role in the creation of products that not only meet consumer needs but also contribute to a sustainable future.

In short, this section emphasizes that the transformation of chemistry concepts into marketable wonders isn't a linear process—it's an intricate dance. A successful chempreneur is not just a master of chemical reactions but also a visionary who dances in step with emerging trends. Just as a skilled dancer combines steps seamlessly, the chempreneur seamlessly combines chemistry's potential with the dynamics of trends, creating a harmonious symphony that resonates in the market. With the knowledge gleaned from Qiu et al., you possess a toolkit to infuse green innovation with the prowess of chemistry, thereby crafting products that not only capture consumer attention but also stand the test of time.

3.4.   The Chemistry of Competitors and Competitive Advantage

"In the world of marketable chemistry, knowledge of competitors is as crucial as the knowledge of compounds."

Stepping into the realm of marketable chemistry requires more than just understanding chemical reactions; it demands a profound comprehension of the competitive landscape. This section delves into the notion that the insights into competitors' strategies are as vital as your grasp of chemical compounds. Varadarajan (2020) offers a compelling perspective on the interplay between customer information resources advantage and competitive advantage—two sides of the same coin that is the chempreneurial journey.

The insights drawn from Varadarajan's work form a dynamic canvas that vividly portrays the juncture where market insights meet strategic advantage. Just as catalysts expedite chemical reactions, knowledge of competitors' moves and strategies expedites your path to success. A chempreneur's arsenal is far from complete without a meticulous analysis of the market landscape. This includes a comprehensive evaluation of competitors' strengths and weaknesses, a discerning study that lays the foundation for crafting a strategic response that not only counters but also propels your own venture forward.

The parallels between chemistry and business strategy are striking. Just as chemists experiment with reaction conditions to yield desired products, chempreneurs experiment with market strategies to yield competitive advantage. Varadarajan's insights encourage us to see competitors not just as rivals but as catalysts that spur our own innovation and improvement. An informed chempreneur doesn't operate in isolation; they engage in a dynamic exchange of strategies, constantly recalibrating their approaches based on the evolving market dynamics.

In essence, this section underscores that the journey from concept to market isn't merely about chemical transformation; it's about strategic transformation. Just as a chemist adapts reaction conditions to optimize outcomes, a chempreneur adapts strategies to optimize success. By leveraging Varadarajan's insights, you're equipped to navigate the intricate web of competitors, transforming their presence from an obstacle into an opportunity. This understanding empowers you to craft a strategic response that not only ensures your chemistry-driven products stand out but also flourish in a competitive market.

3.5. Case Studies: From Molecules to Marketable Wonders

"Real-world stories of chempreneurs remind us that chemistry's marvels extend beyond labs into the hands of consumers."

Amid the laboratory equipment and chemical equations, the most awe-inspiring transformation lies in the journey from abstract concepts to tangible products. This section unearths the power of real-world case studies—testaments to the alchemical prowess of chempreneurs who bring chemistry's wonders to life in the hands of consumers. These stories remind us that chemistry isn't confined to beakers; it extends to the market, influencing everyday lives.

The tales of chempreneurs, as living embodiments of innovation, inspire us to explore the boundaries of what chemistry can achieve. Their stories resonate with the principles of ingenuity and resourcefulness. Take, for instance, the inspiring narrative of a group of chemistry enthusiasts who harnessed their knowledge to develop eco-friendly cleaning products. This case study, an embodiment of chemistry meeting market demands, exemplifies the potent synergy that arises from aligning chemistry's potential with consumer aspirations for sustainability.

As Malhotra, Nunan, and Birks (2020) discuss in their work on marketing research, the development process is not a linear path—it's a journey filled with distinct phases. This case study allows us to dissect the journey these chempreneurs embarked upon, from the initial formulation of their product to the intricate branding decisions that positioned their innovation in the market. Just as chemists carefully combine reactants to achieve the desired outcome, these chempreneurs skillfully orchestrated a sequence of steps, each contributing to the final marvel that graced the market shelves.

Through this case study, we witness the tangible embodiment of the concepts explored in earlier sections. The intersection of market research, innovation, and competitive awareness comes to life, encapsulated in the journey of these chempreneurs. This journey isn't just about chemistry—it's about crafting a narrative that resonates with consumers. The chemistry-driven product becomes more than just a commodity; it's a solution to a problem, a fulfillment of a need, and a realization of an aspiration.

In short, this section reiterates that chemistry's true marvel lies in its transformation into marketable wonders. The case study presented here serves as a testament to the power of chemistry to address contemporary needs, showcasing how chemistry enthusiasts translated their knowledge into a product that resonated with consumers' eco-consciousness. This narrative demonstrates the tangible application of principles discussed in previous sections, offering a blueprint for budding chempreneurs to embark on their journey of turning chemistry concepts into marketable gold.

3.6.   Looking Ahead: Chemistry in Tomorrow's Markets

"As chemistry continues to evolve, tomorrow's marketplaces beckon with uncharted possibilities."

In the alchemical fusion of chemistry and commerce, the landscape is never static—it's a canvas that evolves with time. This section ventures into the unknown, contemplating the potential chemistry holds in shaping the markets of the future. The insights shared by Paul (2020) cast a light on this landscape, guiding our gaze toward emerging markets and the synergies between chemistry's transformative power and the dynamics of burgeoning economies.

Paul's musings on marketing in emerging markets beckon us to peer into the horizon of possibilities. As the global economic landscape shifts, the role of chemistry in driving innovation and marketable wonders becomes even more profound. The intersections between disciplines spawn novel opportunities, positioning chempreneurs at the forefront of change. The transformative potential of chemistry isn't bound by borders; it's a dynamic force that transcends geographies and cultures.

In this ever-evolving tapestry, the principles of sustainable growth, as illuminated by Kim, Kim, and Hwang (2020), hold particular resonance. Sustainable growth is more than just financial gain; it's about fostering customer equity and loyalty. The chemistry-driven success that we seek isn't only rooted in the allure of our products; it's deeply connected to the satisfaction and loyalty of our patrons. This insight reminds us that chemistry's transformation into marketable gold is intricately tied to the relationship we cultivate with our consumers.

The canvas of tomorrow's markets is a space of possibilities, where chemistry-driven products can carve new niches, solve novel problems, and cater to evolving needs. As chemistry continues to evolve, the potential to create innovative solutions aligns with the ever-changing market dynamics. The harmonious blend of innovation and trend anticipation, along with a profound understanding of consumer preferences, will be the key to capitalizing on the uncharted possibilities that await.

To conclude, this section ignites the spark of curiosity, inviting us to gaze into the future of chemistry-driven products. Paul's insights into emerging markets serve as a compass, guiding our understanding of the interplay between chemistry and commerce on a global scale. The insights from Kim, Kim, and Hwang underscore that chemistry's transformational power isn't merely about creating products—it's about nurturing lasting relationships with customers. With these reflections, we stand at the precipice of a new era, armed with the knowledge to turn chemistry into marketable gold in a world where possibilities are as limitless as the elements themselves.

3.7. Conclusion: Your Chemistry-Driven Odyssey

"As you step into the world of chempreneurship, remember that your chemistry expertise is a catalyst for marketable gold."

With the culmination of this chapter, you stand at the threshold of a transformative journey—an odyssey that wields the power of chemistry to craft marketable wonders. The insights unearthed within these pages are more than knowledge; they are your compass, guiding you through uncharted territories where chemical reactions metamorphose into products that resonate with consumers. This conclusion encapsulates the essence of your voyage, inspiring you to take the first step with confidence.

The insights gleaned from this chapter serve as your guiding star—a constellation of strategies that will illuminate your path. You are now poised to step into the shoes of a chempreneur, a role that fuses your chemistry expertise with the dynamism of the market. Embrace the principles laid out before you—comprehensive market research, innovative thinking, competitor analysis, and consumer insight. Just as a chemist measures reactants meticulously, you'll measure each strategic step with precision, each decision informed by the insights shared within these pages.

Your journey will be akin to a complex chemical reaction, with moments of challenge and triumph. The process may not always follow a linear trajectory, but that's the nature of creation. As molecules collide and form new compounds, so too will your ideas collide with market realities to create new products. Yet, remember that each challenge is an opportunity for growth and innovation, much like unexpected reactions leading to unexpected products in the lab.

The lessons drawn from the experiences of successful chempreneurs are invaluable companions on your journey. Their stories remind us that chemistry's wonders extend far beyond the laboratory, manifesting as products that shape the lives of consumers. Just as they transformed ideas into realities, so can you. Draw from their wisdom, learn from their missteps, and adapt their strategies to your own circumstances.

As you step forth, armed with your chemistry expertise, you embark on a chemistry-driven odyssey that spans innovation, creation, and market domination. Whether you're converting a chemical reaction into a cosmetic product that enhances beauty or turning an elemental discovery into an essential commodity that revolutionizes industries, the canvas of chemistry and commerce awaits your creative strokes. The alchemical magic of combining elements into compounds finds its counterpart in the art of transforming chemistry into marketable gold.

In closing, this chapter is but the prologue to your narrative—a narrative that will be shaped by your passion, perseverance, and the wisdom accrued from this exploration. Embrace the essence of chemistry, infuse it with the vitality of market insights, and embark on your odyssey. The stage is set, the elements are at your disposal, and the world awaits your chemistry-driven marvels. Onward, dear chempreneur, to turn your dreams into marketable gold.

Remember, the periodic table may have its elements, but you have the elements of success. Your journey from beakers to billions starts now. Onward, chempreneur!

3.8. References

[1]   Daengs, G. S., Istanti, E., Negoro, R. M., & Sanusi, R. (2020). The aftermath of management actions on competitive advantage through process attributes at food and beverage industries export import in Perak Harbor of Surabaya. *International Journal of Criminology and Sociology*, *9*, 1418-1425. http://eprints.ubhara.ac.id/id/eprint/710

[2]   Kim, W., Kim, H., & Hwang, J. (2020). Sustainable growth for the self-employed in the retail industry based on customer equity, customer satisfaction, and loyalty. *Journal of Retailing and Consumer Services*, *53*, 101963. https://doi.org/10.1016/j.jretconser.2019.101963

[3]   Malhotra, N. K., Nunan, D., & Birks, D. F. (2020). *Marketing Research*. Pearson UK.

[4]   Moisander, J., Närvänen, E., & Valtonen, A. (2020). Interpretive marketing research: Using ethnography in strategic market development. https://doi.org/10.4324/9780203710807-19

[5]   Paul, J. (2020). Marketing in emerging markets: a review, theoretical synthesis and extension. *International Journal of Emerging Markets*, *15*(3), 446-468. https://doi.org/10.1108/IJOEM-04-2017-0130

[6]   Qiu, L., Jie, X., Wang, Y., & Zhao, M. (2020). Green product innovation, green dynamic capability, and competitive advantage: Evidence from Chinese manufacturing enterprises. *Corporate Social Responsibility and Environmental Management*, *27*(1), 146-165. https://doi.org/10.1002/csr.1780

[7]   Rosário, A., & Raimundo, R. (2021). Consumer marketing strategy and E-commerce in the last decade: a literature review. *Journal of theoretical and applied electronic commerce research*, *16*(7), 3003-3024. https://doi.org/10.3390/jtaer16070164

[8]   Varadarajan, R. (2020). Customer information resources advantage, marketing strategy and business performance: A market resources based view. *Industrial Marketing Management*, *89*, 89-97. https://doi.org/10.1016/j.indmarman.2020.03.003

4. Brewing Innovation: Formulating Product Concepts

4.1. Introduction

Imagine a world where the intricacies of chemistry don't just live within the walls of laboratories, but thrive in the bustling marketplace, enriching lives and driving innovation. As Cigdemoglu and Geban (2015) reveal through their context-based approach, the traditional boundaries of chemistry education are expanding, emphasizing the real-world relevance of chemical concepts. This shift isn't just about equations and reactions confined to textbooks; it's about how these concepts interlace with our daily lives, sparking ideas that transcend the academic realm.

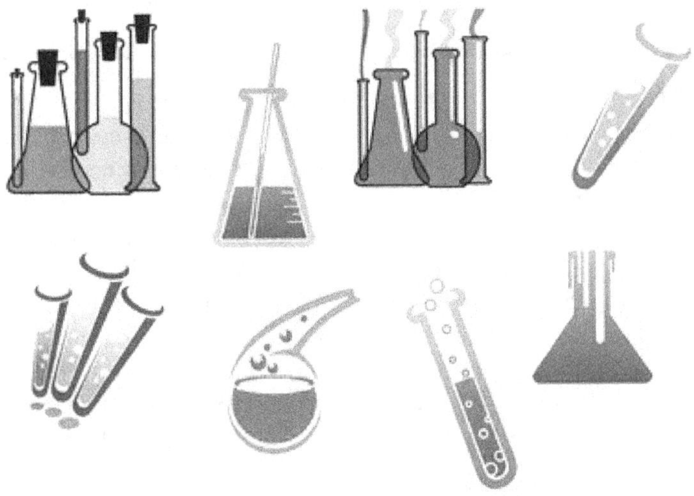

In this chapter, we embark on a journey that carries us far beyond the confines of classroom theories. We journey into a realm where chemical equations and molecular interactions metamorphose into tangible products that influence industries, communities, and cultures. This journey is a testament to the alchemical process of translating abstract chemistry concepts into marketable gold. As Brady, Dürig, Lee, and Li (2017) elaborate in their work on polymer properties, the bridge between laboratory insights and product formulation requires an in-depth understanding of the molecular intricacies that govern material behavior.

We are not merely spectators on this journey; we are explorers armed with the knowledge that our chemistry expertise holds the potential to revolutionize how we experience the world. The sections that follow will take you through the realms of innovation, entrepreneurial success, expert guidance, and practical application. We'll navigate the twists and turns of challenges, traverse the landscapes of emerging trends, and dissect the anatomy of triumph through captivating case studies. It's a voyage of discovery, one that invites you to join the ranks of visionaries who have ventured beyond the chalkboard to transform chemistry into captivating products.

So, let's embark on this adventure—a journey that stretches from theories etched on paper to products held in hand. It's a journey that unearths the artistry within chemistry, the symphony of molecules that harmonize to create products that resonate with the masses. This chapter is your passport to understanding how chemistry is more than an academic pursuit; it's a passport to turning ideas into innovations, equations into tangible realities, and chemistry into marketable gold.

4.2.   The Chemistry of Conceptualization

Before we delve into the exciting realm of chemistry-driven products, it's essential to take a moment to understand how chemistry concepts can be ingeniously transformed into tangible ideas. As highlighted by Cigdemoglu and Geban (2015), the concept of a context-based approach is a beacon illuminating our path. Through this approach, chemistry education extends beyond the theoretical confines of textbooks and laboratories, embracing the dynamic interplay between chemical principles and real-world scenarios. This method isn't just a pedagogical shift; it's a revolution in how we perceive chemistry's role in our lives.

Imagine, for instance, the process of brewing coffee. In the context of chemistry, this simple act involves the dissolution of various compounds, the liberation of volatile aromas, and the intricacies of heat transfer—all fundamental chemical processes. This context-based understanding breathes life into chemical equations, allowing us to envision how they manifest in everyday experiences. Just as a chef infuses recipes with creativity and flair, we can infuse chemistry concepts with innovation, turning them into potential products that can change lives.

Think of this process as a symphony of molecules and reactions, where the conductor is our imagination. We're no longer confined to the theoretical notation of chemistry; we're composing harmonies that resonate in the world of consumer goods. This transformation is akin to brewing a potent concoction of ideas, allowing the reactions to percolate in our minds until they coalesce into innovative products that capture the imagination of consumers. Just as Cigdemoglu and Geban

(2015) suggest, this context-based approach enhances chemical literacy by fostering a deeper understanding of the intricate connections between theoretical knowledge and real-world applications.

In essence, the chemistry of conceptualization involves envisioning chemical concepts not as static formulas but as dynamic elements that interact with the world around us. By embracing this mindset, we're empowered to navigate the exciting journey from equations on paper to transformative products that captivate markets. It's a journey that's both intellectually invigorating and creatively liberating—a journey where chemistry takes on a new identity, one that's grounded in innovation and poised to yield marketable gold.

4.3. From Molecules to Market: The Formulation Process

The journey from classroom concepts to marketable products is indeed a multi-faceted expedition, characterized by intricacies that demand both scientific precision and creative finesse. In many ways, it mirrors the careful choreography that transpires in a culinary kitchen. Just as a chef artfully combines ingredients to create a gastronomic masterpiece, chemists deftly assemble compositions that have the potential to birth groundbreaking products. The insights provided by Brady, Dürig, Lee, and Li (2017) cast a spotlight on the significance of comprehending polymer properties, particularly in the realm of dosage forms, offering a vivid illustration of how chemistry's intricate dance underpins innovations in pharmaceutical sciences.

At the heart of this journey is the process of formulation—a symphony of molecular interactions that culminates in the harmonious creation of a product. It's a process that hinges on the profound understanding of the nuanced behavior of molecules. These molecules, much like dancers in a ballet, engage in precise movements and interactions that influence the ultimate outcome. This orchestration requires a thorough grasp of the intricacies of reactivity, stability, and compatibility—an understanding that resonates with the insights shared by Kotz, Treichel, Townsend, and Treichel (2014) in their exploration of chemical reactivity.

The formulation process is akin to crafting an intricate recipe, where each ingredient plays a role in determining the final flavor. Predicting how these components will interact demands a keen intuition—almost a sixth sense—that only a chemist possesses. This intuition, coupled with rigorous scientific analysis, allows chemists to craft formulations that yield desired outcomes.

Consider the journey from equations transcribed on paper to tangible prototypes held in hand. It's in this transformation that the true essence of chemistry comes to life. The equations that were once confined to the pages of textbooks metamorphose into tangible materials, devices, and products. This metamorphosis is not a mere scientific exercise; it's a testament to the artistry of chemistry. It's the culmination of the chemist's ability to manipulate matter, transforming it into products that have the power to revolutionize industries and enhance lives.

In essence, the formulation process is a bridge—a bridge that connects the theoretical realms of chemistry with the pragmatic landscapes of consumer needs. This bridge doesn't merely facilitate the passage of molecules; it orchestrates a symphony of innovation. As we cross this bridge, we journey from the abstract to the tangible, from equations to prototypes, and from chemistry's theoretical foundations to its tangible manifestations. It's a journey that underscores chemistry's transformative power, showcasing its ability to turn concepts into reality, and reality into marketable gold.

4.4. Stories of Innovation: Entrepreneurs and Their Triumphs

Let's delve into the realm of entrepreneurship, where chemistry concepts are not just academic exercises but the building blocks of transformative market successes. Consider the story of Jane—an exemplar of how chemistry can catalyze remarkable journeys. Jane, an aspiring entrepreneur, set out to bridge the gap between chemistry insights and consumer needs. Drawing from the well of knowledge presented in "The Organic Chemistry of Drug Design and Drug Action" by Silverman and Holladay (2014), Jane embarked on a quest to transform her passion for chemistry into a tangible product.

Armed with her understanding of molecular structures and reactivity, Jane unearthed a natural compound with exceptional skin-rejuvenating properties. Her journey was far from smooth; it required a synthesis of determination, innovation, and scientific insight. The rigors of transforming laboratory formulations into marketable products tested her mettle. Yet, it was Jane's unwavering belief in the transformative potential of chemistry that fueled her perseverance.

Through tireless experimentation and unwavering commitment, Jane succeeded in developing a skincare product that not only delighted customers but also garnered widespread recognition. Her story, a living testament to the power of chemistry, stands as a testament to the possibility of turning scientific insights into tangible market triumphs.

Jane's journey is just a snapshot of the expansive tapestry of chemistry-driven success stories. From sustainable polymers that redefine material science (Fagnani et al., 2020) to biodegradable medical devices that revolutionize healthcare (Wang et al., 2022), these narratives remind us that chemistry is not relegated to laboratories alone. It's a potent catalyst for igniting real-world change, a driving force that propels innovation across industries.

In these stories of entrepreneurial triumphs, chemistry emerges as the cornerstone that bridges the gap between scientific understanding and market demand. It is the spark that ignites innovation, the force that transforms raw ideas into marketable gold. These stories remind us that every chemical reaction, every molecular interaction, and every formulation has the potential to reshape industries, improve lives, and leave an indelible mark on the world.

As we journey through the narratives of these entrepreneurs, we're invited to recognize the transformative power of chemistry. It's a power that transcends the confines of laboratory walls, one that can kindle the flames of creativity and drive us toward meaningful contributions in the market space. These stories challenge us to explore our own chemistry knowledge with an entrepreneurial lens, inspiring us to embark on our own ventures to translate chemistry into marketable success.

4.5.   Expert Insights: The Art of Application

Let's delve into the realm of entrepreneurship, where chemistry concepts are not just academic exercises but the building blocks of transformative market successes. Consider the story of Jane—an exemplar of how chemistry can catalyze remarkable journeys. Jane, an aspiring entrepreneur, set out to bridge the gap between chemistry insights and consumer needs. Drawing from the well of knowledge presented in "The Organic Chemistry of Drug Design and Drug Action" by Silverman and Holladay (2014), Jane embarked on a quest to transform her passion for chemistry into a tangible product.

Armed with her understanding of molecular structures and reactivity, Jane unearthed a natural compound with exceptional skin-rejuvenating properties. Her journey was far from smooth; it required a synthesis of determination, innovation, and scientific insight. The rigors of transforming laboratory formulations into marketable products tested her mettle. Yet, it was Jane's unwavering belief in the transformative potential of chemistry that fueled her perseverance.

Through tireless experimentation and unwavering commitment, Jane succeeded in developing a skincare product that not only delighted customers but also garnered widespread recognition. Her story, a living testament to the power of chemistry, stands as a testament to the possibility of turning scientific insights into tangible market triumphs.

Jane's journey is just a snapshot of the expansive tapestry of chemistry-driven success stories. From sustainable polymers that redefine material science (Fagnani et al., 2020) to biodegradable medical devices that revolutionize healthcare (Wang et al., 2022), these narratives remind us that chemistry is not relegated to laboratories alone. It's a potent catalyst for igniting real-world change, a driving force that propels innovation across industries.

In these stories of entrepreneurial triumphs, chemistry emerges as the cornerstone that bridges the gap between scientific understanding and market demand. It is the spark that ignites innovation, the force that transforms raw ideas into marketable gold. These stories remind us that every chemical reaction, every molecular interaction, and every formulation has the potential to reshape industries, improve lives, and leave an indelible mark on the world.

As we journey through the narratives of these entrepreneurs, we're invited to recognize the transformative power of chemistry. It's a power that transcends the confines of laboratory walls, one that can kindle the flames of creativity and drive us toward meaningful contributions in the market space. These stories challenge us to explore our own chemistry knowledge with an entrepreneurial lens, inspiring us to embark on our own ventures to translate chemistry into marketable success.

4.6. Navigating Challenges: Lessons from the Field

While the stories of triumph inspire us, it's crucial to remember that not every journey from chemistry concepts to marketable products is a seamless one. The tale of Tom stands as a stark reminder of the obstacles that can pepper this path. Tom, a visionary with a passion for innovation, embarked on a mission to translate a cutting-edge chemical concept into a consumer product. His journey, however, was far from straightforward.

Tom's challenges echoed the intricacies of the real world, where the realms of scientific creativity intersect with the regulatory landscape. As outlined in "Chemistry for Pharmacy Students" by Nahar and Sarker (2019), the importance of understanding regulatory hurdles cannot be overstated. Tom learned this lesson firsthand, encountering obstacles that ranged from compliance concerns to safety considerations.

In the pursuit of turning a brilliant chemistry-driven idea into a marketable reality, Tom confronted the complexities of blending creativity with practicality. It became evident that the journey from the lab bench to the marketplace necessitated a thorough understanding of not just scientific principles, but also the legal and regulatory frameworks that govern product development.

Tom's journey serves as a poignant reminder that innovation and creativity must be harnessed within the bounds of regulatory compliance. It underscores the vital importance of conducting due diligence in navigating the intricacies of regulations, quality standards, and safety protocols. This intersection between innovation and regulation is a tightrope that every chemistry-driven entrepreneur must walk.

Tom's story, although marked by challenges, imparts a valuable lesson. It emphasizes the need for aspiring innovators to equip themselves not only with scientific acumen but also with an understanding of the broader context in which their ideas will be brought to life. By embracing the harmony between creative inspiration and regulatory diligence, entrepreneurs can overcome obstacles and propel their chemistry-driven products towards market success.

As we reflect on Tom's journey, we're reminded that while chemistry is a powerful driver of innovation, it's also an endeavor that must be underpinned by a solid foundation of practicality and compliance. By weaving creative ingenuity with regulatory mindfulness, entrepreneurs can navigate the challenges that lie ahead and transform chemistry concepts into products that not only captivate markets but also adhere to the highest standards of safety and quality.

4.7.   A Peek into the Future: Emerging Trends

As we stand at the crossroads of chemistry and innovation, it's imperative to cast our gaze toward the horizon and envision the future landscape of chemistry-driven products. The journey from molecules to market is an ever-evolving one, constantly infused with novel techniques and methodologies. Among these burgeoning trends, the advent of computational methods, as expounded upon by Young (2009), emerges as a beacon of innovation.

Computational methods are ushering in a new era of product development, one characterized by virtual experimentation and digital innovation. Imagine a world where chemistry-driven product ideas can be meticulously tested and optimized within the realm of a computer program, long before a single ingredient is physically mixed. This visionary approach promises to revolutionize the trajectory of product development.

These computational methods, akin to digital alchemy, simulate chemical reactions with astounding precision. They leverage the power of algorithms and computational resources to model molecular interactions, predict outcomes, and optimize formulations—all in a virtual realm. This has far-reaching implications, saving valuable time and resources that would have otherwise been spent on laborious trial-and-error experimentation.

This paradigm shift holds the potential to reshape the innovation landscape. It empowers chemists and entrepreneurs to explore a multitude of possibilities in a fraction of the time, accelerating the pace of discovery and streamlining the journey from concept to product. This capability is especially vital in complex industries such as pharmaceuticals, where the design of new drugs hinges on molecular interactions and properties.

As we embrace this emerging trend, we envision a future where the chemistry of conceptualization and the formulation process converge within the digital realm. The artistry of chemistry extends its tendrils into the virtual space, where molecules dance through algorithms and equations metamorphose into simulations. This convergence has the potential to unlock innovative solutions, enhance efficiency, and elevate the transformative power of chemistry-driven products to unprecedented heights.

In essence, the emergence of computational methods signifies a harmonious fusion of human ingenuity and technological advancement. It augments our ability to turn chemical concepts into tangible marketable products by providing a virtual canvas on which innovation can be painted, assessed, and refined. As we venture into this digital age of chemistry-driven innovation, we're reminded that the journey from beakers to billions is not just a physical one—it's also a digital voyage that promises to redefine how chemistry is harnessed to turn ideas into gold.

4.7.1.   Case Studies: Crafting Success Step by Step

Venturing deeper into the realm of chemistry-driven product development, let's delve into a compelling case study—a narrative that unveils the intricate steps of transforming chemistry principles into tangible marketable products. Our spotlight falls on a start-up that embraced green chemistry principles to conceive a revolutionary household cleaning product.

This case study, as revealed by Grieger and Leontyev (2021), invites us into a world where chemistry meets innovation. At the heart of their approach lies the use of student-generated infographics, serving as bridges between complex chemical concepts and accessible understanding. These infographics fostered comprehension among students, transforming theory into a canvas for innovation.

This particular journey of innovation was marked by the meticulous navigation of each step, each milestone. Just as an architect meticulously plans a structure, the start-up meticulously charted a roadmap, bridging green chemistry ideals with consumer utility. It's a process that encapsulates the essence of chemistry's transformational potential.

From inception to formulation, each phase of this journey is like a step in a choreographed dance. The chemistry of conceptualization, grounded in sustainability and safety, was meticulously crafted into actionable plans. The formulation process took shape through a symphony of molecular interactions, harnessing the potency of green chemistry to yield an effective, eco-friendly cleaning solution.

The journey wasn't just a linear trajectory; it was a mosaic of moments that showcased how chemistry-driven product development is a dynamic interplay of creativity, science, and strategy. The interweaving threads of chemistry literacy, consumer insights, and sustainable ideals culminated in a final product that resonated with the market.

This case study brings the journey to life by breaking it down into digestible steps, akin to a recipe that's both scientific and creative. It's a roadmap that offers insights into the choices, decisions, and considerations that propel chemistry concepts toward marketable gold. As we explore this case study, we're invited to witness the fusion of theory and practice, chemistry and market dynamics, innovation and impact.

Ultimately, this case study underscores that the journey from chemistry principles to marketable products is one that requires not only scientific prowess but also strategic acumen. It is a journey that involves translating theoretical knowledge into actionable steps, leveraging green chemistry ideals to craft solutions that resonate with both consumers and the environment.

As we immerse ourselves in this case study, we recognize that the journey from molecules to market is a tapestry woven with intention, strategy, and innovation. It is a journey that unites the realms of chemistry and entrepreneurship, and as we learn from the steps taken by this start-up, we're armed with insights that can inspire our own ventures into turning chemistry into marketable gold.

4.8.   Practical Tips: Forging Your Own Path

As you set foot on the path of your own chemistry-driven product journey, it's essential to equip yourself with practical wisdom—lessons garnered from the experiences of pioneers who have journeyed before you. These insights, drawn from the well of research and real-world stories, can serve as guiding beacons as you navigate the exciting and challenging terrain of turning chemistry concepts into marketable gold.

1. **Innovate with Purpose:** Your chemistry-driven products should be more than mere innovations; they should be solutions that address real problems or enrich lives. As you embark on your journey, reflect on the stories of entrepreneurs like Jane, who turned scientific insights into transformative skincare products. Just as Jane's product rejuvenated skin, your innovation should rejuvenate industries, communities, or even the planet itself.

2. **Collaborate Widely:** Chemistry is a multidisciplinary endeavor, intersecting with diverse fields. Collaboration isn't just beneficial; it's essential. Engage with experts from various domains to broaden your horizons and infuse your chemistry-driven products with a holistic perspective. The case study presented earlier, which showcased the fusion of green chemistry with consumer needs, stands as a testament to the power of interdisciplinary collaboration.

3. **Safety First:** Amid the excitement of innovation, it's paramount to keep safety at the forefront. Just as Tom's journey emphasized the significance of understanding regulatory hurdles, your product development process must prioritize safety at every stage. The insights from "Polymer Properties and Characterization" by Brady et al. (2017) underline the importance of comprehending material behavior, ensuring that your products not only perform optimally but are also safe for consumers and the environment.

4. **Regulations Matter:** Regulatory compliance is a crucial pillar of success in the chemistry-driven product landscape. The cautionary tale of Tom underscores the risks associated with ignoring regulations. Navigating regulations isn't merely a legal obligation; it's a strategic imperative. The journey from formulation to market is laden with regulatory checkpoints that demand attention and diligence.

As you internalize these practical tips, remember that they are gleaned from the wisdom of those who have journeyed before you. They encapsulate the essence of chemistry-driven product development—a blend of innovation, collaboration, safety, and regulatory mindfulness. These tips are your compass, guiding you toward a journey marked by impact, success, and transformation.

In the pages of this chapter, you've delved into the realms of chemistry's potential, exploring its journey from concepts to products, encountering stories of triumphs and challenges, and envisioning the future of chemistry-driven innovation. Now, armed with insights, practical advice, and the courage to innovate, it's your turn to embark on your own journey of transforming chemistry into marketable gold. The world eagerly awaits the products you'll create, the lives you'll enrich, and the impact you'll make. As you forge your path, remember that the chemistry of possibilities is boundless, and with purpose and determination, you can turn your ideas into reality, and your chemistry concepts into products that shape the world.

4.9.   Reflection and Action: Your Turn

Now, as you stand at the crossroads of inspiration and action, it's time to take a moment to reflect on your own chemistry knowledge and the potential it holds. Just as we've journeyed through the pages of this chapter, consider the equations and concepts that hold within them the seeds of innovation. Recall the insights shared by Cigdemoglu and Geban (2015), where context-based approaches elevate chemical literacy by forging connections between theory and real-world applications.

As you ponder your chemistry education, ask yourself: Which concepts ignite your passion? Which equations stir your curiosity? These are the building blocks that could lead to groundbreaking products. Much like Jane, who harnessed her understanding of natural compounds to create a skincare revolution, you too possess the power to turn your knowledge into tangible solutions.

But don't stop there. Consider the problems that tug at your heartstrings, the challenges you're determined to address. Think about the global issues that demand innovative solutions—sustainability, healthcare, energy, and more. How can chemistry play a role in unraveling these complex challenges? Dive into the insights from "Chemistry & Chemical Reactivity" by Kotz et al. (2014), where the intricate dance of reactivity is unveiled, and apply that dance to the real-world stage of innovation.

As you reflect, remember that every transformative journey begins with a single step, an idea, a spark of curiosity. Just as the entrepreneurs we've encountered embraced their passions and insights, it's your turn to seize the reins of innovation. Your chemistry knowledge is a potent tool—an alchemical recipe for turning ideas into reality.

So, take action. Start by identifying those equations, concepts, and problems that resonate deeply with you. Let your reflections fuel your imagination, igniting the creative fire within. And as you venture forth, remember the lessons from the start-ups, pioneers, and experts we've explored together. Let their stories guide you as you step onto the path of turning chemistry into marketable gold. Your journey is unique, but the potential for impact is limitless. It's your turn to shape the future with your chemistry-driven innovations.

4.10. Further Reading and Exploration

As you embark on your journey of turning chemistry into marketable gold, your quest for knowledge and inspiration can be further enriched through these recommended resources:

1. **"Chemistry & Chemical Reactivity" by Kotz et al. (2014):** This comprehensive guide provides an in-depth exploration of chemical reactivity—a foundational concept that underpins the transformative potential of chemistry-driven products. Delve into the intricacies of molecular interactions, reactions, and the dynamic world of chemicals in motion.

2. **"Computational Drug Design" by Young (2009):** Dive into the realm of computational methods, a field that's reshaping the landscape of product design and innovation. This resource provides insights into how computational approaches can accelerate the process of turning ideas into tangible prototypes, all within the digital realm.

3. **"Developing Solid Oral Dosage Forms" by Brady et al. (2017):** Explore the world of polymer properties, a crucial domain in pharmaceutical formulations. This resource offers a comprehensive understanding of how material science intersects with product design, guiding you through the intricate dance of selecting materials for successful product development.

By immersing yourself in these resources, you'll gain a deeper understanding of the nuances that underpin successful chemistry-driven product innovation. These texts aren't just books; they're lanterns that illuminate the path ahead, providing insights, strategies, and perspectives that can empower you on your journey. As you explore these recommended readings, remember that the pursuit of knowledge is a journey of its own—one that complements your quest to transform chemistry concepts into impactful products.

Let these resources be your companions as you shape your ideas, refine your strategies, and navigate the challenges and triumphs that lie ahead. Just as chemistry is a dynamic field, your journey will be dynamic too, enriched by the insights of experts, the wisdom of pioneers, and the creative spark that resides within you. As you read, reflect, and explore, you'll be equipping yourself with a toolkit that's not just theoretical—it's practical, actionable, and poised to catalyze your own chemistry-driven success story.

4.11. Conclusion: Turning Chemistry into Gold

In drawing the curtains on this chapter, we reflect on a journey that encapsulates the spirit of transformation, innovation, and the boundless possibilities that chemistry holds. From the humble beakers of laboratories to the gleaming halls of market success, the journey from chemistry concepts to marketable products is a voyage that weaves together creativity, science, and the indomitable human spirit.

As we've journeyed through the pages of this chapter, one message resounds with clarity: every chemistry concept, every equation, every insight has the potential to shape products that not only fulfill consumer needs but also leave an indelible mark on industries and societies. The lessons from real-life entrepreneurs, insights from scientific research, and the wisdom of experts all converge to illuminate a truth— your chemistry knowledge is a blueprint for transformation.

So, step onto this path with purpose and enthusiasm. Embrace the challenges, for they are the crucible that forges innovation. Celebrate the triumphs, for they are the milestones that validate your efforts. Just as Jane turned skincare insights into marketable gold and Tom navigated hurdles to shape his vision, you too have the power to infuse your chemistry concepts with life, purpose, and impact.

Your ideas have the potential to become the next big thing, bridging the chasm between scientific theory and consumer delight. As you embark on this adventure, remember that the journey from molecules to market is a narrative of persistence and determination. Equipped with the knowledge you've gathered, the curiosity that fuels your exploration, and the determination that propels you forward, you are poised to turn your chemistry concepts into marketable gold.

In the journey that lies ahead, keep the stories of innovation, the insights from experts, and the reflections on practical tips close to your heart. Remember that the path you tread is unique, but you're not alone. The chemistry of possibilities is boundless, and with each step, you contribute to the legacy of turning ideas into reality, concepts into products, and dreams into market success.

So, let the world witness the alchemy that transpires as you transform chemistry into gold. The world is waiting to be impacted by your creations, your ideas, and your vision. As you step forward, know that you hold the power to shape industries, transform lives, and rewrite the narrative of chemistry's potential. The journey is yours to claim, and with it, the opportunity to turn your chemistry concepts into marketable gold.

Are you ready to brew your own innovation? The world is waiting.

4.12. References

[1] Brady, J., Dürig, T., Lee, P. I., & Li, J. X. (2017). Polymer properties and characterization. In *Developing solid oral dosage forms* (pp. 181-223). Academic Press. https://doi.org/10.1016/B978-0-12-802447-8.00007-8

[2] Cigdemoglu, C., & Geban, O. (2015). Improving students' chemical literacy levels on thermochemical and thermodynamics concepts through a context-based approach. *Chemistry Education Research and Practice, 16*(2), 302-317. https://doi.org/10.1039/C5RP00007F

[3] Fagnani, D. E., Hall, A. O., Zurcher, D. M., Sekoni, K. N., Barbu, B. N., & McNeil, A. J. (2020). Short Course on Sustainable Polymers for High School Students. *Journal of Chemical Education, 97*(8), 2160-2168. https://doi.org/10.1021/acs.jchemed.0c00507

[4] Grieger, K., & Leontyev, A. (2021). Student-generated infographics for learning green chemistry and developing professional skills. *Journal of Chemical Education, 98*(9), 2881-2891. https://doi.org/10.1021/acs.jchemed.1c00446

[5] Kotz, J. C., Treichel, P. M., Townsend, J., & Treichel, D. (2014). *Chemistry & chemical reactivity*. Cengage Learning.

[6] Nahar, L., & Sarker, S. D. (2019). *Chemistry for pharmacy students: general, organic and natural product chemistry*. John Wiley & Sons.

[7] Silverman, R. B., & Holladay, M. W. (2014). *The organic chemistry of drug design and drug action*. Academic press.

[8] Wang, L., Guo, X., Chen, J., Zhen, Z., Cao, B., Wan, W., ... & Ge, Z. (2022). Key considerations on the development of biodegradable biomaterials for clinical translation of medical devices: With cartilage repair products as an example. *Bioactive materials, 9*, 332-342. https://doi.org/10.1016/j.bioactmat.2021.07.031

[9] Young, D. C. (2009). *Computational drug design: a guide for computational and medicinal chemists*. John Wiley & Sons.

5. Safety First: Navigating Regulations

5.1. Introduction

Do you remember the thrill of your first chemistry experiment? The bubbling test tubes, colorful reactions, and the satisfying "pop" when hydrogen gas ignited? That classroom excitement laid the foundation for what chemistry can achieve beyond the walls of academia. Chemistry, as Diaz et al. (2021) emphasize, holds the key to sustainable product development, a concept now firmly rooted in the modern market landscape. From pharmaceutical nanomedicines to digital technologies, chemistry-driven innovations are reshaping industries and influencing consumer preferences.

In this chapter, we delve into the vital journey of turning chemistry concepts into marketable products while navigating the intricate landscape of safety regulations. The importance of this journey is underscored by Cordaillat-Simmons et al. (2020), who highlight the significance of a well-defined regulatory framework for live biotherapeutic products. This framework acts as a safeguard, ensuring that scientific breakthroughs not only dazzle in laboratories but also meet the rigorous standards of safety and compliance demanded by the market.

As Bradford (2020) astutely notes, addressing regulatory and safety considerations in product development is a critical aspect of the modern business environment. The regulatory landscape, often influenced by global trends and agreements, shapes the competitive arena. The chemistry-to-market journey is no longer just about innovation; it's about understanding the intricate dance between scientific creativity and the demands of a regulatory-driven market. Our exploration aims to shed light on this dance and equip you with the insights and tools to navigate it successfully.

Sustainability, a term that once lingered on the fringes, has taken center stage in product development. Diaz et al. (2021) present the implications of sustainable product development in a circular economy. This transition from linear to circular thinking echoes the journey you're about to embark on. It's a journey that encapsulates the transformation of chemistry from a curious classroom endeavor to a force that shapes markets, policies, and the very future of our world.

Through the chapters that follow, we will explore the narratives of pioneers who have translated chemistry concepts into successful marketable products. We will gain wisdom from experts who've navigated the terrain of regulations and innovation. We will analyze real-world examples that showcase the intersection of compliance and marketability. Together, we'll journey from the classroom to the boardroom, armed with the knowledge, inspiration, and practical tools to turn chemistry into marketable gold.

5.2.   Regulatory Safeguards: The Cornerstone of Success

Imagine creating a groundbreaking chemical innovation only to find your path to market blocked by regulatory hurdles. Regulatory frameworks, often referred to as the unsung heroes of innovation, play a pivotal role in shaping the trajectory of scientific advancements. These frameworks are meticulously designed to ensure not only the commercial viability of products but also their alignment with product safety, environmental protection, and public health. The journey from discovery to marketability is indeed a complex one, where the interplay between scientific ingenuity and regulatory compliance is central.

Cordaillat-Simmons et al. (2020) shed light on the paramount significance of a defined regulatory framework in the context of live biotherapeutic products. Their study underscores that adherence to safety protocols and rigorous regulatory standards isn't merely a matter of procedural compliance; rather, it directly impacts market confidence. In the realm of live biotherapeutic products, where the stakes are particularly high due to their potential impact on human health, regulatory adherence becomes a cornerstone of trust and market success.

In the interconnected world of today's global markets, the Brussels Effect, as articulated by Bradford (2020), is an undeniable testament to the far-reaching influence of regulations. The European Union's regulatory standards often serve as a benchmark for global norms, a phenomenon with profound implications for businesses across industries. As we delve into the intricate landscape of product development, this effect serves as a powerful reminder that regulatory considerations are not limited by geographic boundaries; they resonate globally.

Indeed, the process of turning chemistry concepts into marketable products extends beyond scientific innovation. It encompasses the meticulous alignment of every facet of product development, from chemical composition to manufacturing processes, with stringent regulatory mandates. This alignment is what paves the way for market access, enhancing not only the product's viability but also its legitimacy in the eyes of consumers. The chemistry-to-market journey is thus a dance between innovation and compliance, a harmony that ensures both the success of the product and the safety of its users.

5.3. Marketability through Sustainability

Sustainability is no longer a mere buzzword; it has transformed into an imperative that shapes modern product development, particularly in the context of a circular economy. The works of Diaz et al. (2021) shed light on the multifaceted implications of sustainable product development, delving into the intricate considerations of product lifecycles, the various stakeholders involved, and the indispensable role of decision-making support. This aligns seamlessly with the trajectory of our journey, as we explore the transformation of chemistry concepts into marketable products.

Incorporating sustainability into chemical products transcends the realm of eco-consciousness; it emerges as a strategic driver for enhancing both marketability and social responsibility. Diaz et al. (2021) emphasize that modern consumers are not merely looking for products; they're seeking products that align with their values and contribute positively to the world. This shifting consumer landscape underscores that the journey from chemistry to marketability is no longer solely about creating a viable product. Instead, it involves crafting a legacy that resonates across generations, benefitting both present and future societies.

The chemistry-to-market journey is thus an embodiment of sustainable principles. It's about envisioning a product's lifecycle from its inception to its eventual retirement, and ensuring that every phase adheres to sustainability standards. This approach not only amplifies the marketability of the product by appealing to conscious consumers but also elevates the brand's reputation as a responsible corporate citizen. As we traverse through this chapter, the fusion of chemistry and sustainability becomes a beacon that guides us toward not just turning chemistry into gold, but forging a path toward lasting prosperity.

Entrepreneurs embarking on the transformative journey from chemistry concepts to marketable products find themselves walking a tightrope of innovation and compliance. This delicate balancing act is a defining challenge in the chemistry-to-market process, where striking the right equilibrium can determine the success or failure of a venture.

The intricacies of this balancing act are illuminated through the lens of environmental regulations, a driving force that intersects with innovation. Shao et al. (2020) present a compelling argument that environmental regulations, contrary to being roadblocks, can actually act as catalysts for innovation. The constraints posed by these regulations nudge businesses to explore innovative, environmentally friendly alternatives. In this dynamic, the chemistry-to-market journey becomes a space for inventive problem-solving, as entrepreneurs leverage their scientific acumen to find compliant solutions that not only meet regulatory demands but also resonate with consumer demands for eco-consciousness.

However, the dance between innovation and regulation extends beyond mere product development. Trevlopoulos et al. (2021) delve into the intricate interplay between environmental regulations and business performance. Their study uncovers a more holistic impact of these regulations, revealing that their influence reverberates throughout an organization's operations and strategic decisions. This broader perspective underscores that the chemistry-to-market journey isn't just about singular innovations; it's about orchestrating an organizational symphony where compliance and innovation harmonize to drive performance on multiple fronts.

In the context of the chemistry-to-market journey, innovation becomes the engine that propels a product forward, while compliance ensures that the journey is sustainable and fruitful. This intricate dance mirrors the challenges and triumphs faced by entrepreneurs navigating through the complexities of regulations, demonstrating that the chemistry-to-market journey is not a linear path, but a dynamic process of adaptation and innovation.

5.5.   Case Studies: Guiding Lights

The journey from chemistry concepts to marketable products is beautifully exemplified by real-life stories of pioneers who have successfully navigated the intricate terrain of innovation and compliance. These case studies offer us invaluable insights into the challenges, triumphs, and strategic maneuvers that are an integral part of the chemistry-to-market voyage.

Meet Amanda, a trailblazer who harnessed the power of pharmaceutical nanomedicines to transform her breakthrough into a tangible market reality. Halwani (2022) provides a detailed narrative of Amanda's journey, from the earliest stages of discovery to the final product's market debut. Through Amanda's story, we gain an understanding of the meticulous process involved in navigating regulations. Each step, from research and development to manufacturing and distribution, requires a thorough understanding of compliance protocols. Amanda's journey emphasizes the vital role of regulatory diligence, underscoring that meticulous navigation of regulations isn't just a box to check, but a strategic imperative that can determine the product's ultimate success.

Then there's Robert, a visionary entrepreneur who set out to make his mark in the tech-savvy world. Quach et al. (2022) chronicle Robert's path in the realm of digital technology startups, shedding light on the unique challenges he faced. The case study presents a compelling scenario where Robert's aspirations for market impact encountered the complex landscape of privacy tensions. This narrative underscores the reality that the chemistry-to-market journey is rife with unexpected twists and turns. Robert's story teaches us that innovation is not exempt from societal concerns, and entrepreneurs must adeptly navigate both technological advancements and ethical considerations.

These case studies resonate as guiding lights for aspiring entrepreneurs seeking to turn chemistry concepts into marketable gold. Amanda's journey reminds us that innovation flourishes when grounded in compliance, while Robert's experience underscores the intricate ethical tightrope that must be walked in the world of technology. As we immerse ourselves in these narratives, we're privy to the very essence of the chemistry-to-market voyage—its challenges, its rewards, and its potential to shape industries, businesses, and societies.

5.6.   Expert Insights: Navigational Beacons

Navigating the intricate landscape of turning chemistry concepts into marketable products requires not only the wisdom gained from experience but also the insights of experts who have traversed this path before. These experts serve as invaluable navigational beacons, illuminating the way forward and helping us navigate the complexities of regulations and marketability.

Hoekman and Sabel (2019) contribute a profound perspective by highlighting the role of international regulatory cooperation. In a world characterized by global interconnectedness, their insights resonate deeply with our exploration of the chemistry-to-market journey's global impact. Their work underscores that regulations extend beyond national boundaries, often shaping international norms and standards. As we delve into the intricacies of chemistry-driven marketability, the wisdom of Hoekman and Sabel reinforces the fact that the journey is not isolated but entwined with the dynamics of the global market.

Furthermore, Bradford (2020) introduces us to the concept of the *Brussels Effect*, which stands as a testament to the remarkable influence of EU regulations on the world stage. Bradford's insights offer a vivid illustration of how regulations and marketability are inherently intertwined. The reach of EU standards across continents reinforces the idea that addressing regulatory and safety considerations in product development isn't just a local concern; it's a fundamental aspect of successful global market penetration.

These expert insights collectively serve as guiding stars in our journey. The perspectives of Hoekman and Sabel remind us of the significance of regulatory alignment in a borderless world, while Bradford's observations underscore the global ripple effects of regulatory decisions. As we move forward, we draw upon the wisdom of these experts to navigate the intricate dance between innovation and compliance that defines the chemistry-to-market voyage.

5.7.   Your Journey: A Call to Action

As you embark on the journey through the pages of this chapter, you're not just a reader; you're an explorer poised to uncover the secrets of transforming chemistry concepts into marketable gold. Allow the tales of innovation, regulation, and marketability to serve as a catalyst for your own aspirations and dreams. Let these narratives ignite your imagination, inspiring you to consider the potential of your own chemistry-driven brainchild and its transformation into a remarkable, marketable gem.

Take a moment to reflect on the real-world stories that unfold within these pages. The journey of Amanda, who navigated the intricacies of regulatory compliance in the realm of pharmaceutical nanomedicines, or the challenges that Robert encountered as he balanced innovation and ethical considerations in the tech world, each story carries valuable lessons. These lessons are not confined to the words on these pages; they are stepping stones that can guide you as you navigate your own unique chemistry-to-market journey.

Expert insights, such as those offered by Hoekman and Sabel (2019) and Bradford (2020), are compass points that can direct your path. Just as Diaz et al. (2021) illuminate the implications of sustainable product development and Cordaillat-Simmons et al. (2020) emphasize the importance of regulatory diligence, you have the opportunity to infuse your journey with scientific brilliance and regulatory diligence.

Remember that the journey from chemistry to marketability is an art—an intricate dance that harmonizes the brilliance of scientific discovery with the strategic orchestration of compliance. Your journey is not just about creating a product; it's about crafting a legacy that impacts markets, industries, and society at large. As you read, reflect, and internalize the insights presented here, you're not merely observing; you're preparing to take your own bold steps toward transforming chemistry into marketable gold.

5.8.   Exploring Further: Your Toolkit

Before you conclude this chapter, consider it not as an endpoint but as a launchpad into a deeper exploration of the world of regulations, innovation, and marketability. To equip you with the tools and knowledge needed to embark on your own journey of transforming chemistry into gold, we offer a curated toolkit of recommended resources, further reading, and insightful tools.

Delve into the complexities of regulatory landscapes by immersing yourself in the works of Cordaillat-Simmons et al. (2020), Shao et al. (2020), and Trevlopoulos et al. (2021). These studies provide a comprehensive understanding of how regulatory frameworks influence innovation, environmental considerations, and overall business performance.

For those interested in understanding the global impact of regulations, Hoekman and Sabel (2019) shed light on international regulatory cooperation, while Bradford's (2020) exploration of the *Brussels Effect* offers a unique perspective on the worldwide influence of regulatory standards.

To deepen your understanding of sustainability's role in marketability, Diaz et al. (2021) provide insights into sustainable product development in a circular economy. This work can inspire you to not only create innovative products but also align them with the values and preferences of environmentally conscious consumers.

For those seeking a roadmap on navigating regulations and innovation, the case studies of Amanda and Robert provide real-world examples. Halwani (2022) unveils Amanda's journey through the pharmaceutical nanomedicines landscape, emphasizing regulatory navigation, while Quach et al. (2022) introduces us to Robert's world of digital technology startups, marked by privacy concerns and market impact considerations.

As you delve into these resources, you'll amass the knowledge, perspectives, and strategic insights needed to transform your chemistry-driven ideas into marketable gold. Remember, this toolkit is not just a collection of information; it's a catalyst for your own exploration, a stepping stone toward shaping your chemistry-to-market journey.

5.9. Conclusion: Transform Chemistry into Gold

Dear reader, as you conclude this chapter, you are not merely concluding a chapter, but opening the door to a transformative adventure. Armed with a treasure trove of insights, real-world anecdotes, and a heightened understanding of the chemistry-to-market journey, you stand at the cusp of a remarkable opportunity.

Allow the sparks of innovation, kindled by pioneers like Amanda and Robert, to light your path. Draw inspiration from the wisdom of regulatory compliance, intricately woven into every stage of the journey. Just as Cordaillat-Simmons et al. (2020) highlight the importance of regulatory frameworks for market confidence, and Diaz et al. (2021) underscore the role of sustainability in marketability, you are equipped to leverage this dual foundation of innovation and compliance.

Your journey from chemistry concepts to marketable gold is a culmination of scientific brilliance, regulatory diligence, and strategic acumen. The intricacies of regulations, as discussed by experts like Hoekman and Sabel (2019) and Bradford (2020), are not roadblocks, but navigational stars guiding you toward success. The challenges and triumphs illuminated through case studies illustrate that your journey will be marked by strategic maneuvers, ethical considerations, and creative problem-solving, just like Amanda and Robert.

As you step beyond these pages, remember that the journey ahead is uniquely yours. Your chemistry-driven brainchild carries the potential to transform industries, revolutionize markets, and leave an indelible mark on society. Let the amalgamation of innovation and compliance be your guiding force. The world eagerly awaits your alchemical touch, your ability to turn chemistry into gold.

5.10. References

[1]   Bradford, A. (2020). *The Brussels effect: How the European Union rules the world.* Oxford University Press, USA.

[2]   Cordaillat-Simmons, M., Rouanet, A., & Pot, B. (2020). Live biotherapeutic products: the importance of a defined regulatory framework. *Experimental &*

molecular medicine, *52*(9), 1397-1406. https://www.nature.com/articles/s12276-020-0437-6

[3]   Diaz, A., Schöggl, J. P., Reyes, T., & Baumgartner, R. J. (2021). Sustainable product development in a circular economy: Implications for products, actors, decision-making support and lifecycle information management. *Sustainable Production and Consumption*, *26*, 1031-1045. https://doi.org/10.1016/j.spc.2020.12.044

[4]   Halwani, A. A. (2022). Development of pharmaceutical nanomedicines: from the bench to the market. *Pharmaceutics*, *14*(1), 106. https://doi.org/10.3390/pharmaceutics14010106

[5]   Hoekman, B., & Sabel, C. (2019). Open plurilateral agreements, international regulatory cooperation and the WTO. *Global Policy*, *10*(3), 297-312. https://doi.org/10.1111/1758-5899.12694

[6]   Quach, S., Thaichon, P., Martin, K. D., Weaven, S., & Palmatier, R. W. (2022). Digital technologies: tensions in privacy and data. *Journal of the Academy of Marketing Science*, *50*(6), 1299-1323. https://doi.org/10.1007/s11747-022-00845-y

[7]   Shao, S., Hu, Z., Cao, J., Yang, L., & Guan, D. (2020). Environmental regulation and enterprise innovation: a review. *Business strategy and the environment*, *29*(3), 1465-1478. https://doi.org/10.1002/bse.2446

[8]   Strine Jr, L. E., Smith, K. M., & Steel, R. S. (2020). Caremark and ESG, Perfect Together: A Practical Approach to Implementing an Integrated, Efficient, and Effective Caremark and EESG Strategy. *Iowa L. Rev.*, *106*, 1885. https://heinonline.org/HOL/LandingPage?handle=hein.journals/ilr106&div=46&id=&page=

[9]   Trevlopoulos, N. S., Tsalis, T. A., Evangelinos, K. I., Tsagarakis, K. P., Vatalis, K. I., & Nikolaou, I. E. (2021). The influence of environmental regulations on business innovation, intellectual capital, environmental and economic performance. *Environment Systems and Decisions*, *41*, 163-178. https://doi.org/10.1007/s10669-021-09802-6

6. Scaling Dreams: From Lab to Production

6.1. Introduction

In the bustling world of chemistry, where ideas germinate within the confines of laboratories, the journey from theoretical concepts to tangible marketable products is a symphony of creativity, collaboration, and calculated steps. This chapter takes you on a transformative voyage, revealing the intricate process of scaling up production from the cozy realm of experimentation to the grand theater of industry. The alchemical transformation of chemistry concepts into profitable marketable products has captured the imagination of both scientists and entrepreneurs alike.

As we traverse this landscape, we will explore the dynamic partnership between chemists, engineers, and manufacturers to ensure the viability of innovations. This convergence of expertise is well-documented in the literature. Cong and Zhang (2022) underscore the pivotal role of engineers in translating microfluidic devices from laboratory prototypes to industrial-scale production. Their work emphasizes the necessity of collaboration in overcoming the challenges of upscaling complex chemical processes. Similarly, Rogers and Jensen (2019) highlight how continuous manufacturing, a result of the synergy between chemists and engineers, embodies the promises of Green Chemistry. This partnership not only drives efficiency but also aligns with modern trends of sustainable production.

This narrative will be enriched by inspiring stories of entrepreneurs who defied odds to turn their dreams into lucrative marketable gold. Real-life anecdotes provide a tangible connection to the otherwise intricate journey of scaling up. The achievements of these entrepreneurs are a testament to the alchemical fusion of scientific curiosity and commercial acumen. Drawing inspiration from the work of Smanski et al. (2022), who outline the journey from microbial cultures to bioproduct manufacturing processes, we witness the transformation of laboratory innovations into economically viable entities. These stories of resilience and innovation motivate aspiring chemists and entrepreneurs to embark on their own transformative journeys.

From formula to factory, let's embark on a journey that unfolds the essence of turning chemistry into a tangible reality. The path from laboratory innovation to industrial realization is a narrative shared by the pioneers in the field, as captured in the references presented. Through a seamless blend of creative storytelling and meticulous research, this chapter aims to be a beacon for those seeking to navigate the intricate landscape of turning chemistry into marketable gold. As we proceed, we'll dive deeper into the various aspects of this journey, exploring not only the scientific intricacies but also the strategic decisions, challenges, and triumphs that accompany this remarkable transformation.

6.2. A Symphony of Collaboration: Chemists and Engineers Unite

The story begins in the laboratory, where chemists craft their visions using beakers and vials. But to breathe life into these creations, a harmonious collaboration with engineers is essential. As elegantly illustrated by Cong and Zhang (2022), translating microfluidic devices from laboratory prototypes to scale-up production is akin to a dance between chemistry and engineering. Engineers bring their specialized expertise in designing processes that not only flourish in the controlled laboratory environment but can also be meticulously replicated on an industrial scale.

The significance of this dynamic partnership cannot be overstated. Cong and Zhang's study (2022) delves into the complexities of microfluidic devices, which are intricate systems that require precision and reliability for successful scaling. Engineers possess the skill set to analyze, optimize, and adapt these lab-scale phenomena into large-scale, real-world applications. Their intricate understanding of fluid dynamics, materials science, and manufacturing processes serves as the bridge between the realm of scientific curiosity and the practical realm of manufacturability.

Rogers and Jensen (2019) echo this sentiment in the context of continuous manufacturing, emphasizing the interplay between chemistry and engineering. This symbiotic relationship is pivotal, as chemists' discoveries are like raw gemstones, while engineers craft them into refined jewels ready for the market. The iterative feedback loop between these disciplines ensures that the scientific underpinnings are not lost in translation during the transition from bench to production floor.

The success stories of chemistry-driven products often owe their triumphs to this partnership. The examples set by Cong and Zhang (2022) and Rogers and Jensen (2019) underline the collaborative spirit that propels groundbreaking ideas into the marketplace. This union of minds, encompassing creativity and technical prowess, is the cornerstone of turning chemistry concepts into tangible reality. As we proceed in our exploration, this chapter will continue to shed light on the intricate details of this collaboration, illustrating how it evolves at each stage of the journey from laboratory innovation to industrial marvel.

6.3. Continuous Manufacturing: The Green Chemistry Revolution

Enter the world of continuous manufacturing, a revolution that marries chemistry with environmental sustainability. As illuminated by Rogers and Jensen (2019), this paradigm shift brings forth a transformation in the way chemistry-driven products are produced. The principles of Green Chemistry, which focus on minimizing the environmental impact of chemical processes, are seamlessly integrated into the scaling process.

The conventional batch processes, often associated with resource-intensive practices and wastage, are reimagined through continuous operations. This shift not only enhances efficiency but also significantly reduces waste generation. Rogers and Jensen's research (2019) underscores the intricate connection between these principles and the scaling of production. The reduction of waste aligns with eco-conscious trends and echoes the global call for sustainable practices across industries.

The impact of this transformation stretches far beyond the laboratory walls. By embracing the principles of Green Chemistry, the chemistry-driven products become agents of change in the quest for a greener future. The work of Rogers and Jensen (2019) stands as a testament to how scientific innovation can harmonize with environmental stewardship. As we journey through the chapters ahead, this environmental consciousness will continue to weave its way into the narrative, highlighting the potential of chemistry not just as a creator of products, but also as a catalyst for positive ecological transformations.

6.4. Circular Production: Challenges and Triumphs

The journey doesn't stop at efficiency; circularity takes the stage. As illuminated by Despeisse et al. (2021), this chapter unveils the remarkable potential of circular and efficient production systems. Here, chemistry enters into a dynamic tango with sustainability, forging a partnership that transcends conventional industrial practices.

Despeisse et al.'s research (2021) provides a comprehensive exploration of real-world industrial cases where circularity is achieved. This isn't just a theoretical concept; it's a strategic approach to production that redefines the role of chemistry in the marketplace. The paradigm shift involves reimagining waste as a resource and embracing recycling as a cornerstone of production. This transition is pivotal in the journey from lab-scale experimentation to industry-scale production.

Circular production resonates deeply with the ethos of sustainability, weaving principles of environmental stewardship into the fabric of chemistry-driven products. As Despeisse et al. (2021) illustrate, this transformation isn't without its challenges. Overcoming obstacles and implementing circular systems requires ingenuity and collaboration among various stakeholders. Yet, the rewards are substantial, as circular production heralds a new era where chemistry-driven products not only serve as commodities but also as ambassadors of sustainability.

The narrative will continue to explore these facets, delving into the stories of those who have successfully navigated the challenges of circular production. The chapters ahead will highlight how circularity intertwines with chemistry and amplifies the impact of products, underscoring their potential to reshape industries while simultaneously fostering a more sustainable future.

6.5. Bioindustrial Manufacturing: From Microbes to Marketable Gold

From the microscale to the macroscale, bioindustrial manufacturing unveils the art of harnessing living organisms for mass production. As illustrated by Smanski et al. (2022), this chapter delves into the remarkable journey of converting microbial cultures into marketable bioproducts. This transformation is not just a scientific feat; it's a testament to the boundless possibilities that chemistry offers when combined with the power of biology.

Central to this journey is the introduction of Bioindustrial Manufacturing Readiness Levels (BioMRLs), a shared framework presented by Smanski et al. (2022). This framework serves as a compass, guiding the transition of biotechnological concepts from the confines of the laboratory to scalable industrial practices. This structured approach ensures that the path from the laboratory to the market is well-defined, minimizing uncertainties and maximizing the potential for successful commercialization.

The evolution from a single microbial culture to a bioproduct that shapes markets is a remarkable showcase of the potential that chemistry-driven innovations hold. Smanski et al. (2022) emphasize the strategic interplay of science, engineering, and entrepreneurship that drives this journey. This chapter will further explore the intricacies of this process, unveiling the stories of those who have navigated this path successfully. As we journey through the case studies and practical insights ahead, the transformation of microbial concepts into tangible marketable gold will emerge as a shining example of chemistry's power to reshape industries and societies.

6.6.   Navigating the Pharmaceutical Landscape

Chemistry-driven products span diverse sectors, and among them, pharmaceuticals stand as a cornerstone. Szkodny and Lee (2022) lead us on a comprehensive journey through the historical perspectives and future directions of biopharmaceutical manufacturing. This chapter unveils the intricacies of translating chemical discoveries into lifesaving drugs—a process that underscores the profound impact chemistry has on human health.

The pharmaceutical landscape is an arena where chemistry's potential truly shines. Szkodny and Lee's exploration (2022) delves into the historical evolution of biopharmaceutical manufacturing, revealing how chemical innovation has paved the way for groundbreaking treatments. This historical context is essential for understanding the trajectory of this critical industry, where the synthesis of molecules meets the needs of patients and healthcare systems alike.

The path from bench to bedside is paved with challenges and triumphs, as Szkodny and Lee (2022) illuminate. The translation of a chemical compound into a pharmaceutical product is a journey that demands scientific rigor, regulatory compliance, and ethical considerations. The quest for safety, efficacy, and accessibility underscores the responsibility that accompanies the development of chemistry-driven products in the pharmaceutical domain.

As we venture through this chapter and the chapters beyond, the narratives of biopharmaceutical manufacturing will serve as a poignant reminder of the human dimension of chemistry. The contributions of chemists to healthcare are not just technical feats but vital components of a broader ecosystem that touches lives and shapes the future of medicine.

6.7. Emerging Reaction Technologies: Pioneering the Future

As we journey towards the future, Cohen et al. (2023) illuminate a fascinating landscape of emerging reaction technologies in pharmaceutical development. The marriage of electrochemistry, photochemistry, and biocatalysis doesn't just push the boundaries of chemistry-driven products; it redraws the limits of what was once thought possible.

Cohen et al.'s insights (2023) underscore the transformative potential of innovative techniques that are redefining the pharmaceutical landscape. Electrochemistry, for instance, offers new avenues for selective reactions that were previously challenging or impossible to achieve using conventional methods. Photochemistry harnesses the power of light to drive chemical transformations, while biocatalysis leverages the exquisite specificity of biological catalysts to create complex molecules with precision.

The fusion of these techniques lays the foundation for products that not long ago were merely the stuff of dreams. The boundaries between imagination and reality are becoming increasingly porous as chemistry-driven products venture into realms that were once reserved for science fiction. This chapter, along with the ones that follow, will illuminate the frontiers of chemistry's potential, inviting you to explore how these emerging technologies can shape the trajectory of your own journey.

6.8. Process Intensification: Efficiency as the North Star

Efficiency reigns supreme in the world of chemistry-driven products. As expounded by Müller et al. (2022), process intensification is the guiding principle that propels the biopharma industry forward. It's not merely a goal; it's a way of life that underpins the journey from laboratory curiosity to industrial titan.

Müller et al.'s investigation (2022) into process intensification offers a profound insight into the biopharma industry's mindset. Efficiency isn't a one-time endeavor but an ongoing commitment that spans the spectrum from development to full-scale production. Synergistic approaches are the currency of this efficiency-driven culture—where every step, every reaction, and every resource is optimized to the highest degree.

This relentless pursuit of efficiency doesn't merely streamline operations; it defines the trajectory of products. The transition from laboratory novelties to industrial powerhouses is fueled by the industry's unwavering dedication to process intensification. It's the secret sauce that allows chemistry-driven products to not just survive but thrive in the real-world marketplace.

The chapters that follow will delve deeper into the strategies and innovations that drive this pursuit of efficiency. As you explore these pages, consider how you can integrate these insights into your own journey, ensuring that every endeavor you undertake is a testament to the power of efficiency in transforming chemistry into marketable gold.

6.9.   Beyond Products: Circular Economy Principles

The journey doesn't conclude with product development; it extends to the broader context of a circular economy. Meath et al. (2022) offer a glimpse into this extended journey by unveiling the infrastructure CoLab—a platform designed to orchestrate an industry-level transition to circular economy principles.

Meath et al.'s exploration (2022) highlights the significance of circular economy principles that extend beyond individual products. The infrastructure CoLab embodies a visionary approach that transcends isolated product lifecycles, embracing a holistic view that considers the long-term impacts of chemistry-driven products. This platform acts as a nexus where industry leaders, researchers, and policymakers convene to chart a course towards a more sustainable future.

Circular economy principles emphasize the interconnectedness of chemistry-driven products with societal and environmental paradigms. The lifecycle of a product is no longer linear but cyclical, where resources are regenerated and waste is minimized. Meath et al.'s insights demonstrate how chemistry-driven products can be catalysts for change that reverberate far beyond their initial creation.

As we explore this chapter and beyond, the circular economy principles will continue to weave through the narrative. They serve as a reminder that the journey of chemistry-driven products doesn't conclude with the creation of marketable innovations. It's a journey that extends to fostering a symbiotic relationship with the environment, society, and the future—a journey that ultimately transforms chemistry into a driving force for positive change.

6.10. The Blueprint of Success: Enzymes and Probiotics

Zooming in on specific products, Speight et al. (2022) take us on a detailed exploration of platforms designed to accelerate the biomanufacturing of enzyme and probiotic animal feed supplements. This case study serves as a microcosm of the larger journey from laboratory concepts to thriving marketable products, offering a close-up view of the strategies and considerations that transform chemistry into reality.

The insights shared by Speight et al. (2022) dissect the journey from discovery to manufacturing, unraveling the intricacies that define the success of such endeavors. This detailed examination unveils the strategies employed to ensure the scalability and commercial viability of enzyme and probiotic products. The case study not only provides a glimpse into the scientific underpinnings but also highlights the practical aspects of navigating regulations, optimizing production processes, and meeting market demands.

The strategies and considerations outlined by Speight et al. (2022) are invaluable resources for aspiring chemists and entrepreneurs. By examining this blueprint of success, readers can glean insights into the challenges faced and overcome in the journey from laboratory to marketplace. This case study serves as a roadmap, offering tangible takeaways that can be applied to diverse chemistry-driven products, enabling the transformation of innovative concepts into thriving, marketable realities.

6.11. Rethinking Construction: Industry 4.0 and Chemistry

Chemistry's impact transcends industries, even reaching the realm of construction. In a striking example, Gomaa et al. (2023) redefine rammed earth construction for the era of Industry 4.0. This case study serves as a vivid illustration of how chemistry wields its transformative power to reshape traditional practices and industries that seem worlds apart.

Gomaa et al.'s exploration (2023) delves into the intersection of chemistry and technology, illuminating how these seemingly disparate disciplines collaborate to revolutionize construction methods. Rammed earth, a time-honored building technique, is reimagined through the lens of Industry 4.0, where automation, data analytics, and advanced materials converge. This convergence not only enhances the efficiency and sustainability of construction but also showcases the pervasive influence of chemistry on diverse sectors.

This case study highlights how chemistry plays a pivotal role in the evolution of construction. Chemistry-driven innovations, whether they involve materials science or process optimization, are catalysts for change that extend beyond laboratory walls. They seep into traditional practices, challenging conventions and paving the way for more efficient, sustainable, and technologically advanced solutions.

As we delve deeper into this chapter and the chapters beyond, keep in mind the far-reaching influence of chemistry. Whether in laboratories or construction sites, chemistry has the power to reshape industries, redefine processes, and create a future where innovation and sustainability are intrinsically intertwined.

6.12.   Your Journey Awaits: From Dreamer to Creator

As our journey nears its conclusion, consider the incredible transformations that chemistry-driven products undergo. From the minute, almost imperceptible reactions that occur in laboratories to the commanding presence these products hold in the market, the journey of chemistry is nothing short of awe-inspiring. The chapters you've explored have been a guided tour through this remarkable voyage.

Reflect on the practical advice, case studies, and insights shared in this chapter. Draw inspiration from the pioneering entrepreneurs who ventured into uncharted territories, turning their ideas into thriving marketable gold. The real-life stories presented in this book resonate as proof that with dedication and determination, chemistry concepts can indeed become impactful realities.

The exercises and prompts scattered throughout the chapters are not mere suggestions; they are your personal guideposts to mapping your own journey from concept to market. Just as Szkodny and Lee (2022) delved into biopharmaceutical manufacturing, or Gomaa et al. (2023) redefined construction, you too can be the architect of your own chemistry-driven product, creating a transformative impact on the world around you.

Remember, turning chemistry into marketable gold requires not just knowledge, but passion, perseverance, and a touch of alchemy. The fusion of creativity and science, of innovation and collaboration, is the crucible that will shape your journey. As you step forward from these pages, let the stories, insights, and practical wisdom of this book serve as your companions on the path from dreamer to creator, and from concept to market. Your journey awaits—forge ahead with the knowledge that chemistry's potential knows no bounds.

As we close this chapter, let's direct our gaze towards the future—an uncharted expanse that holds the promise of new discoveries and transformative innovations. Emerging trends and technologies beckon, and at the forefront of this realm stands chemistry, a beacon of innovation that continues to push the boundaries of what's possible. The chapters you've navigated through have equipped you with the knowledge and inspiration to step confidently into this frontier.

Consider the insights presented by Cohen et al. (2023), who shed light on emerging reaction technologies, or Müller et al. (2022), who delve into process intensification. These glimpses into cutting-edge research and practical applications are just the tip of the iceberg. What groundbreaking concepts will you pioneer? How will your journey intertwine with the chemistry-driven products of tomorrow? The horizon stretches endlessly, and you hold the power to shape it.

The world eagerly awaits the alchemical transformations you will catalyze. The impact of chemistry-driven products isn't confined to laboratories or industrial settings—it reverberates through societies, economies, and ecosystems. The future is shaped by those who dare to dream, innovate, and translate their visions into reality. The references and research-based insights shared in this book serve as your guideposts, offering glimpses of what's possible and fueling your imagination.

As you step forward from this chapter, remember that you're not alone in this journey. You join a legacy of scientists, entrepreneurs, and visionaries who have harnessed the power of chemistry to create products that shape the world. Armed with the knowledge, inspiration, and research-based understanding you've gained, you're poised to chart unknown territories, explore new horizons, and leave an indelible mark on the ever-evolving landscape of chemistry-driven innovation. The journey is yours—embrace it with the courage to imagine, innovate, and transform.

To continue your voyage of turning chemistry into marketable gold, a wealth of knowledge awaits your exploration. Delve deeper into the references mentioned in this chapter to unlock new layers of understanding in the art of scaling up chemistry-driven products. These references are gateways to a world of insights, experiences, and expertise that will empower you on your journey.

Embark on a journey of discovery by immersing yourself in the works of Cong and Zhang (2022), who provide perspectives on translating microfluidic devices to scale-up production, or Rogers and Jensen (2019), who offer insights into the promises of continuous manufacturing in Green Chemistry. These are just a few of the stepping stones that can lead you to a profound grasp of the dynamics that shape the transformation of chemistry concepts into marketable realities.

Equip yourself with tools, techniques, and inspiration by traversing the pages of Smanski et al. (2022) on Bioindustrial Manufacturing Readiness Levels (BioMRLs), or Müller et al. (2022) on process intensification in the biopharma industry. These resources offer blueprints and strategies that can illuminate your path, enabling you to navigate the intricacies of bringing your ideas to life on an industrial scale.

As you dive into these resources, remember that you're joining a community of learners, thinkers, and creators who are shaping the world through their pursuit of chemistry-driven innovations. Each reference is a treasure trove of insights waiting to be uncovered, an opportunity to expand your knowledge and horizons. Your journey is a tapestry woven from the wisdom of those who have come before you, the stories of those who have succeeded, and the collective aspiration to transform chemistry into marketable gold.

6.15.   Conclusion: Embark on Your Alchemical Adventure

As you bid adieu to this chapter, let the wisdom gained resonate within you—the journey from beakers to billions is a mosaic of creativity, collaboration, and unwavering persistence. The pages you've explored have been more than just words; they've been windows into a world where chemistry becomes tangible gold. The stories of entrepreneurs who transformed their ideas into marketable reality are not mere tales—they are blueprints, guideposts for the adventure that lies ahead.

Reflect on the insights shared by Despeisse et al. (2021) on achieving circular and efficient production systems, or the transformative potential of emerging reaction technologies unveiled by Cohen et al. (2023). These references aren't just academic citations; they're keys that unlock doors to possibilities, inspiring you to shape your own journey in the realm of chemistry-driven products.

Let this chapter be the spark that ignites your journey—an adventure that fuses your passion for chemistry with the art of transforming dreams into marketable reality. The path won't always be straightforward; challenges will arise, and uncertainties will test your resolve. But remember, the entrepreneurs who defied odds to turn their visions into gold faced similar trials. Their stories are reminders that with dedication, creativity, and the willingness to collaborate, remarkable feats are achievable.

As you set forth on your alchemical adventure, carry with you the insights, research-based details, and inspiration garnered from this chapter. Keep the images of scaling up production, embracing emerging technologies, and shaping the future of chemistry-driven products firmly in mind. The journey you're embarking upon is one that intertwines your aspirations with the transformative power of chemistry. The world is waiting for your innovations, your solutions, and your contributions. The alchemical adventure awaits—will you rise to the challenge?

6.16. References

[1] Cohen, B., Lehnherr, D., Sezen-Edmonds, M., Forstater, J. H., Frederick, M. O., Deng, L., ... & Diwan, M. (2023). Emerging Reaction Technologies in Pharmaceutical Development: Challenges and Opportunities in Electrochemistry, Photochemistry, and Biocatalysis. *Chemical Engineering Research and Design.* https://doi.org/10.1016/j.cherd.2023.02.050

[2] Cong, H., & Zhang, N. (2022). Perspectives in translating microfluidic devices from laboratory prototyping into scale-up production. *Biomicrofluidics*, *16*(2). https://doi.org/10.1063/5.0079045

[3] Despeisse, M., Chari, A., González Chávez, C. A., Chen, X., Johansson, B., Igelmo Garcia, V., ... & Polukeev, A. (2021, August). Achieving circular and efficient production systems: Emerging challenges from industrial cases. In *IFIP International Conference on Advances in Production Management Systems* (pp. 523-533). Cham: Springer International Publishing. https://doi.org/10.1007/978-3-030-85910-7_55

[4] Gomaa, M., Schade, S., Bao, D. W., & Xie, Y. M. (2023). Rethinking rammed earth construction for industry 4.0: Precedent work, current progress and future prospect. *Journal of Cleaner Production*, 136569. https://doi.org/10.1016/j.jclepro.2023.136569

[5] Meath, C., Karlovšek, J., Navarrete, C., Eales, M., & Hastings, P. (2022). Co-designing a multi-level platform for industry level transition to circular economy principles: A case study of the infrastructure CoLab. *Journal of Cleaner Production*, *347*, 131080. https://doi.org/10.1016/j.jclepro.2022.131080

[6]   Müller, D., Klein, L., Lemke, J., Schulze, M., Kruse, T., Saballus, M., ... & Zijlstra, G. (2022). Process intensification in the biopharma industry: Improving efficiency of protein manufacturing processes from development to production scale using synergistic approaches. *Chemical Engineering and Processing-Process Intensification*, *171*, 108727. https://doi.org/10.1016/j.cep.2021.108727

[7]   Rogers, L., & Jensen, K. F. (2019). Continuous manufacturing–the Green Chemistry promise?. *Green chemistry*, *21*(13), 3481-3498. https://doi.org/10.1039/C9GC00773C

[8]   Smanski, M. J., Aristidou, A., Carruth, R., Erickson, J., Gordon, M., Kedia, S. B., ... & Tomczak, M. (2022). Bioindustrial manufacturing readiness levels (BioMRLs) as a shared framework for measuring and communicating the maturity of bioproduct manufacturing processes. *Journal of Industrial Microbiology and Biotechnology*, *49*(5), kuac022. https://doi.org/10.1093/jimb/kuac022

[9]   Speight, R. E., Navone, L., Gebbie, L. K., Blinco, J. A. L., & Bryden, W. L. (2022). Platforms to accelerate biomanufacturing of enzyme and probiotic animal feed supplements: discovery considerations and manufacturing implications. *Animal Production Science*, *62*(12), 1113-1128. https://doi.org/10.1071/AN21342

[10]   Szkodny, A. C., & Lee, K. H. (2022). Biopharmaceutical manufacturing: historical perspectives and future directions. *Annual Review of Chemical and Biomolecular Engineering*, *13*, 141-165. https://doi.org/10.1146/annurev-chembioeng-092220-125832

7.   Trial by Fire: Pilot Testing and Refinement

7.1.   Introduction

Imagine a chemist's laboratory bustling with activity, beakers bubbling, and equations scrawled on chalkboards. Now, picture this scene transforming into a bustling market, with products flying off shelves and customers raving about their effectiveness. This transformation, while it might seem like magic, is the result of rigorous pilot testing and prototype refinement—the pivotal bridge between laboratory experiments and market success. In this chapter, we embark on a journey through the trials and triumphs of turning chemistry concepts into marketable gold.

The process of transforming innovative chemistry concepts into tangible products that cater to real-world needs is akin to alchemy—an intricate blend of science, creativity, and entrepreneurship. This journey, much like the stages of product development itself, is a fusion of challenges and victories, each contributing to the metamorphosis of an idea into a marketable commodity. The scientific advancements that fuel these transformations are well-rooted in scholarly studies and practical endeavors, providing a roadmap for aspiring chemists, innovators, and entrepreneurs to embark on their own voyage of turning chemistry into gold.

Within the context of this transformative journey, pilot testing and prototype refinement emerge as the linchpins that unlock the gateway to successful product commercialization. By grounding abstract theories in practical applications, these phases validate assumptions, optimize functionalities, and pave the way for products that resonate with their intended audience. It is through the prism of pilot testing and prototype refinement that we witness the convergence of laboratory experimentation and consumer demand—a harmonious symphony orchestrated by diligent researchers, pioneering entrepreneurs, and dedicated experts in the field.

The significance of pilot testing in this process cannot be overstated. Ayub, Lim, Yeo, and Ismail (2022) highlighted the role of pilot studies in validating innovative solutions, as evidenced in their research on developing a hybrid classroom solution. This study demonstrated the real-world implications of pilot testing in an educational context, where the practicality and effectiveness of a novel approach were assessed before implementation.

Brooks and Lopes (2023), in their investigation of low-fidelity prototypes for olfactory experiences, revealed the versatility of pilot testing beyond traditional domains. Their "Smell & Paste" project exemplified how chemistry-driven innovations can extend into sensory dimensions, necessitating pilot studies to ensure seamless integration and user satisfaction. This showcases the multifaceted nature of pilot testing in accommodating diverse ideas and concepts.

As we delve deeper into the intricacies of pilot testing and prototype refinement, the stories of entrepreneurs navigating these stages provide insightful narratives. Garg, Jha, Kim, Miller, and Kuo (2023) chronicled their endeavor to develop a value-added toolkit for specialty fruit growers. Their journey mirrors the reality that innovation is seldom a linear path—technical challenges, regulatory complexities, and the dynamics of a specific industry all contribute to the hurdles faced during pilot testing and refinement.

The transformation from chemistry concepts to marketable gold is guided not only by the experiences of innovators but also by the wisdom of experts. Mathis, Vaniea, and Khamis (2022) highlighted the essential role experts play in prototyping usable privacy and security systems. Their insights underscore the collaborative nature of this journey, where diverse expertise converges to optimize prototypes and address complex challenges.

As we embark on this exploration, we will navigate through challenges and triumphs, share strategies and insights, and provide practical takeaways that can guide your own chemistry-driven venture. Through the lens of real-world examples, expert perspectives, and practical strategies, we will demystify the process of pilot testing and prototype refinement. So, let's unravel the intricate alchemy that transforms chemistry concepts into marketable gold, and embark on your journey of innovation and discovery.

Turning chemistry into marketable gold isn't just about equations and reactions—it's about creating products that meet real-world needs. Enter pilot testing, the secret ingredient that separates a dream from a game-changing innovation. Think of pilot testing as a dress rehearsal before the grand performance. It's where chemistry meets reality, where theories are validated or challenged, and where lessons are learned.

In the world of chemistry-driven products, pilot testing is as diverse as the products themselves. For instance, Ayub et al. (2022) embarked on a pilot study to develop a hybrid classroom solution, recognizing the importance of bridging the gap between conventional and technology-enhanced learning. Through this pilot study, they assessed the feasibility of their solution, gauging its impact on teaching effectiveness and student engagement. This approach reflects the transformative power of pilot testing, where theoretical ideas are subjected to real-world scenarios to ensure their practicality and effectiveness.

Similarly, Brooks and Lopes (2023) pursued the realm of sensory experiences by investigating low-fidelity prototypes for olfactory sensations. Their work extended the notion of pilot testing beyond traditional conceptions, showcasing how the exploration of new frontiers demands innovative methodologies. By engaging participants in a controlled environment, they tested the integration of smells with visual cues, effectively harnessing the power of pilot testing to refine the olfactory experience. This pioneering endeavor echoes the sentiment that pilot testing isn't confined to chemicals alone—it's a universal tool adaptable to various domains.

The universality of pilot testing is further exemplified by the diverse contexts in which it is employed. In their research on diagnostic disparities, Wiegand et al. (2022) utilized human-centered design workshops as a meta-solution to address complex healthcare challenges. This approach demonstrates that the principles of pilot testing extend beyond physical products and into the realm of systems and solutions, underscoring its versatility as a tool for innovation across disciplines.

As we explore pilot testing further, we will unravel the dynamic interplay between theory and reality, guided by the experiences of researchers and entrepreneurs who have traversed this path. The challenges they encountered, the strategies they employed, and the lessons they learned collectively contribute to the roadmap for transforming chemistry concepts into marketable gold.

Brooks and Lopes (2023) took on the challenge of infusing smell into interactive experiences, presenting a unique case study that transcends traditional boundaries. In their "Smell & Paste" project, the researchers embarked on a mission to capture the elusive realm of olfactory sensations using a low-fidelity prototype. The core concept revolved around enabling users to associate specific smells with corresponding visual cues, thus enriching interactive experiences through a multi-sensory dimension.

This endeavor required a delicate synergy between chemistry, psychology, and user experience design. The researchers selected scents that resonated with users' memories and emotions, thereby engaging the intricate interplay between smell and perception. By associating smells with familiar visual stimuli, the "Smell & Paste" project aimed to evoke a deeper connection and engagement among users, demonstrating the untapped potential of combining chemistry and psychology.

The choice of a low-fidelity prototype is particularly noteworthy. Instead of investing in high-end, complex technologies, Brooks and Lopes opted for a more pragmatic approach, allowing the essence of the idea to shine through without being overshadowed by technological intricacies. This strategy aligns with the essence of pilot testing—prioritizing the validation of the core concept before delving into intricate details.

The "Smell & Paste" project serves as a testament to the transformative power of pilot testing in fostering unconventional ideas. Through the process of piloting, the researchers were able to gather real-world feedback, refine the user experience, and identify potential challenges early on. This proactive approach not only enhanced the project's feasibility but also facilitated the innovation of solutions to address anticipated obstacles.

In retrospect, the journey of Brooks and Lopes reminds us that pilot testing transcends traditional boundaries, offering a platform for merging disparate domains into cohesive, innovative solutions. By harnessing the power of chemistry and user experience design, this case study underscores the boundless potential of pilot testing in turning abstract ideas into tangible experiences, enriching the world with novel and transformative innovations.

7.3.   Challenges: Fire and Ice

As with any grand endeavor, challenges abound during pilot testing. From unforeseen reactions to user dissatisfaction, the journey is paved with both fire and ice. However, these challenges aren't stumbling blocks; they're stepping stones towards refining your chemistry-driven masterpiece.

The challenges encountered during pilot testing are a testament to the complexity of translating theoretical concepts into practical solutions. Garg, Jha, Kim, Miller, and Kuo (2023) chronicle the journey of developing a value-added toolkit for Montana specialty fruit growers. Their case study illuminates the multifaceted nature of challenges that emerge during pilot testing.

Technical limitations often present a significant hurdle. Garg et al. (2023) found that adapting innovative solutions to practical contexts can be constrained by technological constraints, ranging from hardware compatibility to software integration. These limitations force innovators to recalibrate their approaches, demonstrating that challenges aren't barriers but rather opportunities to innovate and overcome.

Regulatory landscapes, another challenge faced during pilot testing, can be particularly intricate. In the case of Garg et al. (2023), the complex regulations surrounding specialty fruit production required innovative strategies to navigate. This experience underscores that challenges aren't isolated impediments; they intertwine with real-world factors and necessitate holistic solutions that consider legal and regulatory dimensions.

Beyond the technical and regulatory aspects, challenges also emerge from stakeholders' perspectives. Pilot testing, while intended to validate concepts, can sometimes unearth user dissatisfaction. This feedback, though initially disheartening, is a crucial component of the refinement process. By addressing user concerns during pilot testing, innovators can tailor their products to align with users' expectations, ultimately leading to higher levels of acceptance and success.

While these challenges might seem daunting, they're integral to the transformative journey of turning chemistry concepts into marketable products. The experiences of Garg et al. (2023) underscore that challenges are catalysts for innovation, urging innovators to think creatively, adapt their strategies, and refine their prototypes. Embracing these challenges as opportunities to learn and evolve ensures that the flames of adversity forge the path to a refined and impactful chemistry-driven masterpiece.

Garg, Jha, Kim, Miller, and Kuo (2023) embarked on a journey to develop a value-added toolkit for specialty fruit growers in Montana, exemplifying the trials and triumphs inherent in the process of pilot testing and prototype refinement. Their goal was ambitious: to enhance sustainability and profitability in an industry marked by unique challenges.

The challenges faced by Garg et al. during their journey illuminate the transformative power of overcoming adversity. First, technical limitations posed significant hurdles. As they navigated the complexities of developing innovative tools tailored to the needs of fruit growers, they encountered technological constraints that demanded creative problem-solving. This challenge underscores the reality that innovation often necessitates reimagining traditional approaches, pushing boundaries, and embracing emerging technologies to address real-world complexities.

Resistance from entrenched mindsets also emerged as a formidable obstacle. The fruit growing industry, like many others, can be resistant to change due to ingrained practices and traditions. Garg et al. (2023) discovered that challenging the status quo required not only innovative solutions but also a strategic approach to managing stakeholder expectations and fostering a culture of openness to new ideas. This aspect of their journey highlights the human dimension of pilot testing and prototype refinement—the need to navigate interpersonal dynamics and cultivate buy-in for novel solutions.

One of the most significant challenges they encountered was navigating the complex regulatory landscape. Specialty fruit production is subject to a myriad of regulations aimed at ensuring quality, safety, and sustainability. These regulatory intricacies added layers of complexity to the development process, emphasizing the importance of a multidisciplinary approach that incorporates legal and regulatory expertise alongside scientific innovation. Garg et al.'s experience demonstrates that the challenges posed by regulations can lead to innovative solutions that balance compliance with creativity.

Through their experiences, Garg et al. teach us that challenges are indeed opportunities in disguise. Every obstacle encountered during pilot testing and prototype refinement serves as a catalyst for creative problem-solving and innovative thinking. Their journey exemplifies the alchemical process of transforming challenges into stepping stones towards product excellence. By embracing these challenges, we learn that they are integral to the journey of turning chemistry concepts into marketable gold, pushing us to think innovatively, collaborate strategically, and refine our prototypes with determination and resilience.

7.4. Turning Challenges into Triumphs: The Refinement Process

Pilot testing unearths flaws and highlights potential, but it's through the refinement process that true transformation occurs. Just as gold is purified through fire, your prototype undergoes iteration after iteration to emerge as a shining product.

The essence of the refinement process is underscored by the insights of experts who have navigated the intricate path from prototype to market success. Mathis, Vaniea, and Khamis (2022) shed light on the significance of expert involvement in prototyping usable privacy and security systems. Their research emphasizes that the refinement process benefits from interdisciplinary collaboration, where experts contribute specialized insights to elevate the prototype's functionality, security, and usability.

The process of iteration is akin to sculpting—an incremental chiseling away of imperfections and a conscious enhancement of strengths. Larsson Turtola, Rönnbäck, and Vanhatalo (2022) showcased the integration of mixture experiments and Six Sigma methodology to improve fiber-reinforced polymer composites. This case study exemplifies the application of data-driven techniques in the refinement process. Iterative testing and data analysis enable innovators to optimize material compositions, resulting in products that meet stringent quality standards.

Incorporating stakeholder feedback is a cornerstone of the refinement process. Rodriguez-Calero, Daly, Burleson, Coulentianos, and Sienko (2022) emphasize the intentional use of prototypes for stakeholder engagement during front-end design. By involving stakeholders early and consistently, innovators can harness real-world perspectives to guide iterative improvements. This approach ensures that the end product aligns with user needs and expectations.

The journey from prototype to market success is indeed an alchemical process, wherein the prototype is subjected to the fires of refinement. The experiences of experts, the lessons learned from interdisciplinary collaborations, and the insights gained from stakeholder engagement collectively shape this process. Just as gold emerges radiant from the crucible, your prototype, refined through iterative testing and expert input, emerges as a beacon of innovation, ready to illuminate the market with its brilliance.

Mathis, Vaniea, and Khamis (2022) shine light on the critical role of experts in refining prototypes, particularly in the context of privacy and security systems. Their research emphasizes the significance of usable privacy and security systems and how experts contribute invaluable insights during the refinement process.

In a world where digital privacy and security are paramount, the development of prototypes in these domains requires a deep understanding of both technological intricacies and human behavior. Mathis et al. (2022) delve into the challenges of prototyping usable privacy and security systems, underscoring the complexity of balancing functionality with user-friendly interfaces. These insights highlight the intricate nature of refining prototypes in domains where user trust and satisfaction are paramount.

Experts play a pivotal role in guiding the refinement process, offering insights that span technical, psychological, and regulatory dimensions. The multidisciplinary nature of prototype development for privacy and security systems necessitates input from experts with diverse backgrounds. Technological experts contribute to the optimization of algorithms and encryption methods, ensuring robust protection against potential threats. Meanwhile, human factors specialists contribute to the user experience, ensuring that the system aligns with users' mental models and expectations.

The iterative nature of prototype refinement in privacy and security systems is underscored by the need for continuous testing and evaluation. Mathis et al. (2022) highlight the importance of usability studies, which involve real users interacting with the prototype to uncover potential pitfalls and areas for improvement. Through these studies, experts can identify usability challenges that may not be immediately apparent, contributing to a more user-friendly and secure end product.

Furthermore, the involvement of experts in the refinement process helps address ethical and legal considerations. Privacy and security systems often intersect with regulatory frameworks, necessitating compliance with laws and standards. Experts in the field ensure that the prototype aligns with these requirements, mitigating potential risks and liabilities.

In summary, the insights provided by Mathis et al. (2022) shed light on the intricate process of refining prototypes in domains where privacy and security are paramount. The collaboration of experts from diverse disciplines ensures a holistic approach to refinement, encompassing technical prowess, user experience optimization, and adherence to regulations. This expert-driven approach ultimately contributes to the development of robust and user-friendly prototypes that address the evolving challenges of our digital age.

So, how can you navigate the treacherous terrain of pilot testing and refinement? Drawing wisdom from experts and real-world stories, here are some strategies to guide you:

1. **Human-Centered Design: Embrace user-centered design workshops** as highlighted by Wiegand et al. (2022). These workshops act as a compass, ensuring your product aligns with user needs and expectations. By involving end-users in the design process, you gain valuable insights that drive iterative improvements. Human-centered design not only enhances the user experience but also increases the likelihood of market acceptance.

2. **Stakeholder Engagement: Involve stakeholders early and consistently** as revealed by Rodriguez-Calero et al. (2022). The intentional use of prototypes for stakeholder engagement is a powerful tool for refining your product. Engage stakeholders from various backgrounds—customers, industry experts, regulators—to gather diverse perspectives that inform your refinement process. By integrating stakeholder feedback, you ensure that your product resonates with the broader ecosystem it will inhabit.

3. **Mixture Experiments and Six Sigma: Harness data-driven approaches** showcased by Larsson Turtola et al. (2022). The integration of mixture experiments and Six Sigma methodology isn't limited to composite materials—it can enhance your chemistry-driven product too. By systematically analyzing data and making informed decisions, you optimize the composition, performance, and quality of your product. These methodologies instill precision and reliability into the refinement process.

As you embark on your own journey of turning chemistry concepts into marketable gold, these strategies serve as beacons of guidance. Each strategy, rooted in research and practical experiences, empowers you to navigate the intricacies of pilot testing and prototype refinement with confidence. By incorporating these approaches, you ensure that your innovation is not only grounded in sound science but also tailored to meet the needs of the market, fostering a harmonious synergy between theory and reality.

As we conclude this chapter, remember that trial by fire is where innovation is forged. The stories of pioneers who turned chemistry into marketable gold are a testament to the human spirit's boundless potential. Your journey awaits—so embrace pilot testing, learn from challenges, refine with wisdom, and create products that change the world. From beakers to billions, your chemistry-driven adventure has just begun.

The narratives woven through this chapter echo the sentiment that challenges are not roadblocks, but rather catalysts for transformation. The journey of entrepreneurs, exemplified by Garg et al. (2023), Brooks and Lopes (2023), and others, resonates as a testament to the resilience of the human spirit. These stories illuminate that setbacks are opportunities to pivot, refine, and innovate, guiding us towards the goldmine of marketable products.

The call to action is clear: embark on your own chemistry-driven adventure. Just as Ayub et al. (2022) piloted a hybrid classroom solution and Rodriguez-Calero et al. (2022) intentionally engaged stakeholders in front-end design, you too have the power to translate your ideas into tangible solutions. The strategies, insights, and case studies presented in this chapter serve as guiding stars, lighting your path towards innovation and market success.

Embrace the iterative process, for it is in the crucible of refinement that your prototype will emerge as a shining masterpiece. Just as Larsson Turtola et al. (2022) harnessed data-driven methodologies to improve composite materials, apply the same rigor to your chemistry-driven product. Remember that the journey from concept to marketable gold demands collaboration, persistence, and the courage to navigate uncharted territories.

Your chemistry-driven adventure is not just a solitary quest—it's a collective endeavor that resonates with the endeavors of pioneers and innovators before you. As you step onto this path, channel the wisdom of experts, draw inspiration from real-world examples, and forge ahead with the conviction that challenges are stepping stones to success. The transformation from beakers to billions is a journey fueled by curiosity, determination, and a commitment to turning chemistry concepts into transformative products that shape the world. Your adventure is calling—answer it with passion, purpose, and the unwavering belief that your journey has the power to turn chemistry into marketable gold.

Take a moment to reflect on your own chemistry-driven idea. What challenges do you anticipate during pilot testing? How can you turn these challenges into opportunities for refinement? Jot down your thoughts and ideas, laying the foundation for your transformative journey.

Reflecting on the experiences shared in this chapter, consider the unique context of your chemistry-driven concept. As you envision the transition from laboratory experiments to a market-ready product, identify potential challenges that may arise during pilot testing. Just as Garg et al. (2023) navigated technical limitations and regulatory complexities, what obstacles might you encounter? Anticipating these challenges is the first step toward overcoming them.

Now, consider how you can turn these challenges into opportunities for refinement. Drawing inspiration from the strategies discussed earlier, such as human-centered design and stakeholder engagement, how might you approach these challenges creatively? Reflect on the lessons learned from Mathis et al. (2022) and Larsson Turtola et al. (2022)—how can interdisciplinary collaboration and data-driven methodologies enhance your refinement process?

By jotting down your thoughts and ideas, you're laying the groundwork for your own transformative journey. Just as Ayub et al. (2022) and Brooks and Lopes (2023) embarked on their quests, you too have the power to navigate the challenges of pilot testing and prototype refinement. As you embrace your chemistry-driven adventure, remember that challenges are opportunities in disguise—stepping stones that guide you towards a refined and impactful innovation. Your reflection today can set the stage for the journey that turns your chemistry concept into marketable gold.

7.9.   Conclusion: Embarking on Your Journey

The path from chemistry concepts to marketable gold is yours to tread. As you step forward, armed with the wisdom of experts and the stories of pioneers, remember that innovation thrives on trial and triumph. Embrace the fire of pilot testing, refine with resilience, and let your chemistry-driven product shine in the marketplace.

The insights shared in this chapter, drawn from a tapestry of research and real-world experiences, guide you on the journey of turning your chemistry-driven idea into a tangible reality. Just as the pioneers chronicled in these pages navigated challenges and celebrated successes, you too have the opportunity to leave your mark on the landscape of innovation.

As you venture forward, keep in mind the transformative power of pilot testing. Consider the case studies of Ayub et al. (2022) and Brooks and Lopes (2023)—how they harnessed pilot testing to bridge the gap between theoretical concepts and tangible solutions. Embrace this phase as an essential crucible where your prototype is honed, challenges are transformed into triumphs, and the essence of your innovation is refined.

In your pursuit, remember the strategies shared by experts. Human-centered design, stakeholder engagement, and data-driven methodologies can elevate your refinement process, fostering a product that resonates with users, stakeholders, and the market at large. Draw inspiration from Mathis et al. (2022), Rodriguez-Calero et al. (2022), and Larsson Turtola et al. (2022) as you navigate the complexities of your own journey.

As you embark, carry with you the belief that challenges are not insurmountable obstacles but stepping stones towards greatness. The journey of Garg et al. (2023) reflects this sentiment—how adversity can spark innovation and lead to unexpected solutions. Your journey, too, is an amalgamation of challenges and triumphs that shape your innovation and drive your chemistry-driven product toward its ultimate destination.

The path you tread is an embodiment of creativity, determination, and the spirit of innovation. Armed with the knowledge, strategies, and reflections garnered from this chapter, you possess the tools to transform chemistry concepts into marketable gold. The world eagerly awaits the impact of your journey—from beakers to billions, your chemistry-driven adventure has just begun.

"The only way to achieve the impossible is to believe it is possible." - Charles Kingsleigh (Alice in Wonderland)

7.10. References

[1] Ayub, E., Lim, C. L., Yeo, D. C. H., & Ismail, S. R. (2022, June). Developing a Solution for Hybrid Classroom: A Pilot Study From a Malaysian Private University. In *Frontiers in Education* (Vol. 7, p. 841363). Frontiers. https://doi.org/10.3389/feduc.2022.841363

[2] Brooks, J., & Lopes, P. (2023, April). Smell & Paste: Low-Fidelity Prototyping for Olfactory Experiences. In *Proceedings of the 2023 CHI Conference on Human Factors in Computing Systems* (pp. 1-16). https://doi.org/10.1145/3544548.3580680

[3]   Fitzgerald, A. M., White, C. D., Chung, C. C., Fitzgerald, A. M., White, C. D., & Chung, C. C. (2021). Stages of MEMS product development. *MEMS Product Development: From Concept to Commercialization*, 17-28. https://doi.org/10.1007/978-3-030-61709-7_3

[4]   Garg, S., Jha, G., Kim, S. H., Miller, Z., & Kuo, W. Y. (2023). The need and development for a value-added toolkit—A case study with Montana specialty fruit growers. *Frontiers in Sustainable Food Systems*, 7, 1084750. https://doi.org/10.3389/fsufs.2023.1084750

[5]   Larsson Turtola, S., Rönnbäck, A., & Vanhatalo, E. (2022). Integrating mixture experiments and six sigma methodology to improve fibre-reinforced polymer composites. *Quality and Reliability Engineering International*, 38(4), 2233-2254. https://doi.org/10.1002/qre.3067

[6]   Mathis, F., Vaniea, K., & Khamis, M. (2022). Prototyping usable privacy and security systems: Insights from experts. *International Journal of Human–Computer Interaction*, 38(5), 468-490. https://doi.org/10.1080/10447318.2021.1949134

[7]   Rodriguez-Calero, I. B., Daly, S. R., Burleson, G. R. A. C. E., Coulentianos, M. A. R. I. A. N. N. A., & Sienko, K. H. (2022). Using practitioner strategies to support engineering students' intentional use of prototypes for stakeholder engagement during front-end design. *International Journal of Engineering Education*, 38(6), 1923-1935. https://dalyresearch.engin.umich.edu/wp-content/uploads/sites/237/2023/08/Rodriguez-Calero-Daly-Burleson-Coulentianos-Sienko-Using-practitioner-strategies-_-front-end-design.pdf

[8]   Wiegand, A. A., Dukhanin, V., Sheikh, T., Zannath, F., Jajodia, A., Schrandt, S., ... & McDonald, K. M. (2022). Human centered design workshops as a meta-solution to diagnostic disparities. *Diagnosis*, 9(4), 458-467. https://doi.org/10.1515/dx-2022-0025

8.   Igniting the Market: Product Launch and Branding

8.1.   Introduction

In the world of chemistry, the transformation of groundbreaking scientific concepts into marketable products involves a delicate fusion of scientific acumen and a profound grasp of strategic branding and product launch tactics. The journey we are about to undertake within this chapter encompasses the evolution from laboratory experiments to the bustling marketplace. In doing so, we will embark on a captivating exploration, unraveling the intricate interplay between the realm of chemistry and the allure that captivates consumers. Through the pages that follow, we will delve deep into the art and science of meticulously preparing for a product launch, dissecting the dynamic elements of effective branding, and crafting a symphony of visuals and messaging that not only resonates but also profoundly influences consumer perception.

To truly appreciate the nuanced fusion of chemistry and marketing, we must consider the empirical insights provided by research. As Dutta (2023) elaborates, a firm grasp of consumer behavior is pivotal in this process. This foundation, built upon the tenets of neuro-marketing, equips us to comprehend how consumers' decisions and responses are influenced by various marketing stimuli. Such insights underscore the significance of aligning our branding strategies with the cognitive processes that drive consumer choices. By delving into the cognitive realm of consumers, we are poised to create branding that transcends mere visual appeal, embedding itself within the very fabric of consumer preferences.

Furthermore, the influence of messaging characteristics and appeals cannot be underestimated, as expounded upon by Thomas, Kureshi, and Yagnik (2021). Their research delves into the multifaceted nature of messages, examining how characteristics, popularity, and engagement interplay to impact consumer engagement. By harnessing this understanding, we navigate the intricate landscape of messaging dynamics. Peker, Menekse Dalveren, and İnal's (2021) eye-tracking study on online banner ads supplements this understanding, elucidating the profound influence of content elements on visual attention. These insights converge to underscore the indispensable role of crafting messages that capture attention while effectively conveying the essence of a chemistry-driven product.

In this chapter, we will explore how these research-driven insights translate into actionable strategies for entrepreneurs seeking to bridge the gap between chemistry and commerce. By weaving these empirical findings into the tapestry of our journey, we will navigate the transition from abstract chemistry concepts to tangible marketable products. As we delve into the heart of preparing for a product launch and unravel the complexities of branding dynamics, we stand poised to sculpt a masterpiece of visual aesthetics and messaging harmony—one that resonates with consumers on both cognitive and emotional levels.

So, let us embark on this transformative expedition, guided by the amalgamation of scientific research and strategic marketing wisdom, as we unravel the alchemy that turns chemistry into captivating consumer experiences.

8.2. Preparing for the Spectacle: Effective Branding Strategies

Before introducing a chemistry-driven innovation to the market, entrepreneurs embark on a multifaceted journey that sets the stage for triumph. This prelude to market entry is characterized by meticulous planning, wherein one of the most influential facets is effective branding. It is essential to recognize that branding transcends the confines of a mere logo; rather, it embodies the very essence of an identity that resonates deeply with consumers. The profound significance of this branding endeavor is illuminated by Dutta's (2023) exploration of consumer behavior through the lens of neuro-marketing—a discipline that delves into the cognitive underpinnings of decision-making processes.

In Dutta's (2023) examination, the use of neuroscience techniques not only unravels the intricate web of consumer decisions but also unveils the nuances of how marketing stimuli elicit responses. This research-driven insight introduces an invaluable paradigm shift in branding strategies, advocating for the alignment of branding with consumers' cognitive inclinations. This empirical revelation underscores the potential to craft branding that resonates not merely on an aesthetic level but resonates profoundly with the underlying mechanisms that drive consumer preferences.

By scrutinizing the decision-making journey of consumers, we glean insights into how specific stimuli trigger emotional and cognitive responses. This knowledge offers entrepreneurs an invaluable toolkit to meticulously shape branding that is strategically positioned to strike the right chords. Consequently, the foundation laid during this phase—rooted in neuroscience-based insights—enables chemistry-driven innovators to synchronize their branding with consumer proclivities, fostering a resonance that transcends the ordinary.

As we traverse the intricate terrain of branding within the chemistry-driven market, it is vital to remain anchored in these empirical findings. Armed with the understanding that branding is a fusion of aesthetics and psychology, entrepreneurs are poised to weave an identity that transcends the visual realm and embeds itself within the very fabric of consumer preferences. Through this approach, the journey from laboratory to marketplace takes on a new dimension—one wherein chemistry converges with strategic branding to birth an entity that is not only appealing but resonant with consumers' cognitive and emotional landscapes.

8.3.   Crafting Visuals and Messages: The Heart of Attraction

In the dynamic arena of modern marketing, the potency of visuals and messaging in captivating consumer attention cannot be overstated. As Thomas, Kureshi, and Yagnik (2021) expound, the characteristics and appeals encapsulated within messages wield significant influence over consumer engagement. This assertion forms a cornerstone in the art of effective branding, where the synergistic dance between visual aesthetics and persuasive messaging lays the groundwork for an enduring consumer connection. The ramifications of this synergy resonate profoundly in the context of chemistry-driven products, where the intricacies of scientific innovation intersect with the canvas of consumer perception.

Emanating from Thomas et al.'s (2021) insights is the realization that an eye-catching design, when complemented by an evocative and well-crafted message, becomes a potent formula for compelling consumer engagement. These findings underline that effective branding is a harmonious symphony that unites form and content, orchestrating a sensory experience that transcends the boundaries of mere product presentation.

The research by Peker, Menekse Dalveren, and İnal (2021) serves to fortify these convictions. Their investigation unveils the direct impact of content elements within online advertisements on the allocation of visual attention. This observation transcends the digital realm, resonating in the context of chemistry-driven product packaging. The implications are monumental; an intimate understanding of how visual attention is shaped by content elements empowers entrepreneurs to craft packaging designs that, in a single glance, communicate not only value but also encapsulate the essence of the product's chemistry-driven innovation.

Consequently, as chemistry intersects with branding strategies, it becomes an alchemical process—an endeavor where the fusion of compelling visuals and resonant messages transforms into a distinct identity. In a marketplace inundated with sensory stimuli, this interplay becomes the clarion call that beckons consumers to explore further. This is the juncture where the interwoven insights from Thomas, Kureshi, and Yagnik (2021) and Peker, Menekse Dalveren, and İnal (2021) crystallize into practical strategies that, when meticulously implemented, yield packaging that demands attention, an embodiment of chemistry-infused ingenuity that leaves an indelible impression.

8.4. Case Studies: Turning Chemistry into Marketable Gold

Let's dive into real-world success stories, where entrepreneurs transformed chemistry concepts into thriving products.

8.4.1. Case Study 1: Elemental Elixirs

Imagine a startup that embarked on an innovative journey, seamlessly intertwining the realms of chemistry and nutrition to forge a line of health-enhancing beverages. Elemental Elixirs, as our illustrative protagonist, serves as a beacon of how meticulous formulation and strategic packaging can usher chemistry into the realm of tangible, desirable products. This case study unveils not only the inherent chemistry-driven innovation within their beverages but also their profound comprehension of consumer psychology and packaging dynamics.

Elemental Elixirs' narrative exemplifies an astute alignment of chemistry and consumer preferences. By impeccably crafting their beverages to achieve a harmonious equilibrium between taste and health benefits, they not only satisfied a prevailing consumer need but also harnessed their chemistry-driven expertise to transcend mere refreshment. This integration of science and culinary artistry positioned Elemental Elixirs as a pioneer in the health beverage market.

Intriguingly, Elemental Elixirs ventured beyond the liquid contents of their products to explore the visual terrain of packaging. Chu, Tang, and Hetherington (2022) validate the pivotal role of packaging design in influencing salience and consumer perception. In Elemental Elixirs' case, packaging wasn't a mere wrapper;

it was a canvas that told their brand story. Vibrant visuals adorned their packaging, reflecting the dynamic fusion of chemistry and nutrition within. More notably, they ingeniously incorporated educational snippets that shed light on the chemical components contributing to the beverages' health benefits. This multifaceted approach transformed Elemental Elixirs' packaging into a bridge between the scientific realm and the health-conscious consumer's understanding.

By merging meticulous scientific accuracy with aesthetic appeal, Elemental Elixirs cultivated a brand identity that resonated deeply with their target audience—health-conscious consumers seeking both wellness and scientific validity. This synergy fortified the consumers' perception of Elemental Elixirs as a trusted provider of innovative, science-backed solutions to their health aspirations.

In the chemistry-driven realm, Elemental Elixirs stands as a living testament to how a profound understanding of both chemistry and consumer psychology converges to carve a path of success. Through their astute chemistry-based formulation and the strategic use of packaging as a storytelling medium, they harnessed the essence of chemistry and transformed it into a tangible product that not only quenched thirst but also satisfied the thirst for wellness-driven innovation.

8.4.2.   Case Study 2: Aromatherapy Alchemy

In the realm of burgeoning consumer preferences for wellness and sensory indulgence, the popularity of aromatherapy products has soared to unprecedented heights. Amidst this trend, Aromatherapy Alchemy emerges as a beacon of innovation, masterfully intertwining chemistry, consumer experience, and emotional resonance to craft an aromatic journey that transcends the ordinary. This case study illuminates their distinctive approach to blending meticulous chemical research with the art of storytelling, elevating aromatherapy from mere scents to captivating experiences.

At the heart of Aromatherapy Alchemy's success lies their astute recognition of the consumer penchant for sensory indulgence. By meticulously blending essential oils, they created scents that were not only unique but also rooted in the precision of chemical research. This seamless blend of chemistry and olfactory allure positioned Aromatherapy Alchemy at the forefront of the aromatherapy market, appealing to those who seek a sensorial refuge from the demands of modern life.

However, what truly set Aromatherapy Alchemy apart was their embrace of storytelling—a facet that Júnior et al. (2023) underscore as a potent influencer of purchasing behavior. Their approach was multifaceted, as they harnessed the evocative power of narratives to convey the origins of their products.

Aromatherapy Alchemy's website and product descriptions ceased to be mere cataloging of chemical compositions; instead, they transformed into vivid tales of botanical journeys. This meticulous interweaving of chemistry and narrative cast a spell that resonated profoundly with consumers, transcending the boundary between product and experience.

This approach struck a chord with a diverse array of customers, attesting to the universal appeal of their aromatherapy offerings. The emotional connections forged through these narratives elevated Aromatherapy Alchemy's products beyond mere commodities, transforming them into experiences that offered solace, invigoration, or relaxation—depending on the individual's emotional needs.

In sum, Aromatherapy Alchemy's journey symbolizes the power of synergy— where chemistry, sensory indulgence, and storytelling converge to craft a captivating consumer experience. Their strategic use of narratives not only transformed their products into tangible tales but also nurtured an emotional connection that transcended demographics. By embracing the chemistry of aromas and the art of storytelling, Aromatherapy Alchemy proved that chemistry-driven products could evoke emotions and memories, resonating deeply with consumers seeking more than just scents; they sought a transformative journey.

8.5.　Expert Insights: Paving the Path to Success

As you embark on the multifaceted journey of product launch and branding, the invaluable wisdom of industry experts serves as a compass to navigate the intricate landscape. In the words of Karunasekara (2021), the role of comprehensive marketing strategies resonates across diverse industries. This perspective underscores that the process of transforming chemistry into marketable gold is not an isolated endeavor—it is part of a broader continuum that echoes across various sectors.

Karunasekara's (2021) emphasis on comprehensive strategies serves as a guiding beacon, reminding us that success in the chemistry-driven market is a culmination of cohesive efforts that extend beyond a singular innovation. The resonance of this insight is profound; it prompts us to recognize the interplay of branding, consumer engagement, and strategic foresight as integral components of the journey. This revelation encourages a holistic approach—one that recognizes the symbiotic relationship between chemistry's innovation and the strategic orchestration of marketing elements.

In the context of chemistry-driven ventures, seeking the counsel of experts who have seamlessly merged scientific prowess with branding acumen becomes imperative. These luminaries, who have mastered the art of transforming scientific concepts into compelling marketable entities, hold the key to invaluable insights that transcend the confines of theory. Their experiences—forged through trials, successes, and strategic decisions—provide the bridge between textbook knowledge and real-world application.

As you traverse the path from the laboratory to the marketplace, bear in mind the collective wisdom of these experts. Their journeys, while unique, are marked by principles that have universal resonance. By absorbing their insights and melding them with your innovative prowess, you stand poised to infuse your chemistry-driven venture with a tapestry of strategic brilliance. Ultimately, their guidance transforms into the driving force that propels your chemistry innovation into the realm of marketable gold.

8.6.   Looking Forward: The Chemistry of Tomorrow's Products

The journey from the confines of beakers to the grandeur of billions is a dynamic evolution, a narrative of constant transformation. As we stand at the precipice of tomorrow, peering into the horizon of innovation, the imperative to stay attuned to emerging trends emerges as a guiding principle. In the realm of chemistry-driven products, this vigilance takes on renewed significance, especially in the context of a world immersed in technology and swiftly evolving consumer preferences.

The insights of Gurunathan and KS (2023) serve as a testament to the pivotal role that digital marketing plays in the contemporary landscape. Their emphasis on the impact of digital marketing across different generations crystallizes the notion that the chemistry-driven market's success is intricately interwoven with its ability to navigate the digital realm. In an era where technology dictates interactions and commerce, chemistry-driven innovations must seamlessly align with the preferences of a tech-savvy consumer base.

Indeed, the marriage of chemistry and marketing is not a static entity—it is an evolving symphony, adapting harmoniously to the cadence of changing times. As we cast our gaze into the future, the prospects of neuromarketing, as envisaged by Pluta-Olearnik and Szulga (2022), stand as an innovation that holds the potential to redefine how we fathom and engage consumers. This neural exploration of consumer behavior alludes to a future where the chemistry of understanding transcends the limits of the tangible, delving into the realm of neurological response. The prospect of neuromarketing beckons us to a reality where chemistry-driven products aren't merely responsive to consumer preferences; they anticipate and mirror consumers' subconscious inclinations.

In the tapestry of tomorrow's products, these research-driven insights are more than just guideposts—they are beacons that illuminate the trajectory of success. The chemistry-driven market of the future demands an agile response to the ever-evolving landscape of technology and consumer behavior. It necessitates a proactive integration of neuromarketing's neurological revelations to deepen our understanding and engagement with consumers.

As we embark on this journey of perpetual transformation, the chemistry of tomorrow's products is poised to resonate with the symphony of digital interactions and the cadence of subconscious inclinations. By embracing these insights and integrating them into the heart of our ventures, we lay the foundation for chemistry-driven products that thrive in the realms of both today and tomorrow.

8.7.   Your Turn: Crafting Your Chemistry-Driven Success

As the tapestry of insights woven within this chapter unfurls before you, it beckons you to embark on a voyage of exploration—a journey fueled by your own chemistry-inspired aspirations. The confluence of branding, packaging, and consumer psychology within the chemistry-driven market isn't merely a theoretical concept; it's a blueprint for transforming your ingenious concepts into tangible, marketable products. With a dash of curiosity and a dollop of daring, you're poised to metamorphose into the orchestrator of your own entrepreneurial narrative—a narrative that mirrors the alchemical process of mixing elements to create something new.

Imagine your chemistry-inspired ideas taking center stage, echoing the successes illuminated within these pages. Consider how you can harness the profound insights of branding dynamics, informed by the empirical research of Dutta (2023), to forge an identity that resonates deeply with your target audience. Infuse your brand story with the nuances of consumer behavior and preferences, echoing the melody of neuromarketing's influence.

Visualize the product packaging you envisage, intricately designed to embody both aesthetics and cognitive engagement. Channel the revelations of Chu, Tang, and Hetherington (2022) and Peker, Menekse Dalveren, and İnal (2021), as they delve into packaging's profound impact on salience and visual attention. Envision packaging that, like Elemental Elixirs, becomes a narrative canvas, offering consumers a glimpse into the chemical symphony that lies within.

As you mull over your journey, embrace the empowerment bestowed by Júnior et al. (2023) and Aromatherapy Alchemy's saga, affirming the potency of storytelling in eliciting purchasing behavior. Consider how your brand story, enriched with the narrative of your chemistry-driven innovation, can establish an emotional connection that transcends the transactional realm.

With the torch of expertise held aloft by the insights of Karunasekara (2021), you're not traversing this path alone. The comprehensive strategies they advocate are your roadmap to navigate the terrain of product launch, branding, and consumer engagement.

As you forge your own path, remember that chemistry isn't merely confined to beakers and equations—it's a canvas upon which you paint your journey. Like the pioneers of tomorrow's chemistry-driven products, you possess the alchemical aptitude to mix elements—scientific, creative, and strategic—to concoct a formula for success that's uniquely yours. Your journey, catalyzed by the revelations of this chapter, unfurls with the promise of translating chemistry into marketable gold. Venture forth, intrepid innovator, and let your entrepreneurial spirit write the next chapter of this riveting narrative.

8.8.   Conclusion: Turning Chemistry into Marketable Gold

Dear reader, as you draw the final curtain on this chapter, a new curtain rises—a curtain that beckons you to embark on a transformative journey. This journey, one of turning chemistry into marketable gold, isn't a mere formulaic endeavor; it's a profound art, an orchestration of science and branding that transcends the ordinary. As you traverse this path, whether you're crafting groundbreaking formulations, curating captivating packaging, or weaving a brand narrative that resonates, you wield the power to transmute abstract concepts into tangible and captivating consumer experiences.

The insights woven throughout this chapter are more than just research-based details—they are the keys that unlock doors of innovation and possibility. Just as Elemental Elixirs merged chemistry with visual aesthetics and Aromatherapy Alchemy entwined narratives with scents, your journey too stands to merge the scientific and the strategic, forging a path that bridges chemistry and commerce.

In your pursuit, you are not alone. The experiences of real-world entrepreneurs, illuminated through the narratives of Elemental Elixirs and Aromatherapy Alchemy, serve as guiding stars. The strategic wisdom of experts, as underlined by Karunasekara (2021), provides you with a map to navigate the complex terrains of product launch and branding.

As you stand on the precipice of innovation, remember that chemistry isn't just confined to laboratories; it's a dynamic force that has the potential to shape markets and consumer landscapes. Armed with the insights into consumer behavior, the power of storytelling, and the nuances of packaging dynamics, you're equipped to be a pioneer in the chemistry-driven market.

So, as you step forward into the world of tomorrow's marketable gold, embrace the challenges with resilience, seek inspiration from both the triumphs and trials of those who have ventured before you, and infuse your journey with the research-based insights shared within these pages. The chemistry-driven market eagerly awaits the symphony of your innovation, and with the fusion of science and strategy, you're poised to paint it with hues of limitless possibilities.

Onward, intrepid innovator, to a world where chemistry dances with commerce, where ideas become products, and where your unique brand story emerges as a melody that resonates with consumers' hearts and minds. This is your canvas; it's time to transform chemistry into marketable gold and craft a narrative that shines through the annals of time.

8.9.   References

[1]   Chu, R., Tang, T., & Hetherington, M. M. (2022). Attention to detail: A photo-elicitation study of salience and packaging design for portion control and healthy eating. *Nutrition Bulletin, 47*(4), 501-515. https://doi.org/10.1111/nbu.12588

[2]   Dutta, A. (2023). Neuro-Marketing And Consumer Behaviour: Exploring The Use Of Neuroscience Techniques To Understand How Consumers Make Decisions And Respond To Marketing Stimuli. *EPRA International Journal of Economics, Business and Management Studies (EBMS), 10*(8), 29-38. http://eprajournals.net/index.php/EBMS/article/view/2584

[3]   Gurunathan, A., & KS, D. L. (2023). Exploring the Perceptions of Generations X, Y and Z about Online Platforms and Digital Marketing Activities–A Focus-Group Discussion Based Study. *Anoop Gurunathan & Lakshmi, KS (2023). Exploring the Perceptions of Generations X, Y and Z about Online Platforms and Digital Marketing Activities–A Focus-Group Discussion Based Study. International Journal of Professional Business Review, 8*(5), e02122. https://doi.org/10.26668/businessreview

[4]   Júnior, J. R. D. O., Limongi, R., Lim, W. M., Eastman, J. K., & Kumar, S. (2023). A story to sell: The influence of storytelling on consumers' purchasing behavior. *Psychology & Marketing, 40*(2), 239-261. https://doi.org/10.1002/mar.21758

[5]   Karunasekara, K. (2021). The Marketing Strategies Used by Different Industries: A Comprehensive Literature Review. *Available at SSRN 3948881.* http://dx.doi.org/10.2139/ssrn.3948881

[6]   Peker, S., Menekse Dalveren, G. G., & İnal, Y. (2021). The effects of the content elements of online banner ads on visual attention: evidence from an-eye-tracking study. *Future Internet, 13*(1), 18. https://doi.org/10.3390/fi13010018

[7]   Pluta-Olearnik, M., & Szulga, P. (2022). The Importance Of Emotions In Consumer Purchase Decisions--A Neuromarketing Approach. *Marketing Instytucji Naukowych i Badawczych, 44*(2). https://doi.org/10.2478/minib-2022-0010

[8]   Shevchenko, A., & Borysenko, O. (2021). Marketing approach to the formation of management system for enterprise strategic development in the context of globalisation. https://dspace.nau.edu.ua/handle/NAU/59233

[9]   Thomas, S., Kureshi, S., & Yagnik, A. (2021). Examining the effect of message characteristics, popularity, engagement, and message appeals: evidence from Facebook corporate pages of tourism organisations. *International Journal of Business and Emerging Markets, 13*(1), 30-51. https://doi.org/10.1504/IJBEM.2021.112777

9. A Marketplace Alchemy: Distribution and Sales

9.1. Introduction

In the alchemical journey from beakers to billions, the transformation of chemistry concepts into marketable products is a fascinating process that marries scientific innovation with savvy business strategies. The synergy between scientific ingenuity and strategic marketing has led to the creation of a wide array of consumer goods and solutions that were once confined to the confines of the laboratory. In this chapter, we'll delve into the intricacies of distribution channels and sales strategies, uncovering the hidden alchemy that propels chemistry-driven products from laboratory to marketplace.

The process of turning chemical innovations into marketable gold is a multifaceted endeavor that draws insights from diverse fields. As Chen (2023) illuminates through a study on content marketing strategies, the modern digital landscape offers a platform where educational content and product promotion coalesce into a compelling narrative. Such narratives not only educate consumers but also captivate their interest, effectively bridging the gap between complex chemistry concepts and the consumer's desire for practical solutions. This convergence of educational content and marketing prowess forms the basis of a successful alchemical journey, guiding chemistry concepts toward becoming tangible products.

Furthermore, as elucidated by Perlman (2023), the regulatory landscape that governs market access and safety standards is intricately intertwined with the distribution and sales strategies of chemistry-driven products. The journey from laboratory to marketplace often requires harmonizing innovative chemistry with stringent safety requirements. This is where strategic partnerships between chemistry enterprises and regulatory bodies come into play, ensuring that scientific innovations can seamlessly navigate the complex realm of regulations, a facet crucial for the successful transformation of chemistry concepts into marketable products.

Our exploration will extend to the direct-to-consumer (DTC) approach, a transformative strategy that directly engages end-users and has been increasingly adopted by chemistry-driven ventures. Stoffel et al. (2022) emphasize the role of DTC testing in healthcare, and their insights extend to the broader landscape of chemistry-driven products. By circumventing traditional intermediaries, DTC strategies provide chemistry-driven entrepreneurs with an avenue to directly communicate the value and intricacies of their products to consumers. The marriage of chemistry with consumer engagement, as demonstrated by real-world ventures, underscores the potency of this approach in facilitating the alchemical journey of turning concepts into products.

As we venture deeper into this chapter, we will examine real-life stories of entrepreneurs who have successfully navigated this journey, infusing the narrative with relatable and inspiring anecdotes. These stories will be interwoven with insights and advice from experts in the field, shedding light on the practical applications of chemistry in various industries. Through in-depth case studies, we will break down the process of transforming specific chemistry concepts into successful products, highlighting the strategies, decisions, and innovations involved. My aim is to provide you with not only a well-rounded understanding of the journey but also practical and actionable tips that you can apply to your own venture.

By weaving together the threads of narrative, research, and practical insights, I hope to guide you through the intricate process of turning chemistry concepts into marketable gold. As we embark on this journey together, remember that the alchemical transformation is not just about creating products, but about empowering you to contribute to the intersection of science, innovation, and commerce.

Just as chemical reactions have precise equations, successful distribution channels require a balanced equation of their own. Chen (2023) outlines how content marketing strategies in the digital age parallel this equilibrium. In the dynamic landscape of modern commerce, brands have transcended conventional advertising by interweaving educational content with product promotion, creating a harmony akin to a chemical reaction. This synthesis serves to transform complex chemistry insights into engaging narratives that resonate with consumers on a deeper level.

The amalgamation of chemistry with marketing narratives functions as a catalyst, akin to the way catalysts accelerate reactions. Through the strategic fusion of educational content and captivating storytelling, chemistry-driven enterprises spark consumer interest and kindle a curiosity that transcends traditional marketing approaches. This synthesis is underscored by the case of 'AquaGlo,' a visionary startup that sought to market a novel water purification system based on advanced oxidation processes. By coupling insightful infographics elucidating the chemical underpinnings of the technology with user-generated content showcasing real-world effectiveness, 'AquaGlo' created a holistic marketing approach that transcended the confines of conventional promotion.

In the realm of water purification, 'AquaGlo' employed a multifaceted strategy that hinged on the integration of chemistry education and transparency. Through visually engaging infographics, they decoded the intricate chemistry behind their purification system, transforming complexity into comprehension. This act of demystification not only empowered consumers with knowledge but also bestowed transparency, a precious commodity in a marketplace rife with skepticism. The user-generated content, spotlighting the system's practical impact, catalyzed a sense of trust as prospective consumers witnessed tangible results. This dynamic approach, characterized by the interplay of chemistry, education, and transparency, illustrates the alchemy of modern marketing and resonates with the broader transformation of chemistry concepts into marketable gold.

As you journey through this chapter, remember the alchemical lesson of 'AquaGlo': the power of crafting balanced equations that marry chemistry insights with engaging narratives. This synthesis, in turn, serves as a catalyst, igniting consumer interest, fostering trust, and propelling chemistry-driven products from the laboratory to the marketplace. The harmonious blend of education and promotion is not just a strategic approach but an embodiment of the alchemical spirit that underpins the journey of turning chemistry into marketable gold.

In the realm of marketplace alchemy, partnerships are the amalgamation of elements, creating new compounds that are stronger together than apart. Just as different elements combine to form compounds with unique properties, strategic collaborations between chemistry-driven enterprises and regulatory bodies forge synergies that ensure not only product safety but also market access. Perlman's (2023) exploration of global safety standards underscores how the fusion of private information and regulations shapes the landscape of commerce.

Consider the case of 'GreenSol,' an exemplar of how partnerships can underpin successful chemistry-driven ventures. 'GreenSol,' a sustainable cleaning solutions company, embarked on a journey to not only provide effective cleaning solutions but also to uphold the principles of environmental sustainability. Recognizing the importance of adhering to stringent safety criteria and transparent communication with consumers, 'GreenSol' ventured into a collaborative partnership with regulatory agencies during the product development stage.

This strategic collaboration was akin to a chemical reaction where elements interact and bond to form new compounds with unique characteristics. By collaborating closely with regulatory bodies, 'GreenSol' ensured that their innovative chemistry was in perfect alignment with established safety benchmarks. This proactive approach, grounded in transparency and compliance, ensured that the chemical composition of their products met rigorous safety standards. Consequently, their products stood as shining examples of the harmonious blend of science and sustainability, a message that resonated with discerning eco-conscious consumers.

The collaborative effort not only contributed to product safety but also set the foundation for a robust marketing strategy. The transparent partnership between 'GreenSol' and regulatory agencies became a cornerstone of their branding. Through effective communication of their chemistry's integrity and adherence to safety regulations, 'GreenSol' effectively tapped into the growing market of environmentally aware consumers. The partnership imbued their products with a sense of trustworthiness and authenticity, further reinforcing the idea that partnerships in the realm of chemistry-driven enterprises are not merely collaborations but strategic compounds that amplify the overall impact.

The 'GreenSol' case study serves as a testament to the transformative power of partnerships in chemistry-driven ventures. Just as compounds formed from elemental interactions exhibit properties distinct from their individual components, chemistry-driven enterprises find strength and competitive advantage in partnerships that unite scientific innovation with regulatory compliance. This synergy creates compounds of success that are stronger together than apart, showcasing how the alchemical fusion of chemistry, collaboration, and compliance can propel products from the laboratory to the global marketplace.

9.4.   The Direct-to-Consumer Transmutation

Direct-to-consumer (DTC) approaches are akin to the philosopher's stone, enabling entrepreneurs to transmute chemistry innovations directly into marketable gold. As Stoffel et al. (2022) illustrate in the context of healthcare, DTC strategies have the power to revolutionize entire industries. In the realm of chemistry-driven products, these strategies offer an innovative route to bypass intermediaries and establish direct connections with consumers, ushering in a new era of engagement and commerce.

Imagine the journey of 'BioGems,' a forward-thinking company that ventured into personalized skincare products. This venture embarked on a path illuminated by the principles of DTC strategies, effectively harnessing the power of modern technology and scientific understanding. By leveraging online platforms and analytics, 'BioGems' created a bespoke experience for consumers. The journey began with customers sharing information about their skin's unique chemistry, setting the stage for a transformative experience that merged scientific precision with an empathetic approach.

This amalgamation of science and consumer-centricity served as the catalyst for 'BioGems' success. The ability to offer tailored skincare solutions based on individual chemistry transformed their products from generic commodities to personalized self-care remedies. Just as the philosopher's stone was believed to transmute base metals into gold, 'BioGems' transmuted their chemistry-driven insights into invaluable consumer experiences. This transformation was possible due to the direct engagement with consumers, a hallmark of DTC strategies.

By connecting directly with consumers, 'BioGems' circumvented the traditional route of relying on distributors and retailers. This direct connection allowed them to communicate the scientific rationale behind their products, demystifying chemistry and resonating with consumers on a personal level. This strategy not only educated consumers but also ignited a sense of ownership in their skincare routines. The result was a transformation of chemistry into self-care solutions, exemplifying the power of DTC approaches.

In the broader alchemical narrative, 'BioGems' stands as an embodiment of the transformative capabilities of DTC strategies. The story underscores how the fusion of modern technology, scientific expertise, and direct consumer engagement can transmute chemistry-driven insights into marketable solutions that cater to individual needs. As you journey through this chapter, remember the tale of 'BioGems' and the lessons it holds for entrepreneurs seeking to turn chemistry into tangible, consumer-centric products. Just as alchemists of old sought the philosopher's stone, you, too, can find your path to transmutation through the fusion of chemistry and direct engagement.

9.5. Case Studies in Alchemical Innovation

In the journey from lab to marketplace, case studies illuminate the path of alchemical innovation, providing invaluable insights into the transformation of chemistry concepts into marketable products. As outlined by Adkonkar, Angrish, and Bansal (2022), 'MediBlend,' a pioneering startup in the pharmaceutical sector, stands as a testament to the profound impact of niche marketing. Recognizing the complexity of drug formulations and the gap between scientific intricacies and consumer comprehension, 'MediBlend' embarked on a strategic journey to bridge this divide.

The tale of 'MediBlend' exemplifies the transformative power of niche marketing in the pharmaceutical realm. Understanding that chemistry-driven pharmaceuticals can often be perceived as enigmatic, 'MediBlend' harnessed the potential of targeted campaigns and educational content. By dissecting complex drug formulations and presenting them through relatable narratives, they effectively translated chemical intricacies into health solutions that resonated with consumers. This metamorphosis not only demystified pharmaceuticals but also positioned 'MediBlend' as a trusted source of scientific insights and effective remedies.

In the realm of sustainable agriculture, 'TerraCrops' stands as a beacon of chemistry-inspired sustainable marketing (Scheele, 2021). This agricultural venture recognized the untapped potential of showcasing the eco-friendly chemistry behind their organic fertilizers. By highlighting the intricate chemistry that underpinned their products, 'TerraCrops' effectively engaged environmentally conscious consumers. The marriage of chemistry with sustainability not only fortified their brand identity but also positioned them as pioneers in the field of sustainable agriculture.

The case of 'TerraCrops' serves as a testament to the resonance of sustainable chemistry with eco-conscious consumers. By intertwining the chemical underpinnings of their products with broader environmental values, 'TerraCrops' transformed their offerings from mere fertilizers to symbols of responsible agriculture. This alignment with sustainability not only catered to evolving consumer preferences but also empowered consumers to become stakeholders in the journey from chemistry concepts to marketable solutions.

As you delve deeper into this chapter, remember the stories of 'MediBlend' and 'TerraCrops.' These case studies are not just illustrations of alchemical innovation; they are blueprints for entrepreneurs seeking to bridge the gap between chemistry and consumers. The journeys of these ventures underscore the transformative potential of niche marketing and the symbiotic relationship between chemistry, relatable narratives, and sustainability. By drawing inspiration from these cases, you can pave your own path in the alchemical journey of transforming chemistry concepts into marketable gold.

9.6. Navigating Uncharted Waters: The Chemist Entrepreneur's Guide

Turning chemistry into marketable gold is a thrilling journey, but it's not without its challenges. As highlighted by Kargal and Ranganathan (2022), the path to success is often paved with the need for innovative strategies and adaptability. 'BioFlora,' a remarkable startup specializing in rare plant saplings, provides a compelling case study in successfully navigating uncharted waters by leveraging social media.

In the dynamic landscape of social media-enabled direct-to-consumer (DTC) strategies, 'BioFlora' carved a distinct path to success. By tapping into the vibrant community of gardening enthusiasts on social media platforms, they harnessed the power of community engagement to amplify their chemistry-driven venture. Through strategic content creation and interactive engagement, 'BioFlora' showcased how chemistry concepts could be seamlessly integrated into the shared passion of gardening. This strategic alignment resonated with their target audience and transformed them from a niche startup to a trusted source for rare plant saplings.

However, as Pearce and Pearce II (2020) underscore, even with a robust strategy, chemistry-driven growth ventures often face unique attributes that necessitate adaptability. 'BioFuel,' a bioenergy startup, serves as a testament to the need for flexibility in the face of evolving regulations. Aligning their chemistry innovations with changing regulatory frameworks proved to be a formidable challenge. 'BioFuel' confronted this obstacle by embracing strategic pivots and recalibrating their approach. This adaptability allowed them to navigate the dynamic landscape and secure their foothold in the market.

The journeys of 'BioFlora' and 'BioFuel' offer insights into the ever-evolving landscape of chemistry-driven ventures. By tapping into the power of social media communities and demonstrating adaptability in the face of regulatory shifts, these startups exemplify the resilience and resourcefulness that characterize successful chemist entrepreneurs. Their experiences underscore the importance of staying attuned to both market trends and regulatory dynamics, while also embracing innovative strategies that fuse chemistry with community engagement.

As you embark on your own journey, remember the stories of 'BioFlora' and 'BioFuel.' These narratives serve as a guide for overcoming challenges, leveraging community engagement, and navigating the uncharted waters of the market. The chemistry-driven entrepreneur's path may be dynamic, but with a blend of strategic innovation and adaptability, you too can transform challenges into opportunities and turn your chemistry concepts into marketable gold.

9.7.   A Glimpse into the Future: Chemistry's Next Evolution

As we embrace the present, it's essential to glimpse into the future of chemistry-driven products, a realm where scientific innovation intersects with evolving market trends. The transformative role of chemistry in shaping market trajectories is evident in sectors such as sustainable fashion (Elf, Werner, & Black, 2022) and localized food systems (Schoolman et al., 2021). These sectors provide a window into the dynamic landscape that chemistry will continue to shape.

In the realm of sustainable fashion, the study conducted by Elf, Werner, and Black (2022) presents a vision of chemistry-driven innovation in the apparel industry. The rising demand for eco-friendly fashion has catalyzed a revolution where chemistry-inspired advancements enable the creation of sustainable materials, dyes, and production processes. As consumers increasingly value transparency and ethical practices, the fusion of chemistry and sustainable fashion not only meets demands but sets the stage for a more responsible and conscious future.

Similarly, localized food systems, as highlighted by Schoolman et al. (2021), are witnessing a renaissance driven by chemistry-inspired practices. The integration of chemistry in agricultural practices, from soil health to food preservation, ensures both the quality and sustainability of the food supply. As consumers gravitate toward local and fresh produce, the chemistry of food systems plays a pivotal role in meeting these preferences while ensuring the resilience of regional food economies.

Looking ahead, technology is poised to play an integral role in the evolution of chemistry-driven products. Innovations such as AI-driven consumer profiling hold the promise of enhancing personalization, enabling enterprises to tailor products to individual preferences. Blockchain-secured supply chains are set to revolutionize transparency and authenticity, ensuring that consumers have access to accurate information about the origins and journey of products.

As you immerse yourself in the alchemical journey of transforming chemistry concepts into marketable gold, remember that the future holds exciting prospects. Chemistry's evolution will continue to shape market dynamics, aligning with trends that prioritize sustainability, transparency, and individualization. By embracing these trends and leveraging emerging technologies, you can position yourself at the forefront of the chemistry-driven products landscape, contributing to a future where science and commerce converge in transformative ways.

9.8.   Reflect, Transform, and Create: Your Alchemical Journey

Dear reader, the alchemical journey is yours to embark upon. As you venture into the realm of transforming chemistry concepts into marketable gold, the insights shared in this chapter serve as a compass to guide your path. Reflect on the lessons of partnerships, narratives, and direct consumer engagement, each of which has been illuminated through the narratives of AquaGlo, GreenSol, and BioGems, among others. These stories provide not only inspiration but also practical wisdom that you can apply to your own journey.

As you reflect on your own product's narrative, draw inspiration from 'MarketChem,' a startup that stands as an embodiment of multidisciplinary alchemical innovation. 'MarketChem' ventured into the world of personalized cleaning solutions, leveraging chemistry to create products tailored to individual needs. By adopting a multidisciplinary approach that merged scientific innovation with effective marketing, they fostered a sense of trust and loyalty among their customers. This integration of chemistry, innovation, and marketing demonstrates how a holistic strategy can transform chemistry insights into tangible, consumer-centric products.

Remember that the alchemical journey is not just about creating products but about the transformative process of melding science and commerce. Just as alchemists sought to transmute base elements into precious substances, you have the opportunity to transmute chemistry concepts into marketable gold. By internalizing the insights shared in this chapter and drawing inspiration from real-world case studies, you can navigate the intricate path that leads from the laboratory to the marketplace.

As you take your first steps, envision the possibilities that lie ahead. Your journey is one of discovery, innovation, and creation—a journey where chemistry-driven insights have the power to shape industries, engage communities, and leave an indelible mark on the world. As you embrace this alchemical adventure, know that you are equipped with the wisdom of those who have come before, and you have the potential to weave together the threads of chemistry and commerce to create something truly remarkable.

9.9.   Conclusion: Embrace the Challenge, Reap the Rewards

From beakers to billions, the alchemical journey is a transformative odyssey that requires not only scientific acumen but also the courage to venture into uncharted territories. As we draw to a close in this chapter, I invite you to delve further into the world of chemistry-driven innovation through the resources shared below. These resources are your compass, guiding you toward a deeper understanding of the intricate relationship between science and commerce.

Expand your knowledge by exploring the works of scholars and experts who have illuminated the pathways of successful chemistry-driven ventures. Dive into the research conducted by Chen (2023) on content marketing strategies, Perlman (2023) on global safety standards, and Stoffel et al. (2022) on direct-to-consumer testing. Each of these studies offers unique insights into the strategies, challenges, and opportunities that await those who dare to blend chemistry with entrepreneurship.

Engage with like-minded entrepreneurs and innovators who share your passion for turning chemistry concepts into marketable gold. Join forums, attend conferences, and participate in discussions that revolve around the intersection of science and commerce. Learn from the experiences of those who have embarked on their own alchemical journeys, and draw inspiration from their successes and setbacks.

As you set forth on your own alchemical journey, remember that the world eagerly awaits your unique touch. By embracing the challenges, you are poised to reap the rewards that come with transforming chemistry into tangible solutions that cater to consumer needs. The formula for success lies in a potent blend of scientific innovation, strategic partnerships, and effective marketing. This is a journey of transformation, exploration, and limitless possibilities—one that has the power to shape industries, improve lives, and leave an enduring mark on the world.

So, as you conclude this chapter, I encourage you to step boldly into the realm of chemistry-driven entrepreneurship. Equip yourself with knowledge, collaborate with fellow visionaries, and let your chemistry-driven vision take flight. With the right formula, unwavering determination, and the alchemical spirit that propels innovation, you have the potential to turn chemistry into marketable gold and forge a legacy of transformation that resonates for generations to come.

9.10. References

[1] Adkonkar, A., Angrish, A. K., & Bansal, S. K. (2022). A Paradigm Shift in Pharmaceutical Marketing. *Paradigm Shift in Marketing and Finance, 107*.

[2] Chen, Y. (2023). Comparing content marketing strategies of digital brands using machine learning. *Humanities and Social Sciences Communications, 10*(1), 1-18. https://www.nature.com/articles/s41599-023-01544-x

[3] Elf, P., Werner, A., & Black, S. (2022). Advancing the circular economy through dynamic capabilities and extended customer engagement: Insights from small sustainable fashion enterprises in the UK. *Business Strategy and the Environment, 31*(6), 2682-2699. https://doi.org/10.1002/bse.2999

[4] Kargal, R. G., & Ranganathan, S. (2022). Social-Media Enabled Direct-To-Consumer Sales Of Areca-Nut Saplings: Case Study. *Fostering Resilient Business Ecosystems and Economic Growth: Towards the Next Normal, 34*.

[5] Mishra, R. (2023). Study on the role of Below-the-line Advertising agencies in Pharmaceutical Industry. *resmilitaris, 13*(2), 3681-3702. https://resmilitaris.net/menu-script/index.php/resmilitaris/article/view/2892

[6] Nguyen, B., & Tran, T. (2020). Digital marketing strategy for a medium-sized sustainable fashion brand: Case: Népra Oy. https://www.theseus.fi/handle/10024/346314

[7] Paintsil, A. (2019). *Consumer engagement with modern luxury direct-to-consumer brands on social media: A study of glossier*. University of Delaware.

[8] Pearce, D. D., & Pearce II, J. A. (2020). Distinguishing attributes of high-growth ventures. *Business Horizons, 63*(1), 23-36. https://doi.org/10.1016/j.bushor.2019.10.003

[9] Perlman, R. L. (2023). *Regulating Risk: How Private Information Shapes Global Safety Standards*. Cambridge University Press.

[10] Rouault, G. (2021). Developing Sustainability Marketing Strategies: A Case Study of Crocs. *Papers of the Research Society of Commerce and Economics, 62*(1), 213-221.

[11]   Scheele, L. (2021). Sustainable marketing and business: prospects and challenges in agribusiness. https://cardinalscholar.bsu.edu/items/a64d4594-ed68-415d-8629-328aa9628454

[12]   Schofield, C. A., Ponzini, G. T., & Becker, S. J. (2020). Evaluating approaches to marketing cognitive behavioral therapy: does evidence matter to consumers?. *Cognitive Behaviour Therapy*, *49*(4), 257-269. https://doi.org/10.1080/16506073.2019.1682654

[13]   Schoolman, E. D., Morton, L. W., Arbuckle Jr, J. G., & Han, G. (2021). Marketing to the foodshed: Why do farmers participate in local food systems?. *Journal of Rural Studies*, *84*, 240-253. https://doi.org/10.1016/j.jrurstud.2020.08.055

[14]   Stoffel, M., Greene, D. N., Beal, S. G., Foley, P., Killeen, A. A., Shafi, H., & Terrazas, E. (2022). Direct-to-Consumer testing for routine purposes. *Clinical chemistry*, *68*(9), 1121-1127. https://doi.org/10.1093/clinchem/hvac106

10. Crafting Success Stories: Marketing and Promotion

10.1. Introduction

Imagine a world where beakers bubble with more than just colorful liquids and test tubes hold more than mere reactions. In this chapter, we embark on a fascinating journey that seamlessly bridges the gap between the meticulously controlled confines of laboratories and the dynamic realm of bustling markets. Here, the very essence of chemistry concepts undergoes a metamorphosis, evolving into tangible products that not only satisfy needs but also captivate the imagination of consumers. This transition from lab to marketplace exemplifies the intricate dance between scientific ingenuity and consumer desire.

As we delve into this captivating narrative, it becomes evident that success is not solely a product of scientific prowess; rather, it is the harmonious symphony of science and strategy. Just as a chemical reaction requires precise proportions and specific conditions, crafting a compelling marketing strategy necessitates a meticulous understanding of the audience, the competitive landscape, and the prevailing trends. The alchemical fusion of chemistry and marketing is a realization that the principles governing a product's formulation are intrinsically linked to the principles that drive its promotion.

This exploration takes us beyond the boundaries of traditional academia, echoing the insights of Igorevna (2023), who discerned how innovative marketing technologies revolutionized the music industry. This shift underscores the universal application of effective marketing techniques across diverse domains, from music to chemistry-driven products. Bhatia and Gupta's exploration of the influence of public relations on lifestyle branding reinforces the notion that the world beyond laboratories is as much about perception and image as it is about scientific accuracy. In this journey, chemistry-driven products cease to be mere commodities; they metamorphose into vehicles of aspiration, embodiment of values, and reflections of identities.

Intriguingly, the transition from lab to market parallels the transformation that occurs on the virtual landscape. As highlighted by Mou (2020), social media platforms like TikTok and Instagram have emerged as potent catalysts, effectively transmuting obscure notions into viral trends. The phenomenon extends beyond entertainment, as evidenced by Sundaram, Sharma, and Shakya's (2020) research, which illustrates the power of social media advertisement in brand building. This digital revolution has brought the world closer, enabling chemistry-driven products to transcend geographical boundaries and resonate with global audiences.

This journey also echoes the pioneering spirit of entrepreneurs who dared to venture beyond their laboratories, armed with innovative marketing strategies. Ahmed and Abdulkareem (2023) offer a glimpse into the entertainment industry, where big data analytics dissect audience behavior and fuel content recommendations. The intersection of science and marketing is unmistakable, with analytical insights illuminating pathways to capture consumer attention effectively. Adeola, Hinson, and Evans (2020) further reaffirm that the digital generation is deeply influenced by impactful social media strategies, laying a foundation for chemistry-driven products to establish meaningful connections.

In the world of chemistry-driven products, branding goes beyond mere aesthetics; it represents an amalgamation of science and storytelling. Harju's (2023) insights into the impact of branding and social media marketing in the sports apparel industry parallel the significance of evoking emotions and narratives that transcend the laboratory's boundaries. This dynamic interplay beckons entrepreneurs to adopt the role of storytellers, weaving narratives that resonate with the values and aspirations of their audience.

In the grand tapestry of transforming chemistry into marketable gold, this chapter sets the stage for an awe-inspiring spectacle. As we navigate through the pages that follow, we shall uncover the strategies, stories, and secrets that underpin the journey of turning chemistry concepts into marketable marvels. Just as an alchemist meticulously combines elements to create gold, we, too, shall craft a narrative that synthesizes the essence of chemistry with the art of marketing, ultimately forging a path to success.

Turning chemistry concepts into marketable gold is an art that goes beyond the laboratory. It's about understanding not just molecules and reactions, but also the pulse of the market and the desires of consumers. Crafting a successful marketing strategy begins with aligning your product with your target audience's needs and aspirations (Igorevna, 2023). This process mirrors the careful balance required in chemical reactions, where precise proportions are essential for success.

As revealed by Igorevna (2023), innovative marketing technologies have played a pivotal role in promoting music projects, igniting global trends and captivating audiences. This intersection of innovation and marketing applies seamlessly to the chemistry-driven products arena, where transformative ideas can capture the imagination of consumers. Just as musical compositions are marketed to resonate with particular audiences, chemistry-driven products must evoke a sense of connection and utility among their potential users.

Delving deeper into the realm of consumer perception, Bhatia and Gupta's research unravels the intricate influence of public relations on lifestyle branding. They highlight how strategic communication can mold brand identity, presenting products as more than their functional value—rather, they become symbols of a lifestyle, aspiration, or ethos. In the context of chemistry-driven products, this understanding underscores the need to communicate not just the product's attributes but also the story and values it represents.

The dynamic interplay between chemistry and marketing is akin to the synergy of chemical reactions, where catalysts enable transformations. Similarly, a well-crafted marketing strategy acts as a catalyst, accelerating the journey from lab to market success. Understanding the nuances of consumer behavior is key, as illustrated by Mou's (2020) research on social media marketing campaign strategies. Platforms like TikTok and Instagram have revolutionized marketing dynamics, offering a stage where chemistry-driven products can shine through engaging visuals and compelling narratives. In this realm, creativity acts as a catalyst, sparking interactions and fostering a sense of curiosity.

Sundaram, Sharma, and Shakya (2020) reinforce the power of social media advertisement, illustrating how carefully designed content can resonate deeply with audiences and build brand loyalty. This resonates in the chemistry-driven product landscape, where well-crafted marketing materials can illuminate the science behind the innovation while also engaging potential users on a personal level. By leveraging these platforms, chemistry-driven entrepreneurs can demystify complex concepts and foster genuine connections.

In the modern world, where information flows at an unprecedented pace, perception and communication strategies are pivotal. Bhatia and Gupta's exploration of lifestyle branding serves as a testament to the power of perception in shaping consumer preferences. As chemistry-driven entrepreneurs, it is essential to recognize that the market perception of your product—its brand—is as influential as its scientific attributes. Aligning your brand with the values and aspirations of your target audience, while weaving in the scientific narrative, creates a compelling fusion that resonates in the modern marketplace.

10.3. The Social Media Alchemy

In the age of social media, where attention spans are fleeting and trends are born and fade in a blink, creating buzz around your product has become a captivating art form (Mou, 2020). Mou's study on social media marketing campaign strategies accentuates the transformative potential of platforms like TikTok and Instagram, platforms that have redefined how products are introduced to the world. The chemistry-driven products realm is no exception to this phenomenon, as the captivating visual nature of these platforms aligns perfectly with the need to communicate complex concepts succinctly.

As detailed by Mou (2020), the succinctness of short-form videos resonates with the fast-paced nature of modern communication. TikTok and Instagram encapsulate this dynamic, serving as stages where chemistry-driven products can sparkle in the spotlight. These platforms allow entrepreneurs to showcase their products through compelling visuals that distill intricate scientific concepts into bite-sized, engaging content. The result is an amalgamation of science and creativity, resonating with audiences across diverse demographics.

The influence of social media goes beyond mere exposure; it encompasses the very essence of brand building. Sundaram, Sharma, and Shakya (2020) underscore the power of social media advertisements in not only capturing attention but also in laying the foundation for enduring brand loyalty. This observation is of paramount importance for chemistry-driven products, where authenticity and meaningful narratives can cultivate a loyal user base.

By leveraging the potential of social media, chemistry-driven entrepreneurs can communicate the value proposition of their products, weaving the scientific journey into the broader fabric of consumer experience. This is the alchemy of modern marketing—transmuting scientific complexity into compelling narratives, transforming potential users into brand advocates, and harnessing the virality inherent to these platforms to ensure that your chemistry-driven creation is not just understood, but celebrated.

While social media is an essential ingredient, advertising remains a cornerstone of marketing success (Rathore, 2019). Rathore's exploration of innovative fashion marketing strategies serves as a beacon, illuminating how creativity can catalyze revolutions within industries. Indeed, this same principle resonates within the realm of chemistry-driven products, where clever advertising campaigns possess the remarkable ability to transcend traditional marketing paradigms.

Rathore's research reinforces the idea that advertising is not just about promoting a product; it's about weaving a compelling narrative that resonates with consumers' aspirations and desires. In the world of chemistry-driven products, this means showcasing not only the physical attributes of the innovation but also the scientific journey that led to its creation. By intertwining the science behind the product with the human story of innovation, entrepreneurs can create a narrative that evokes curiosity and excitement, much like the anticipation stirred by an engaging movie trailer.

Consider Rathore's insights as a template for transforming your chemistry-driven product into a captivating story. Imagine an advertising campaign that not only showcases the technical intricacies but also introduces the individuals who envisioned and brought it to life. By personifying the chemistry and presenting it as an embodiment of human ingenuity, advertising campaigns can elevate the perception of chemistry-driven products beyond the laboratory, making them relatable and inspiring.

Just as Rathore's exploration extends beyond conventional fashion marketing, chemistry-driven entrepreneurs can harness this philosophy to revolutionize how their products are perceived. Clever advertising campaigns become a bridge between the science and the consumer, kindling a fire of interest that burns brighter as the story unfolds. Through this narrative alchemy, advertising transforms from a promotional tool to an immersive experience—one where chemistry concepts metamorphose into engaging stories, and potential customers are not merely observers, but active participants in the journey.

10.5. Stories That Sell: Entrepreneurial Journeys

Behind every successful chemistry-driven product, there's an entrepreneur with a vision—a vision that transforms scientific concepts into tangible solutions that impact lives. Let's step into the shoes of these modern alchemists, drawing inspiration from their journeys as they navigate the intricate intersection of chemistry and marketing.

Ahmed and Abdulkareem's (2023) entrepreneurial odyssey in the entertainment industry exemplifies the transformative potential of big data analytics. Their journey, rooted in data-driven decisions, underscores the importance of understanding audience behavior to maximize revenue. Just as they dissected audience preferences to tailor content recommendations, chemistry-driven entrepreneurs can harness data to create personalized marketing strategies. By understanding consumer preferences and behavior, entrepreneurs can refine their messaging and target their marketing efforts with laser precision.

Adeola, Hinson, and Evans (2020) shed light on the synthesis of successful social media strategies for the digital generation. Their insights provide a roadmap for resonating with today's tech-savvy consumers, emphasizing the power of authenticity and relatability. In the realm of chemistry-driven products, this authenticity translates to showcasing the human story behind the innovation. Entrepreneurs can connect with their audience by revealing the individuals and passion that drive the scientific journey. By weaving the human narrative into marketing campaigns, chemistry-driven products evolve from sterile concepts to relatable and inspiring solutions.

Ahmed and Abdulkareem's and Adeola, Hinson, and Evans' narratives remind us that success stories are not limited to a specific industry; rather, they are founded on universal principles. Chemistry-driven entrepreneurs are, at their core, storytellers—crafting narratives that bridge the gap between the technical intricacies of their products and the emotional aspirations of their audience. By embracing data-driven insights and authentic storytelling, entrepreneurs become the architects of compelling marketing strategies that resonate deeply and drive success.

10.6.   Building Brands: Beyond the Lab Coat

A strong brand is more than just a label; it's a fusion of science and storytelling that creates a lasting impression. Harju's (2023) exploration of the impact of branding and social media marketing in the sports apparel industry underscores the critical role of consistency and authenticity. In a world inundated with information and options, a clear and compelling brand message becomes the beacon that guides consumers through the maze of choices. This principle holds true for chemistry-driven products, where the marriage of science and brand identity shapes consumer perception and loyalty.

Harju's insights emphasize the importance of consistency in brand messaging. Just as a chemical reaction requires precise conditions for a successful outcome, a successful brand relies on a consistent narrative that aligns with the product's essence. Chemistry-driven entrepreneurs can draw from this wisdom by ensuring that their branding speaks coherently about both the scientific innovation and the values it embodies. By weaving these elements into a seamless brand story, entrepreneurs create a memorable and distinctive identity that resonates with consumers.

Authenticity emerges as a cornerstone in Harju's exploration, mirroring the findings of Adeola, Hinson, and Evans (2020) about the resonance of authenticity in social media strategies. Authenticity is the bridge that connects the scientific authenticity of the product with the genuine emotions of consumers. Chemistry-driven products have a unique opportunity to leverage this authenticity—by sharing not only the technical attributes but also the passion, dedication, and human story behind their creation.

The ever-expanding digital landscape amplifies the significance of a compelling brand message. Just as Harju's research indicates the role of social media in amplifying brand impact, chemistry-driven entrepreneurs can harness these platforms to extend their reach and engage with consumers on a global scale. By presenting their products as more than mere scientific innovations, entrepreneurs can cultivate an emotional connection that transcends geographical boundaries.

In a world where competition is fierce and information is abundant, a well-crafted brand message serves as a rudder, steering the perception of chemistry-driven products in the desired direction. By blending science with storytelling and aligning branding with authenticity, chemistry-driven entrepreneurs can carve their own unique space in the market—a space that resonates with consumers and sets their products apart from the competition.

10.7. Navigating Challenges and Emerging Trends

The journey from beakers to billions is a thrilling odyssey, yet it's not without its challenges—challenges that chemistry-driven entrepreneurs must navigate with insight and resilience. Regulatory hurdles, competition, and the shifting tides of consumer preferences can create formidable roadblocks along the way. Acknowledging and understanding these challenges is essential for devising strategies that ensure the successful transformation of chemistry concepts into marketable gold.

Ahmed and Abdulkareem's (2023) recognition of the significance of staying informed about emerging trends echoes resoundingly in this context. By keeping a vigilant eye on the evolving landscape, entrepreneurs can anticipate shifts in consumer behavior and preferences. Just as they harnessed the power of big data analytics to analyze audience behavior, chemistry-driven entrepreneurs can leverage data to foresee trends that may impact their products. This proactive approach empowers entrepreneurs to adapt their marketing strategies in real-time, ensuring their chemistry-driven products remain relevant and appealing to the target audience.

Incorporating sustainable and ethical practices has transcended the realm of being just a trend—it's now an imperative that resonates deeply with conscientious consumers (Ahmed & Abdulkareem, 2023). The modern consumer is not merely interested in the product itself; they're invested in the ethical values and sustainability ethos upheld by the company. Chemistry-driven entrepreneurs can harness this trend by ensuring that their products adhere to ethical and sustainable standards. By integrating eco-friendly practices into the product's narrative and highlighting these aspects in their marketing strategies, entrepreneurs can tap into the growing consumer demand for responsible consumption.

It's important to note that the challenges and trends are interconnected. For instance, as regulatory frameworks evolve to accommodate new technologies and innovations, staying informed about these changes becomes imperative (Ahmed & Abdulkareem, 2023). Navigating regulatory hurdles with finesse requires chemistry-driven entrepreneurs to blend scientific expertise with a keen understanding of the legal and compliance landscape. By proactively addressing regulatory concerns, entrepreneurs can position their products as not just innovative but also compliant, instilling consumer confidence.

The journey from beakers to billions is not linear; it's a dynamic process that demands adaptability and forward-thinking. Chemistry-driven entrepreneurs who embrace the lessons from Ahmed and Abdulkareem's insights and incorporate sustainable practices will find themselves well-equipped to navigate challenges and capitalize on emerging trends. By fusing science with strategic awareness, entrepreneurs can steer their ventures through the currents of change, ultimately arriving at the shores of success.

10.8.   Case Studies: Pioneering the Transformation

Let's journey into the heart of entrepreneurship by delving deeper into real-life case studies that illuminate the path from chemistry concepts to successful marketable products. By examining these case studies, we gain invaluable insights into the intricate process of bridging the gap between innovation and consumer engagement, thereby transforming theoretical concepts into tangible realities.

Drawing inspiration from Ahmed and Abdulkareem's (2023) data-driven success story in the entertainment industry, we witness the transformative power of analytics in the entrepreneurial landscape. Ahmed and Abdulkareem harnessed big data analytics to understand audience behavior and optimize content recommendations, ultimately maximizing revenue. In the context of chemistry-driven products, this approach could involve leveraging data to pinpoint target demographics, optimize marketing channels, and fine-tune product positioning. By extrapolating this methodology, entrepreneurs can guide their marketing efforts with precision, ensuring that their chemistry-driven innovations reach the right audiences at the right time.

Adeola, Hinson, and Evans (2020) provide a roadmap for digital engagement by synthesizing successful social media strategies. Their exploration delves into the strategies that resonate with the digital generation—authenticity, relatability, and engaging content. By studying their insights, chemistry-driven entrepreneurs can craft social media campaigns that connect on a personal level, humanizing their innovations and fostering emotional connections with potential users. These case studies offer a glimpse into how seemingly abstract chemistry concepts can be communicated effectively through digital channels, providing a blueprint for captivating online audiences.

Furthermore, Rathore's (2019) exploration of innovative fashion marketing strategies offers a profound lesson in creativity's potential to revolutionize industries. Rathore's insights extend seamlessly to chemistry-driven products, emphasizing that innovation isn't confined to the laboratory. By injecting creativity into marketing campaigns, entrepreneurs can captivate audiences and challenge traditional marketing norms. Rathore's case study serves as a reminder that embracing innovation doesn't solely pertain to product development—it's a philosophy that should permeate every aspect of entrepreneurship, including marketing and promotion.

As we journey through these case studies, we realize that they are not mere success stories; they are blueprints for transforming ideas into marketable gold. The entrepreneurs who pioneered these paths grappled with challenges, harnessed innovation, and crafted strategies that aligned with consumer desires. Their journeys provide us with a lens through which we can decode the complexities of the chemistry-driven product landscape. By assimilating their strategies, adapting them to our unique contexts, and infusing our entrepreneurial spirit, we set ourselves on a trajectory to forge our own successful path from chemistry concepts to thriving marketable products.

As we embark on the intricate journey of crafting a marketing strategy for your chemistry-driven product, it's crucial to recognize that your path is uniquely yours. The world of chemistry-driven products is as diverse and dynamic as the elements on the periodic table, and your entrepreneurial journey will be shaped by your innovation, determination, and the insights gleaned from research and experience.

Embrace the spirit of experimentation, drawing inspiration from the scientific method itself. Rathore's (2019) exploration of innovative fashion marketing strategies reveals that creativity and risk-taking are potent catalysts for reshaping industries. Just as researchers iterate and refine their experiments, entrepreneurs can iterate and refine their marketing strategies, learning from each attempt and adapting their approach accordingly. This iterative process allows for optimization, enabling chemistry-driven entrepreneurs to discover what resonates most effectively with their target audience.

Failures, far from being setbacks, are stepping stones to success. In the world of chemistry, failed experiments often provide valuable insights that lead to breakthroughs. Similarly, the world of marketing is marked by trial and error. The case studies we've explored, from Ahmed and Abdulkareem (2023) to Adeola, Hinson, and Evans (2020), remind us that success is often built upon a foundation of lessons learned from failures. Each misstep is an opportunity to refine your approach, align with your audience's preferences, and come closer to creating a resonant marketing strategy.

Celebrate your successes along the way. Just as chemistry involves the synthesis of elements to create compounds, your marketing strategy is a synthesis of strategies, insights, and efforts that culminate in success. Every milestone achieved is a testament to your dedication and ingenuity. Harju's (2023) exploration of the impact of branding and social media marketing underscores the value of consistency and authenticity in building brand equity. By weaving your achievements into a consistent narrative, you create a compelling story that resonates with consumers and stakeholders alike.

Remember that the essence of chemistry is the formation of bonds—connections between atoms that lead to the creation of compounds with unique properties. In the same vein, your marketing strategy is about forging connections—with consumers who relate to your story, collaborators who share your vision, and the world that awaits the transformation your chemistry-driven product promises. By infusing your strategy with authenticity, data-driven insights, and the spirit of innovation, you are not just crafting a marketing plan; you are embarking on a journey to turn your chemistry concepts into marketable gold—a journey that is distinctly yours and brimming with potential.

10.10. Take Action: Your Alchemical Challenge

Take a moment to reflect on the chemistry-driven concept that ignites your passion. Picture its intricate scientific intricacies and envision the potential it holds for transforming lives. Now, as you stand at the crossroads of science and entrepreneurship, consider how you can transmute its scientific essence into a compelling story that resonates with your target audience.

Drawing inspiration from the references in this chapter, you're poised to infuse innovation into your marketing strategy, mirroring the pioneers who ventured into the worlds of music (Igorevna, 2023), lifestyle branding (Bhatia & Gupta), social media marketing (Mou, 2020), fashion (Rathore, 2019), big data analytics (Ahmed & Abdulkareem, 2023), and more. The stories of these visionaries are your guiding stars, illuminating the path from laboratory brilliance to market success.

Consider how you can leverage social media platforms to capture the attention of a global audience, as illuminated by Sundaram, Sharma, and Shakya (2020). Visualize short-form videos that distill your complex concept into bite-sized, engaging content, just as Mou (2020) highlighted. Embrace the authenticity that resonates with consumers, as demonstrated by Adeola, Hinson, and Evans (2020), to create a narrative that evokes curiosity and emotional connection.

Harju's (2023) insights emphasize the significance of branding and authenticity in building consumer loyalty. Infuse your marketing plan with these principles, ensuring that your brand message not only communicates the scientific innovation but also reflects the values and ethos that underpin your chemistry-driven concept.

The journey ahead is one of transformation and growth. As you craft your marketing strategy, remember that the fusion of science and strategy is the alchemy that turns ideas into marketable gold. Your journey is uniquely yours, just as every compound forged in a laboratory possesses its distinct properties. Take action today—translate your passion into a compelling story, integrate innovative marketing techniques, and embark on your own odyssey from beakers to billions. Your chemistry-driven venture has the potential to not only captivate the world but also leave an indelible mark on the landscape of innovation. Your journey starts now.

In the grand tapestry of innovation, the journey from beakers to billions encapsulates an exhilarating, challenging, and transformative odyssey. As we conclude this chapter, brimming with insights from experts and illuminated by real-world success stories, it's essential to recognize the profound impact that you, as an entrepreneur, possess in shaping this narrative. Armed with knowledge and driven by the spirit of possibility, you hold the alchemical power to transmute chemistry concepts into marketable gold.

The knowledge gained from references such as Igorevna (2023) and Bhatia and Gupta underscores the strategic importance of crafting a compelling marketing strategy that resonates with your target audience. Just as music projects and lifestyle brands are tailored to evoke specific emotions and connections, your chemistry-driven product has the potential to capture the imagination and address the needs of consumers in a novel and impactful way.

The wisdom gleaned from Mou (2020) and Sundaram, Sharma, and Shakya (2020) guides you in harnessing the transformative force of social media and innovative advertising campaigns. The captivating visuals, short-form videos, and engaging content strategies explored in these references serve as tools to communicate the scientific journey of your product, fostering genuine connections and fostering curiosity among potential users.

The exploration of branding by Harju (2023) and the insights from Ahmed and Abdulkareem (2023) remind us that authenticity, consistency, and data-driven insights are the pillars upon which enduring success is built. By weaving a compelling brand narrative that authentically reflects both the scientific and human dimensions of your product, you can establish a strong presence in the market while addressing evolving trends and consumer preferences.

As you stand at the threshold of this remarkable journey, remember that you are more than an entrepreneur; you are an alchemist. Your chemistry-driven product holds the potential to ignite a spark of curiosity, create lasting connections, and influence lives. Embrace this power and channel your creativity, innovation, and determination into crafting a marketing strategy that showcases not only the science but also the story, values, and potential of your creation.

In the end, the world awaits your alchemical transformation—a transformation that extends beyond laboratory walls and product specifications. It's a transformation that resonates in the hearts and minds of consumers, collaborators, and the global market. Your journey from beakers to billions is an ode to the fusion of science and entrepreneurship, a testament to the power of turning chemistry into marketable gold. With your strategy as the catalyst and your passion as the driving force, you are poised to illuminate the market and redefine what is possible in the world of chemistry-driven products. The world is eager to witness your transformation—go forth and let your chemistry-driven product shine.

10.12. References

[1] Adeola, O., Hinson, R. E., & Evans, O. (2020). Social media in marketing communications: A synthesis of successful strategies for the digital generation. *Digital transformation in business and society: Theory and cases*, 61-81. https://link.springer.com/chapter/10.1007/978-3-030-08277-2_4

[2] Ahmed, A., & Abdulkareem, A. M. (2023). Big Data Analytics in the Entertainment Industry: Audience Behavior Analysis, Content Recommendation, and Revenue Maximization. *Reviews of Contemporary Business Analytics*, 6(1), 88-102. https://orcid.org/0000-0002-5515-3800

[3] Bhatia, A. K., & Gupta, A. The Influence of Public Relations on Lifestyle Branding. *Innovations and Practices in Mass Communication*, 49.

[4] Harju, M. (2023). Impact of branding & social media marketing in the digital era: Sports apparel brands. https://www.theseus.fi/handle/10024/802772

[5] Igorevna, K. A. (2023). Innovative Marketing Technologies in Promoting Music Projects: International Experience Analysis. *European science*, (1 (65)), 89-94.

[6] Mou, J. B. (2020). *Study on social media marketing campaign strategy--TikTok and Instagram* (Doctoral dissertation, Massachusetts Institute of Technology). https://dspace.mit.edu/handle/1721.1/127010

[7] Rathore, B. (2019). Chic Strategies: Revolutionizing the Industry through Innovative Fashion Marketing. *International Journal of New Media Studies: International Peer Reviewed Scholarly Indexed Journal*, 6(2), 23-33. https://www.ijnms.com/index.php/ijnms/article/view/121

[8] Sundaram, R., Sharma, D. R., & Shakya, D. A. (2020). Power of digital marketing in building brands: A review of social media advertisement. *International Journal of Management*, 11(4). https://papers.ssrn.com/sol3/papers.cfm?abstract_id=3600866

11. Feedback Loop: Listening to the Customer

11.1. Introduction

As we embark on a captivating expedition through the intricate world of transforming intricate chemistry concepts into highly sought-after marketable products, one pivotal factor rises above all: the invaluable input of customer feedback. Picture a bustling chemistry lab, alive with a symphony of experiments and exhilarating discoveries. In the pages that follow, we delve into the remarkable narratives of visionary entrepreneurs and relentless innovators who masterfully weave these scientific revelations into products that not only captivate the market's imagination but also address its needs. Our focal point: the indispensable and often underestimated role of customer feedback within this awe-inspiring journey of metamorphosis.

Every chemistry experiment is a canvas upon which various compounds, catalysts, and reactions intermingle to create new possibilities. Similarly, in the dynamic realm of business, customer feedback provides the brushstrokes that steer the evolution of products toward unprecedented heights. Alzoubi et al. (2022) illuminate the transformative potential of open innovation, exemplified by BLE technology, in enhancing marketing strategies, customer satisfaction, and loyalty. This synergy between technological advancement and customer-centricity harmonizes seamlessly with the ethos of chemistry-driven innovation.

Just as a chemist deciphers the subtle interplay of elements, so do entrepreneurs unravel the intricate nuances of consumer preferences. Ali et al. (2021) navigate this intersection by exploring how service quality in the hospitality industry intricately threads its way through the tapestry of customer satisfaction. In this chapter, we journey side by side with these pioneers, unveiling the artistry behind translating customer insights into remarkable market offerings.

In the world of molecules and compounds, each bond forged or broken has a distinct impact on the resulting product. Similarly, entrepreneurs forge relationships with their clientele, with customer feedback serving as the very backbone of this partnership. Shokouhyar et al. (2020) illuminate the influential post-purchase interaction, underscoring how after-sales service quality profoundly shapes customer contentment. Just as a chemical equation's elements collaborate to yield a specific outcome, the elements of customer feedback collaboratively guide product evolution.

This voyage doesn't just recount the successes; it paints the complete picture, encompassing the myriad challenges and triumphs faced during the process of transforming ideas into tangible marketable gold. As we navigate the intriguing narratives of product development, the interplay of chemistry and customer insight shines like a beacon of guidance, revealing the alchemical process by which entrepreneurs transmute raw concepts into valuable commodities.

11.2.   The Chemistry of Customer Satisfaction

In the world of chemistry, reactions follow distinct pathways, each leading to a unique product. Just as atoms combine in precise arrangements to yield diverse compounds, the business landscape thrives on the synthesis of innovative ideas. Similarly, in the intricate world of transforming chemistry concepts into tangible marvels, the role of customer feedback takes center stage.

Alzoubi et al. (2022) provide illuminating insights into this synergy between innovation and customer satisfaction. Their exploration of the impact of open innovation and BLE technology on marketing strategies underscores the power of these modern tools in amplifying customer contentment and fostering loyalty. These technological enablers parallel the role of catalysts in chemical reactions, accelerating the process of refining products to meet consumer desires.

Just as a skilled chemist adjusts reaction conditions to optimize yields, entrepreneurs heed the voice of the customer to enhance their offerings. The progression of chemical reactions occurs through stepwise transformations, and similarly, product evolution relies on iterative feedback loops. These loops function as the equilibrium state in a reaction, constantly readjusting and optimizing based on the dynamic interplay of customer preferences and evolving market trends.

The synergy between chemistry and business is palpable as we traverse the realm of innovation. Much like chemists observe the evolution of reactions over time, entrepreneurs keenly monitor the trajectory of their products in the market.

Alzoubi et al.'s (2022) findings draw a parallel between the progressive advancement of chemical reactions and the gradual refinement of marketing strategies, underpinned by customer-centric input. This interplay fosters a harmonious symphony where customer feedback guides the strategic maneuvers of entrepreneurs, much like chemical reactions navigate a predetermined pathway.

As chemists manipulate variables to steer reactions toward desired outcomes, entrepreneurs tinker with product attributes to align with customer preferences. This dynamic process, much akin to chemical reactions, elucidates the fascinating journey from initial concept to tangible product. Like the fusion of reactants in a test tube, customer feedback fuses with innovation to yield not only products but an enduring connection between consumers and their coveted commodities.

11.3.   From Lab to Market: A Successful Transformation

Consider the captivating journey of Lara, an entrepreneur who metamorphosed her fervor for sustainable cleaning products into a thriving business venture. Commencing her odyssey from the confines of her basement laboratory, Lara embarked on a meticulous endeavor to craft eco-friendly detergents that resonated with her vision. However, the true alchemical transformation unfolded when she opened a conduit for customer feedback, demonstrating the harmonious convergence of chemistry and commerce.

Lara's narrative finds resonance in the work of Ali et al. (2021), who delved into the intricate relationship between service quality and customer satisfaction within the hospitality industry. Much like Lara, entrepreneurs within the hospitality sector recognize the significance of customer experience, a sentiment that spans the intersection between chemistry and customer engagement. Through meticulous attention to detail and an unwavering commitment to customer preferences, Lara pioneered a movement that resonates with eco-conscious consumers.

Aligned with the findings of Shokouhyar et al. (2020), Lara employed customer feedback as a compass for navigating the seas of market demands. By actively soliciting insights through surveys and leveraging the expansive reach of social media, she instilled her products with a distinct customer-oriented essence. The evolution of her formulations and packaging stands as a testament to the ever-evolving nature of chemical reactions, where slight modifications lead to profound transformations.

Lara's journey echoes the sentiments of Alzoubi et al. (2022), who elucidate the indispensable role of open innovation and technological advancements in bolstering marketing strategies. The success of her brand attests to the prowess of customer feedback as a catalyst for innovation. In the crucible of customer engagement, Lara harnessed the reactions between consumer preferences and her formulations, culminating in a flourishing enterprise at the vanguard of the green cleaning revolution.

Just as chemical compounds align in intricate arrangements to yield distinct molecules, Lara's brand flourished by orchestrating customer feedback and innovative formulations. Her journey stands as a beacon, guiding us through the intricate choreography of chemistry-inspired entrepreneurship. The alchemical fusion of customer insights and innovative formulations, much like the joining of atoms in a chemical reaction, illuminated a path to success that encapsulates the very essence of chemistry-driven product evolution.

11.4. Customer-Centric Chemistry: Crafting the Perfect Formula

In the realm of innovation, entrepreneurs share a kinship with chemists who deftly manipulate reaction conditions to yield desired outcomes. The symmetry between these disciplines is poignantly echoed by the insightful work of Shokouhyar et al. (2020), who underscore the profound impact of after-sales service quality on customer satisfaction. Just as chemical reactions unfold through the orchestration of multiple variables, so does the journey of product evolution, guided by the harmonious interplay of customer preferences.

Consider a chemistry equation laden with variables; each element represents a distinct customer preference, akin to a reactant in a chemical reaction. The outcome, much like the final product, emerges as a result of carefully balancing these factors. This analogy is vividly exemplified in the cosmetic industry, where products cater to a spectrum of preferences. Companies, reminiscent of chemists in their laboratories, engage in a continuous cycle of reformulation. In this arena, the dynamic equilibrium of chemistry parallels the dynamic equilibrium between customer needs and product offerings.

The cosmetic industry's ability to recalibrate skincare products aligns with the sentiment of Alzoubi et al. (2022), who emphasize open innovation's contribution to marketing strategies, customer satisfaction, and loyalty. This innovation, akin to adjusting the reagents in a reaction, embodies the principle of customer-centric chemistry. The iterative cycle of reformulation reflects the iterative nature of chemical reactions, wherein each alteration propels the process toward an optimal outcome.

In the marriage of chemistry and customer insight, companies distill customer feedback into the very essence of their products. This ethos, akin to a chemist fine-tuning reaction conditions, leads to the fine-tuning of product attributes based on nuanced preferences. As Shokouhyar et al. (2020) elucidate the importance of post-sales engagement, we glean insights into how the careful balance of variables can yield the desired outcomes of customer loyalty and satisfaction.

The beauty of this narrative lies in its resonance with real-world practices. Just as a chemist's artistry emerges in the lab, entrepreneurs channel their creativity into the art of crafting products that resonate with customers. By embracing the mosaic of customer preferences, they strike a harmonious chord that transcends mere transactions. This blend of chemistry and commerce is not just a formula but a melody, a symphony that echoes the intricate dance of balancing variables for a harmonious result.

11.5.   The Innovation Elixir: From Problem to Solution

The journey of turning chemistry concepts into marketable treasures is a terrain where innovative thinking reigns supreme. Amidst this journey stands Steve, a chemist whose narrative reflects the fusion of science and ingenuity in the face of adversity. Steve's path unveils the pivotal role of innovative problem-solving, a principle echoed in the study of Huang, Lee, and Chen (2019), who delved into the influence of service quality on customer loyalty in the B2B technology service industry. This interplay between innovation and customer satisfaction paints a fascinating portrait of chemistry-driven product development.

Imagine Steve's challenge: crafting an adhesive that bonded metals with unyielding strength. However, his initial formula fell short, evoking customer dissatisfaction. Here, his experience mirrors the insights of Myo, Khalifa, and Aye (2019), who probed the impact of service quality on customer loyalty in the hospitality industry. Just as service quality shapes customer loyalty, the quality of Steve's adhesive determined the loyalty of his customer base.

In the realm of chemistry, a reaction's success hinges on the selection of appropriate reactants and conditions. Similarly, Steve's journey relied on the selection of multidisciplinary collaborators, akin to reactants in a formula. Collaborating with material scientists and engineers echoes the principles elucidated by Latif, Pérez, and Sahibzada (2020) in their exploration of corporate social responsibility and customer loyalty. Steve's interdisciplinary approach demonstrates that like chemical reactions, collaboration catalyzes transformative outcomes.

Steve's collaborative endeavor serves as a testament to the essence of cross-disciplinary collaboration, an aspect emphasized by Setiawati et al. (2019), who explored the role of customer relationship management (CRM) in enhancing customer loyalty. In this narrative, the amalgamation of chemistry and engineering mirrors the symbiotic relationship between CRM practices and customer loyalty. This convergence underscores the notion that just as chemistry is a multidisciplinary endeavor, so is the journey of entrepreneurship and innovation.

Steve's journey offers a profound lesson: innovation thrives when rooted in collaboration and guided by the crucible of customer feedback. The multidisciplinary engagement that enhanced his adhesive's performance mirrors the intricate choreography of a chemical reaction's steps. His story becomes an emblem of how embracing diverse perspectives and disciplines can lead to the transformation of challenges into triumphs.

11.6.   Navigating the Regulatory Labyrinth

In the intricate world of transforming chemistry concepts into marketable commodities, navigating the regulatory landscape emerges as a critical facet, echoing the meticulous adherence of chemical compounds to precise rules. The journey of Sarah, an entrepreneur embarking on the development of an innovative food additive, encapsulates the interplay between innovation and regulatory compliance. Her tale finds resonance in the research of Adak, Pradhan, and Shukla (2022), who conducted a systematic review on sentiment analysis of customer reviews, emphasizing the role of explainable artificial intelligence. This narrative underscores the symbiotic relationship between innovation and adherence to regulations, illuminating the tightrope walk of chemistry-driven product development.

Sarah's journey presents an allegory to the chemical principle of precision and equilibrium. As chemical reactions demand precise proportions, so do regulatory norms mandate strict compliance. When Sarah faced the daunting labyrinth of regulatory barriers, she sought guidance akin to a chemist consulting textbooks to decipher complex equations. Just as sentiment analysis unpicks customer feedback, Sarah's consultations elucidated the nuanced regulations and guidelines that govern the product landscape.

The intricate dance between regulatory compliance and innovation mirrors the synergy explored by Setiawati et al. (2019), who examined the pivotal role of customer relationship management (CRM) in enhancing customer loyalty and brand image. Similarly, Sarah's story showcases that just as CRM fosters loyalty, regulatory compliance fosters consumer trust by ensuring safety and efficacy. Her journey reflects the dynamic interplay between chemistry and regulations, affirming that just as chemical compounds align in harmonious arrangements, products must adhere to regulatory harmonization.

The collaboration between Sarah and regulatory experts mirrors the multidisciplinary engagement advocated by Huang, Lee, and Chen (2019), who explored the influence of service quality on customer loyalty in the B2B technology service industry. This synergy of diverse expertise harmonizes with Sarah's journey, as her collaboration upheld the product's integrity while adhering to intricate regulations. This is a testament to the profound understanding that just as service quality nurtures loyalty, regulatory compliance nurtures consumer confidence.

In this journey of turning chemistry into marketable gold, Sarah's narrative is emblematic of the intricate balance entrepreneurs must strike between innovation and regulatory conformity. Just as a chemist balances reactants to ensure a successful reaction, Sarah's compliance ensured her product's successful journey from concept to market. Her story is a beacon, guiding aspiring entrepreneurs through the maze of regulations, and reaffirming that just as chemistry adheres to its laws, products too must honor the laws that govern their existence.

11.7.   Reflecting on the Journey: Personal Insights

As you set forth on your voyage of transmuting chemistry concepts into invaluable marketable treasures, allow the guiding light of customer feedback to illuminate your path. The significance of this guiding principle echoes with profound clarity through the works of Ali et al. (2021), who ventured into the realm of service quality and customer satisfaction within the hospitality industry. Just as their exploration mirrored the fusion of service quality and customer contentment, your expedition is rooted in the intertwining of chemistry-driven innovation and meeting consumer needs.

Imagine each customer insight as a star in your firmament, collectively forming a North Star that directs your journey. The experience of Adam et al. (2020) in harnessing digital platforms to enhance customer satisfaction and loyalty mirrors the digital landscape you navigate. Their experiences become a constellation of inspiration, guiding your digital marketing strategies with the same ingenuity and precision that characterizes chemistry-driven product development.

The journey ahead mirrors the essence of Setiawati et al. (2019), who emphasized the pivotal role of customer relationship management (CRM) in fostering loyalty and brand image. Their insights draw parallels between the chemistry of CRM and the chemistry of your products. Just as the right balance of elements yields a harmonious compound, the right balance of customer engagement and innovation leads to the creation of marketable gold.

As you reflect on the collective wisdom amassed from the annals of research, remember that your journey's narrative intertwines with those who have trod similar paths. Much like the entrepreneurs who turned ideas into marketable gold with innovation, collaboration, and compliance, your journey is your unique canvas. The stories of Lara, Steve, and Sarah echo through time, resonating with your aspirations as you transmute chemistry into products that captivate the market's imagination.

The profound interplay between customer feedback and chemistry unfolds not only as a narrative but as a life philosophy. Just as chemical reactions proceed with precision, each customer interaction and feedback point guides your path with the same precision, steering you toward a destination where innovation and market dynamics converge.

11.8. Charting a Course for the Future

The tapestry of chemistry-driven product development unfolds with ever-increasing complexity and innovation. As you chart your course toward the future, remember that the realm of customer feedback and product evolution is ever-evolving. The dawning era of data analysis presents a paradigm shift akin to the discoveries in the world of chemistry. With the advent of sentiment analysis, as elucidated by Adak et al. (2022), customer reviews are transformed into a wellspring of insights that guide the trajectory of product development.

Imagine sentiment analysis as a laboratory instrument that dissects customer feedback, revealing nuanced insights previously hidden from view. This transformation mirrors the transitions in chemistry, where the lens of analysis opens up new dimensions in the understanding of reactions. The pioneering work of Adak et al. (2022) underscores the importance of this transition, forging a bridge between the unfiltered voices of customers and the precise trajectory of product evolution.

In the crucible of modern business, sustainability emerges as a driving force, reflecting the ethos of Latif, Pérez, and Sahibzada (2020). Their exploration of corporate social responsibility (CSR) within the hotel industry echoes the parallel between chemistry's commitment to ethical principles and the integration of sustainability into business practices. Just as chemists uphold ethical standards in their research, corporations embrace CSR as a testament to their commitment to both society and customers.

The trajectory from laboratory to real-world application is mirrored in the evolution of customer feedback's impact on product development. Just as chemistry concepts find their place in the world, the insights distilled from customer feedback transition from raw data to informed decisions that shape product offerings. This shift aligns with the transition from theoretical chemistry to the practical applications that enrich our lives.

As the contours of chemistry and business intertwine, you stand at the intersection of innovation and consumer insight. The journey of turning chemistry into marketable gold, much like chemistry itself, is an ongoing narrative of discovery and transformation. As you navigate this terrain, fueled by customer feedback and the boundless realm of data analysis, remember that just as chemistry's evolution shapes our world, your endeavors will shape the market's landscape.

11.9.   Your Eureka Moment: Embrace the Journey

As you forge ahead on your transformative voyage, inching closer to your Eureka moment, the echoes of research stories reverberate with insights that illuminate your path. Recall the case of Setiawati et al. (2019), a beacon of how customer relationship management (CRM) radiates beyond mere transactions, elevating loyalty and brand image. This narrative is not just an illustration but a blueprint to be wielded as you step into the realm of innovation and chemistry-driven product development.

Imagine CRM as a catalyst that initiates a profound reaction, shaping the bonds between consumer and product. Just as Setiawati et al. (2019) unveiled the profound impact of CRM on loyalty and image, your journey parallels this dynamic interplay. Their work mirrors the essence of your transformational narrative, where chemistry evolves into cherished products and customer relationships flourish.

As you journey forward, the tapestry of your actions is woven from the threads of wisdom left by those who have journeyed before you. The importance of integrating feedback loops, a sentiment endorsed by Alzoubi et al. (2022) and Shokouhyar et al. (2020), becomes a refrain guiding your every step. Like a reaction constantly refined by feedback, your journey evolves with each interaction, each insight captured from customer feedback.

Innovation, that elusive alchemy, finds its roots in the pioneering steps of entrepreneurs like Steve, whose story resonates with Huang, Lee, and Chen's (2019) exploration of service quality's influence on customer satisfaction and loyalty. Their work becomes a touchstone for your journey, a reminder that innovation springs from the crucible of customer-centric solutions.

Regulations, often likened to the constants that govern chemical reactions, present themselves as an essential aspect of your voyage. Here, Sarah's narrative of navigating regulatory hurdles aligns with Adak et al.'s (2022) research on sentiment analysis, where compliance shapes the landscape of consumer perception. Just as regulation ensures chemical reactions adhere to principles, regulatory compliance safeguards your products' integrity.

The transformational journey from chemistry to marketable gold, interwoven with consumer insights, is a narrative that unfurls with every endeavor. As you progress, remember that every innovation, every product, is a chapter in a narrative that chemistry and commerce compose together. Your journey is a symphony of ideas, insights, and inspiration, a melody that resonates with the hearts and minds of your consumers.

11.10. Conclusion: Unleash Your Inner Alchemist

As the final curtain falls on this chapter, let the tales of visionaries like Lara, Steve, Sarah, and a constellation of others serve as your guiding stars. The chemistry that unfolds in the transformation of concepts into marketable treasures is a symphony of innovation, led by the rhythm of customer feedback. Much like the skilled alchemist who extracts gold from base metals, you possess the alchemical artistry to transmute raw chemistry into captivating products. This journey, adorned with insights and inspired by a commitment to excellence, mirrors the exploration of Huang, Lee, and Chen (2019), who ventured into the impact of service quality on loyalty. Their study becomes a beacon, illuminating your voyage with the spirit of pursuit.

Imagine yourself as the modern-day alchemist, standing at the intersection of chemistry and commerce. Your journey is akin to an alchemical process, where you refine and combine elements to create something of immense value. Just as Setiawati et al. (2019) illuminated the transformational effects of customer relationship management (CRM), your journey showcases the transformational power of aligning chemistry with customer insights. The crucible of CRM becomes your chamber of transformation, turning ideas into tangible value.

The symphony of your journey echoes with the profound chord struck by Alzoubi et al. (2022), who explored the role of open innovation in refining marketing strategies, customer satisfaction, and loyalty. In your narrative, the innovation is not merely confined to technology or processes; it encompasses the innovation of thought, of perspective, and of embracing feedback as the elixir that propels your journey.

As you stand at the crossroads of innovation and chemistry, remember that your journey's compass is calibrated by the insights gleaned from the pioneers of research. The insights of Shokouhyar et al. (2020) mirror your path, affirming that the influence of after-sales service quality is not confined to a single industry—it resonates through the chambers of every enterprise that strives to win the heart of customers.

Armed with these insights, fortified by the wisdom of experts, and fueled by the fire of your passion, you are poised to embark on your transformational journey. The journey is not solitary; it is a shared narrative, a saga woven by the confluence of chemistry and human insight. Embrace the feedback loop, for in it, you forge the link between the chemistry that fuels your creation and the commerce that propels your success.

The chapter may close, but the narrative continues. You are the protagonist of your story—a story where chemistry becomes not just a scientific endeavor, but a journey of innovation, collaboration, and marketable alchemy. Let this be the start of your tale, where ideas take flight, chemistry meets commerce, and you, the alchemist, turn concepts into marketable gold.

11.11. References

[1]   Adak, A., Pradhan, B., & Shukla, N. (2022). Sentiment analysis of customer reviews of food delivery services using deep learning and explainable artificial intelligence: Systematic review. *Foods*, *11*(10), 1500. https://doi.org/10.3390/foods11101500

[2]   Adam, M., Ibrahim, M., Ikramuddin, I., & Syahputra, H. (2020). The role of digital marketing platforms on supply chain management for customer satisfaction and loyalty in small and medium enterprises (SMEs) at Indonesia. *International Journal of Supply Chain Management*, *9*(3), 1210-1220. https://core.ac.uk/download/pdf/328146431.pdf

[3]   Ali, B. J., Gardi, B., Jabbar Othman, B., Ali Ahmed, S., Burhan Ismael, N., Abdalla Hamza, P., ... & Anwar, G. (2021). Hotel service quality: The impact of service quality on customer satisfaction in hospitality. *Ali, BJ, Gardi, B., Othman,*

BJ, Ahmed, SA, Ismael, NB, Hamza, PA, Aziz, HM, Sabir, BY, Anwar, G.(2021). Hotel Service Quality: The Impact of Service Quality on Customer Satisfaction in Hospitality. International Journal of Engineering, Business and Management, 5(3), 14-28.
https://papers.ssrn.com/sol3/papers.cfm?abstract_id=3851330

[4]   Alzoubi, H., Alshurideh, M., Kurdi, B., Akour, I., & Aziz, R. (2022). Does BLE technology contribute towards improving marketing strategies, customers' satisfaction and loyalty? The role of open innovation. *International Journal of Data and Network Science, 6*(2), 449-460.
https://doi.org/10.5267/j.ijdns.2021.12.009

[5]   Huang, P. L., Lee, B. C., & Chen, C. C. (2019). The influence of service quality on customer satisfaction and loyalty in B2B technology service industry. *Total Quality Management & Business Excellence, 30*(13-14), 1449-1465.
https://doi.org/10.1080/14783363.2017.1372184

[6]   Latif, K. F., Pérez, A., & Sahibzada, U. F. (2020). Corporate social responsibility (CSR) and customer loyalty in the hotel industry: A cross-country study. *International Journal of Hospitality Management, 89*, 102565.
https://doi.org/10.1016/j.ijhm.2020.102565

[7]   Myo, Y. N., Khalifa, G. S., & Aye, T. T. (2019). The impact of service quality on customer loyalty of Myanmar hospitality industry: the mediating role of customer satisfaction. *International Journal of Management and Human Science, 3*(3), 1-11.

[8]   Setiawati, A. P., Susetyorini Susetyorini, U. E., Rusdiyanto, R., Astanto, D., Ulum, B., Khadijah, S. N., ... & Umanailo, M. C. B. (2019). The Role Of Customer Service Through Customer Relationship Management (CRM) To Increase Customer Loyalty And Good Image. *International Journal of Scientific and Technology Research, 8*(10), 2004-2007.

[9]   Shokouhyar, S., Shokoohyar, S., & Safari, S. (2020). Research on the influence of after-sales service quality factors on customer satisfaction. *Journal of Retailing and Consumer Services, 56*, 102139.
https://doi.org/10.1016/j.jretconser.2020.102139

12.   Sustainability Science: Eco-Friendly Marketability

12.1.   Introduction

In the ever-evolving landscape of consumer preferences, a remarkable transformation is taking place – a shift towards sustainability and eco-friendliness. The demand for products that harmonize with the environment while maintaining quality and performance has grown exponentially. Recent empirical investigations by Prakash, Choudhary, Kumar, Garza-Reyes, Khan, and Panda (2019) have illuminated the intricate relationship between consumer values and their attitudes towards eco-friendly packaged products. This surge in interest stems from consumers' altruistic and egoistic values, which are increasingly influencing their purchase intentions, underscoring the significance of aligning products with environmentally conscious ideals.

This chapter, titled "*Sustainability Science: Eco-Friendly Marketability,*" embarks on a journey to explore the intersection of chemistry and marketability within this transformative landscape. The amalgamation of chemistry and marketability isn't just a theoretical abstraction; it's a tangible phenomenon that has given rise to a new wave of eco-friendly innovations. By drawing insights from real-life stories, such as Tuomisto's (2019) groundbreaking exploration of cultured meat, we gain a deeper understanding of how chemistry can spearhead the creation of sustainable alternatives in industries traditionally marked by environmental concerns.

As we delve into this world of innovation, we'll witness entrepreneurs turning chemistry concepts into marketable gold, creating products that not only satisfy consumer needs but also nurture the planet we call home. This nexus of science and commerce is underscored by the findings of Nguyen, Parker, Brennan, and Lockrey (2020), whose exploration of consumer definitions of eco-friendly packaging sheds light on the resonance between sustainable products and consumers' perceptions. The journey that unfolds in this chapter traces the trajectory from lab experiments to successful eco-friendly products, guided by insights from pioneers like Salih and Salimon (2021), who have pioneered the development of eco-friendly green biolubricants from renewable plant oil sources.

In an age where the impact of human activities on the environment looms large, the chemistry-driven solutions explored in this chapter provide a glimmer of hope. Through case studies like Gayathiri, Prakash, Karmegam, Varjani, Awasthi, and Ravindran's (2022) investigation of biosurfactants for sustainable agriculture, we understand that chemistry offers not just individual innovations, but a paradigm shift towards holistic and environmentally responsible practices. This journey isn't just about concepts; it's about tangible products that echo the ethos of sustainability.

The voyage ahead promises to unravel the strategies, challenges, and triumphs of transforming chemistry concepts into marketable eco-friendly products. From eco-design principles that frame the work of Khan, Jhariya, Raj, Banerjee, and Meena (2021) to the segmentation approaches unveiled by Jaiswal, Kaushal, Singh, and Biswas (2020), this chapter aspires to be a beacon for entrepreneurs seeking to navigate this complex terrain. By weaving in insights from Hasan, Ahmad-Hamdani, Rosli, and Hamdan (2021) regarding bioherbicides for sustainable weed management, we glimpse the future potential of chemistry-driven solutions that foster harmony between human progress and ecological integrity.

As we embark on this journey, let us reflect on the powerful potential of chemistry. It is a force that transcends laboratory walls, merging with market dynamics to create products that leave a lasting legacy. The following pages will not only offer insights and practical tips for your own ventures but will also inspire you to see the world through a sustainable lens. The chemistry of eco-friendly marketability beckons – a realm where innovation, responsibility, and success converge for the betterment of our planet and the generations that will inherit it.

12.2.1.   In the Lab and Beyond: The Birth of Green Biolubricants

One compelling example comes from the work of Salih and Salimon (2021), who dived into the realm of biolubricants derived from renewable plant oil sources. Their study delves deep into the chemistry behind these innovative lubricants, standing as a testament to the power of green chemistry. With meticulous research, these scientists harnessed the inherent properties of plant oils to engineer lubricants that not only match but rival their petroleum-based counterparts in performance. Through the transformation of plant oils, chemistry has provided a solution that goes beyond a mere replacement; it has initiated a paradigm shift in the industry.

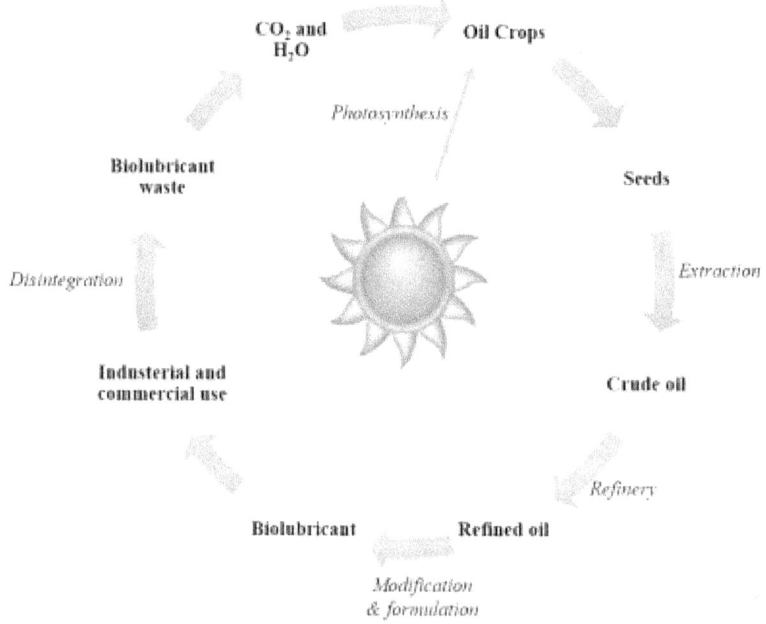

Salih and Salimon's (2021) exploration is marked by a meticulous analysis of plant oil structures, molecular interactions, and their behavior under various conditions. By skillfully manipulating these variables, they managed to create lubricants that not only showcase remarkable performance characteristics but also adhere to the principles of sustainability. The precision and insight of their work underscore the capacity of chemistry to drive innovation that aligns with environmental ideals.

The impact of their research resonates beyond the laboratory walls. By introducing eco-friendly alternatives to traditional lubricants, Salih and Salimon have made a significant stride towards reducing carbon footprints. The implications of their work reach industries where lubricants play a pivotal role in machinery and operations. This pioneering shift is underscored by the findings of Prakash et al. (2019), who discovered a strong alignment between consumer values and eco-friendly products. The marriage of Salih and Salimon's innovation with consumer values emphasizes not just the viability but the marketability of eco-friendly chemistry-driven products.

Moreover, this transformation isn't confined to theory. The products borne from Salih and Salimon's research have transcended the laboratory bench to perform exceptionally well in the real world. Their green biolubricants stand as an embodiment of chemistry's potential to provide solutions that balance performance and environmental responsibility. This resonates with the insights offered by Pahlevi and Suhartanto (2020) regarding the integrated model of green loyalty, where product quality and environmental consciousness synergistically create lasting consumer connections.

In the pursuit of sustainable and eco-friendly solutions, the story of Salih and Salimon's (2021) biolubricants emerges as a beacon of hope. It encapsulates the essence of chemistry-driven innovation – the ability to transform nature's resources into products that not only rival but surpass their conventional counterparts. This transformative journey is a testament to the intricate dance between science, marketability, and environmental stewardship. As we proceed on our exploration, we'll continue to witness such stories of chemistry shaping a greener future for industries and the planet at large.

12.2.2. A Fusion of Values: Consumer Attitudes and Eco-Friendly Packaging

Prakash, Choudhary, Kumar, Garza-Reyes, Khan, and Panda (2019) delved into the complex interplay between consumer values and purchase intentions, shedding light on an intricate dance that shapes the market landscape. Their empirical investigation revealed a fascinating relationship: consumers who hold altruistic and eco-friendly values exhibit significantly stronger positive attitudes towards products packaged sustainably. This discovery unearths a critical aspect of chemistry-driven product development, emphasizing the profound impact of aligning marketing strategies with these deeply ingrained consumer values.

The study by Prakash et al. (2019) is a revelation that goes beyond traditional market research. It peers into the minds of consumers, uncovering the values that underpin their purchasing decisions. The alignment between altruism and eco-friendliness offers entrepreneurs a profound understanding of what resonates with mindful consumers. This understanding, as underscored by the work of Jaiswal, Kaushal, Singh, and Biswas (2020), can serve as a North Star guiding the journey from chemistry concepts to products that genuinely connect with target audiences.

The insights from Prakash et al. (2019) don't merely highlight a correlation; they underscore causation. The strong positive attitudes observed among consumers who prioritize eco-friendliness illuminate the potential of eco-friendly packaging as a gateway to influencing purchase intentions. This reality aligns beautifully with the consumer definition of eco-friendly packaging outlined by Nguyen, Parker, Brennan, and Lockrey (2020), wherein consumers associate sustainability not just with the product itself, but also with the packaging that embodies their eco-conscious values.

For entrepreneurs seeking to transform chemistry concepts into marketable products, Prakash et al.'s (2019) study offers a practical roadmap. By understanding the psychology that drives consumer attitudes, product developers can craft marketing narratives that resonate deeply with the target audience. This approach isn't limited to theory; it's a testament to how chemistry can be translated into a compelling story that captures consumer hearts and minds. The fusion of values and chemistry is the bridge that connects the laboratory to the marketplace, demonstrating that successful products are not just driven by innovation but also by an alignment with values that shape our world.

12.2.3.	Loyalty to Green: The Integrated Model of Green Loyalty

The concept of green loyalty, as introduced by Pahlevi and Suhartanto (2020), offers a profound insight into the psychology of consumers and their relationship with eco-friendly products. This concept serves as a cornerstone that unites environmental consciousness with consumer devotion, transforming mere products into symbols of a sustainable lifestyle. Pahlevi and Suhartanto's examination of this concept in the context of eco-friendly plastic products demonstrates the potential of chemistry-driven innovations to establish enduring connections with consumers.

Pahlevi and Suhartanto's (2020) research delves into the mechanics of green loyalty, unearthing a framework that goes beyond traditional consumer-brand relationships. As we journey through their study, we are presented with a multi-faceted model that emphasizes the interplay between multiple factors. It becomes clear that green loyalty is not solely determined by a product's eco-friendly attributes; rather, it's a dynamic interaction between product quality, environmental considerations, and the dedication of consumers to embrace and advocate for sustainable choices.

In the context of chemistry-driven products, this model acquires even greater significance. Entrepreneurs seeking to transform chemistry concepts into marketable eco-friendly solutions can draw invaluable lessons from Pahlevi and Suhartanto's (2020) findings. By understanding that the allure of a product goes beyond its functional attributes, they can strategically infuse environmental consciousness into their offerings. This approach finds resonance with the work of Hasan, Ahmad-Hamdani, Rosli, and Hamdan (2021), who explored bioherbicides as an eco-friendly tool for sustainable weed management. The convergence of chemical innovation with environmental responsibility is the fulcrum upon which green loyalty pivots.

Furthermore, Pahlevi and Suhartanto's (2020) model bridges the gap between consumer values and sustainable consumption behavior. Just as Prakash et al. (2019) demonstrated the correlation between values and attitudes, Pahlevi and Suhartanto elucidate the transformation of attitudes into steadfast loyalty. This understanding not only enriches the realm of consumer psychology but also empowers entrepreneurs to craft marketing strategies that tap into this intricate dance of chemistry, sustainability, and loyalty.

In a world where environmental concerns are paramount, the integrated model of green loyalty is an embodiment of the harmonious coexistence of chemistry-driven innovations and consumer devotion to sustainability. As we proceed through this exploration, we'll encounter more stories that resonate with this model, reinforcing the notion that chemistry can foster lasting relationships between products and their users, founded on the principles of environmental responsibility.

12.3. From Classroom to Market: Success Stories Unveiled

12.3.1. Cultured Meat: A Sustainable Burger for a Sustainable Planet

The pioneering work of Tuomisto (2019) ushers us into a realm where chemistry and biology intertwine to create a paradigm-shifting solution: cultured meat. Tuomisto's exploration delves into the heart of an environmental conundrum posed by conventional meat production. The profound impact of this research lies in its proposition of a revolutionary alternative that not only harmonizes with the environment but also holds the potential to transform an industry with immense ecological implications.

Tuomisto's (2019) research unpacks the intricate science behind cultured meat, offering a glimpse into the innovative techniques that blend chemistry and biology to cultivate meat without the environmental toll of traditional livestock production. This intersection of disciplines is a testament to the multifaceted nature of sustainability science. The scientific revelations in Tuomisto's work hold the potential to drive a transformative shift in how we produce and consume meat – an insight that aligns beautifully with the exploration of bio-composites by Karimah et al. (2021).

The concept of cultured meat isn't just an abstract idea; it's a tangible pathway to a greener future. By circumventing the resource-intensive aspects of traditional meat production, cultured meat emerges as a solution that resonates with the principles of eco-friendliness. This resonates with Prakash et al.'s (2019) discovery that consumer values influence attitudes towards sustainable products. The alignment between consumer values and the very essence of cultured meat underscores its potential marketability and societal acceptance.

As we delve into Tuomisto's (2019) exploration, we confront the magnitude of environmental benefits that cultured meat offers. The reduction in land and water use, mitigation of greenhouse gas emissions, and alleviation of ethical concerns surrounding animal welfare present a compelling case for its adoption. This realization finds resonance with the research of Salih and Salimon (2021), who unveiled eco-friendly green biolubricants derived from renewable plant oil sources. Both instances exemplify the potential of chemistry to reshape industries and practices for a more sustainable world.

The journey into cultured meat isn't just about science; it's about hope. It's about reimagining industries and practices through the lens of innovation and environmental responsibility. As we navigate this chapter, let us not only marvel at the scientific prowess behind cultured meat but also envision a world where the marriage of chemistry and biology leads to a more sustainable, humane, and ecologically conscious future.

<table><tr><td>12.3.2.</td><td>Harnessing Nature's Power: Biosurfactants in Agriculture</td></tr></table>

Embarking on a journey to the heart of sustainable agriculture, Gayathiri, Prakash, Karmegam, Varjani, Awasthi, and Ravindran (2022) lead us to the fields where biosurfactants emerge as eco-friendly solutions with transformative potential.

Their research unearths a world where naturally derived compounds redefine the landscape of crop cultivation, offering insights that extend beyond the traditional boundaries of chemistry and agriculture.

As we immerse ourselves in their study, we encounter a profound paradigm shift. Biosurfactants, often hailing from microbial sources, emerge as powerful agents of change. These compounds, as explored by Gayathiri et al. (2022), possess the unique ability to enhance crop yields while preserving environmental safety. This journey underscores the dynamic interplay between science and nature, as researchers leverage the intricate chemistry of biosurfactants to unlock nature's potential for sustainable agricultural practices.

The implications of Gayathiri et al.'s (2022) work extend far beyond the confines of the laboratory. Their exploration exemplifies the essence of sustainability science – the pursuit of innovations that not only address immediate challenges but also contribute to a resilient future. This commitment aligns beautifully with the integrated model of green loyalty introduced by Pahlevi and Suhartanto (2020), where the interplay between product quality, environmental consciousness, and consumer devotion fosters lasting connections between products and users.

As we follow Gayathiri et al.'s (2022) research, we encounter tangible examples of biosurfactants transforming soil quality, nutrient uptake, and pest management. The synergy between chemistry and agriculture becomes apparent as we witness the profound impact of these naturally derived compounds. This impact resonates with Hasan, Ahmad-Hamdani, Rosli, and Hamdan's (2021) exploration of bioherbicides, highlighting how chemistry-driven solutions can reshape the way we manage and enhance our natural resources.

Gayathiri et al.'s (2022) study marks a turning point in the journey towards sustainable agriculture. The research illuminates a path where chemistry-driven innovations align with ecological stewardship, demonstrating that the cultivation of our planet's resources can be harmonized with the principles of environmental responsibility. As we traverse these pages, let us not only grasp the scientific significance but also recognize the profound potential of biosurfactants to reimagine how we nurture our planet's bounty.

12.4.1.   Designing for a Greener Tomorrow: Eco-Design Principles

Guiding us through the intricate tapestry of sustainable innovation, Khan, Jhariya, Raj, Banerjee, and Meena (2021) offer a compass that points toward a greener future. Their research introduces us to the realm of eco-designing, where sustainability is woven into the very fabric of products from the outset. This journey isn't merely about making slight adjustments; it's about a paradigm shift that integrates chemistry into sustainable agriculture, highlighting the paramount importance of designing products that resonate with the planet's long-term health.

Khan et al.'s (2021) work is a masterclass in the art of eco-design. It delves into strategies that go beyond cosmetic alterations, emphasizing a holistic approach that considers every facet of a product's life cycle. This depth of thought aligns harmoniously with the concept of green loyalty introduced by Pahlevi and Suhartanto (2020), where the interplay between product quality, environmental consciousness, and consumer devotion underscores the holistic nature of successful sustainability-driven innovations.

The essence of Khan et al.'s (2021) research lies in its ability to align chemistry with sustainable agriculture. It underscores that innovation isn't merely about developing new products; it's about crafting solutions that nourish the planet and its inhabitants. This ethos resonates with the pioneering work of Tuomisto (2019) in the realm of cultured meat – a testament to the potential of chemistry to shape industries for the better.

As we journey through Khan et al.'s (2021) insights, we recognize that sustainable product design isn't confined to a single discipline; it's a collaborative endeavor that transcends boundaries. Just as biosurfactants (Gayathiri et al., 2022) and bioherbicides (Hasan et al., 2021) harmonize chemistry with agriculture, eco-design harmonizes chemistry with design principles. This symphony of disciplines speaks to the interconnectedness of innovation and sustainability.

The chapter doesn't merely present strategies; it presents a philosophy. By embracing eco-design principles, entrepreneurs have the opportunity to weave sustainability into the very DNA of their products. Khan et al.'s (2021) work isn't just a roadmap; it's an invitation to reimagine how products are conceived, developed, and integrated into our lives. As we proceed, let us absorb not only the strategies but also the spirit of eco-design, recognizing that every innovation can be a step towards a greener, more harmonious tomorrow.

Jaiswal, Kaushal, Singh, and Biswas (2020) usher us into the dynamic world of green consumers, where preferences intersect with sustainability aspirations. Their research paints a detailed picture of this diverse landscape through the lens of market segmentation. This exploration isn't confined to a mere study of demographics; it's a revelation of the intricate tapestry of consumer profiles that underscores the importance of connecting chemistry-inspired products with the right audience.

Jaiswal et al.'s (2020) study introduces us to the crux of successful chemistry-driven product marketing – understanding the nuances that shape consumer behavior. By delving into green market segmentation, the research reveals that green consumers aren't a monolithic group. They are a mosaic of values, motivations, and preferences, as highlighted by Prakash et al. (2019) in their investigation of consumer attitudes and eco-friendly packaged products.

The significance of this exploration lies in its practical implications. The research illuminates the pathways for entrepreneurs to create products that resonate deeply with specific segments of green consumers. The synergy between consumer values and chemistry-driven innovations comes to life as we consider the alignment between eco-friendly products and the diverse consumer profiles identified by Jaiswal et al. (2020). This resonates with the integrated model of green loyalty introduced by Pahlevi and Suhartanto (2020), where the interaction of environmental consciousness and product quality fosters lasting consumer connections.

As we immerse ourselves in Jaiswal et al.'s (2020) research, we encounter a treasure trove of insights that guide product development and marketing strategies. This exploration isn't just a theoretical exercise; it's a practical roadmap to ensuring that chemistry-inspired innovations find their rightful place in the market. By understanding the kaleidoscope of green consumers, entrepreneurs can tailor their approaches, resonating with the work of Tuomisto (2019), who demonstrated how tailored approaches can revolutionize industries through concepts like cultured meat.

This chapter unlocks the doors to understanding the diverse landscape of green consumers. It's an invitation to walk in their shoes, to grasp their motivations, and to align chemistry-driven products with their aspirations. The journey ahead is one of precision, empathy, and strategic insight, where chemistry meets psychology to create meaningful connections between products and people who share a common commitment to sustainability.

12.5.1.   Bioherbicides: Nurturing Crops and Ecosystems

Venturing into the realm of sustainable agriculture, Hasan, Ahmad-Hamdani, Rosli, and Hamdan (2021) guide us through the transformative potential of bioherbicides. This segment is a testament to the dynamic interplay between chemistry and agriculture, where innovative solutions are derived from nature to redefine weed management practices. As we delve into their research, we unveil how bioherbicides not only nurture crops but also safeguard the delicate balance of ecosystems, setting the stage for a sustainable revolution in agriculture.

Hasan et al.'s (2021) study transports us to the very heart of bioherbicides, showcasing the power of harnessing nature's arsenal to combat weeds. The exploration of bioherbicides aligns seamlessly with the ethos of eco-friendliness, echoing the research of Gayathiri et al. (2022), who illuminated the potential of biosurfactants in agriculture. Just as biosurfactants work in harmony with soil and plants, bioherbicides embody a philosophy where chemistry becomes an ally in maintaining the delicate equilibrium of ecosystems.

The significance of bioherbicides is underscored by the escalating concerns surrounding conventional herbicides' environmental impact. This exploration mirrors the pioneering work of Tuomisto (2019) in the realm of cultured meat – an acknowledgment of the necessity to shift paradigms for the greater good. Hasan et al.'s (2021) research unveils a greener pathway, one that harmonizes chemistry with sustainable agricultural practices.

The implications of bioherbicides extend far beyond crop protection. By adopting these nature-inspired solutions, agriculture moves towards a more harmonious relationship with the environment. This transformation aligns with the integrated model of green loyalty introduced by Pahlevi and Suhartanto (2020), where the symbiotic relationship between environmental consciousness, product quality, and consumer devotion fosters lasting connections.

As we navigate Hasan et al.'s (2021) findings, we discover that bioherbicides aren't just alternatives; they are the vanguard of a new era in agriculture. This research is an invitation to embrace chemistry's potential as a catalyst for positive change. The story of bioherbicides isn't just a chapter in the book; it's a narrative that embodies the essence of sustainable innovation, reminding us that chemistry has the power to revolutionize industries while nurturing the planet we call home.

12.5.2. From Nature to Product: The Bio-Composite Revolution

Karimah, Ridho, Munawar, Adi, Damayanti, Subiyanto, and Fudholi (2021) beckon us into the world of bio-composites, where chemistry and nature collaborate to create sustainable materials of remarkable versatility. This segment of the chapter peels back the layers of this innovative realm, shedding light on the intricate balance struck between scientific ingenuity and the wealth of natural resources. As we delve into their research, we unravel the fascinating journey from the raw essence of nature to the creation of products that epitomize eco-friendliness, durability, and adaptability.

Karimah et al.'s (2021) exploration is a journey of transformation. It demonstrates how chemistry-inspired innovation can harness the innate potential of natural fibers, fusing them into bio-composites that challenge traditional material paradigms. This exploration aligns harmoniously with the eco-design principles emphasized by Khan et al. (2021), underscoring the essence of crafting sustainable solutions from the outset.

The significance of bio-composites lies in their ability to redefine industries that depend on materials with specific properties. The blend of natural fibers and chemistry, as highlighted by Karimah et al. (2021), presents a potent formula for producing materials that exhibit the ideal balance of strength, flexibility, and eco-friendliness. This resonance between scientific innovation and environmental consciousness echoes the integrated model of green loyalty introduced by Pahlevi and Suhartanto (2020), where the harmony between product quality and consumer values fosters lasting loyalty.

The journey from nature to bio-composite products isn't just a theoretical exercise; it's a practical demonstration of how chemistry can elevate sustainability. This journey mirrors the essence of bioherbicides (Hasan et al., 2021), biosurfactants (Gayathiri et al., 2022), and cultured meat (Tuomisto, 2019) – each illustrating the transformative potential of chemistry-driven innovation in various domains. The narrative of bio-composites is an embodiment of how chemistry can harness the power of nature to create materials that align with the principles of sustainable innovation.

As we immerse ourselves in Karimah et al.'s (2021) research, we encounter a realm where chemistry bridges the gap between science and nature. It's an invitation to recognize that innovation need not disrupt the balance of our ecosystems but can enhance it. The journey of bio-composites becomes an inspiration for entrepreneurs seeking to blend chemistry with sustainability, forging a path towards products that not only meet human needs but also resonate with the planet's wellbeing.

12.6.   Your Eco-Friendly Venture: Steps to Success

12.6.1.   Reflect and Act: Your Personal Eco-Friendly Odyssey

As you traverse the intricate narratives woven within this chapter, take a moment to immerse yourself in the wealth of insights that have been unearthed. Consider the wisdom imparted by entrepreneurs who, like Salih and Salimon (2021), turned chemistry concepts into biolubricants, demonstrating how innovation can be a gateway to environmentally responsible solutions. Contemplate the journey of those who, inspired by the principles of eco-friendliness, ventured into the world of sustainable packaging (Nguyen et al., 2020), recognizing that values can be the cornerstone of product development.

Reflect on the revelations from Pahlevi and Suhartanto (2020), who delved into the integrated model of green loyalty, and consider how your own aspirations align with these principles. As you ponder the delicate dance between consumer values and loyalty, think of the potential impact your chemistry-inspired venture could have on fostering lasting connections with eco-conscious consumers.

Contemplating Tuomisto's (2019) exploration of cultured meat opens up a world of possibilities. Allow the innovation to spark your imagination, igniting ideas of how chemistry can shape industries in ways that resonate with sustainability and ethical consumption.

Amidst the pages that unravel the dynamics of bioherbicides (Hasan et al., 2021) and biosurfactants (Gayathiri et al., 2022), pause to think about the harmony between chemistry and ecology. Consider how your journey might contribute to the health of both agricultural systems and ecosystems, aligning with the ethos of responsible resource management.

As you engage with the concept of eco-design (Khan et al., 2021), reflect on the profound impact of designing products with sustainability as a guiding principle. Consider how you can weave this approach into your own product development process, ensuring that every step resonates with the principles of eco-friendliness and long-term viability.

This chapter isn't just a collection of stories; it's an invitation to shape your own journey. As you reflect on the narratives, insights, and discoveries shared within these pages, envision the role you could play in turning chemistry into marketable gold that aligns with eco-friendly values. Let the lessons, strategies, and success stories guide you as you embark on your own odyssey of transforming chemistry concepts into products that not only fulfill consumer needs but also nurture the planet we all share.

<table>
<tr><td>12.6.2.</td><td>Chart Your Course: Recommended Resources for Sustainable Success</td></tr>
</table>

To empower your pursuit of transforming chemistry into marketable eco-friendly solutions, we present a curated collection of resources that serve as a compass on your journey. As you navigate the uncharted waters of sustainable innovation, these references, tools, and websites will provide you with the knowledge and guidance needed to navigate the intricacies of chemistry-driven product development.

12.7. Further Reading:

1. **"Biointerfacial Research and Applications in Chemistry"** - Delve deeper into the world of biolubricants and renewable plant oil sources through the comprehensive research presented in Salih and Salimon's (2021) study.

2. **"Consumer Behavior and Sustainable Marketing"** - Extend your understanding of consumer values, attitudes, and behaviors towards eco-friendly products with insights from Prakash et al.'s (2019) empirical investigation.

3. **"Green Loyalty and Sustainable Business Models"** - Explore the integrated model of green loyalty as explored by Pahlevi and Suhartanto (2020), understanding the intricate relationship between product quality, environmental consciousness, and consumer devotion.

4. **"Cultured Meat: A Revolution in Sustainable Agriculture"** - Tuomisto's (2019) work on cultured meat provides a deep dive into a groundbreaking alternative to conventional meat production, showcasing the potential of chemistry to revolutionize industries.

12.7.1.   Online Tools:

1. **Eco-Design Toolkits** - Khan et al. (2021) introduce eco-design principles; explore online toolkits that guide you through the process of integrating sustainability into your product design, ensuring that chemistry is harnessed for lasting environmental impact.

2. **Green Consumer Segmentation Tools** - In alignment with Jaiswal et al.'s (2020) insights, utilize online tools that assist in segmenting and understanding green consumers, enabling you to tailor your marketing strategies effectively.

12.7.2.   Websites:

1. **Sustainable Chemistry Innovation Hub** - Stay updated on the latest trends, breakthroughs, and resources in sustainable chemistry through this online hub that aggregates research, case studies, and practical insights.

2. **Green Business Network** - Join a community of like-minded entrepreneurs and professionals focused on sustainable business practices, and gain access to resources, events, and networking opportunities.

3. **Sustainable Agriculture Knowledge Hub** - Dive into the world of sustainable agriculture through an online platform that offers research, case studies, and practical guidance on integrating chemistry-driven innovations into farming practices.

These recommended resources are more than just references; they are the wind in your sails as you navigate the path of transforming chemistry concepts into eco-friendly marketable solutions. Each resource is a stepping stone towards a more sustainable future, a toolkit to equip you with the knowledge and strategies to make a meaningful impact. As you explore these resources, remember that you are not alone on this journey – a wealth of information and support awaits to empower you in turning your ideas into gold that shines with environmental responsibility.

12.8. Conclusion

As we arrive at the culmination of this chapter, let us reflect on the remarkable journey we've undertaken. It is a journey that started with an idea, a mere spark of curiosity, and transformed into a voyage of innovation that bridges the realms of chemistry and marketability. The passage from beakers to billions isn't just a metaphor; it's a testament to the boundless potential of human ingenuity – a reminder that we possess the power to create products that resonate not only with consumers but also with the very fabric of our planet.

Our exploration has illuminated a path paved with knowledge, insight, and inspiration. We've witnessed entrepreneurs who, like Salih and Salimon (2021), turned scientific concepts into eco-friendly biolubricants, and visionaries who, like Karimah et al. (2021), harnessed the synergy of chemistry and nature to forge bio-composites of remarkable versatility. We've delved into the world of green consumers, bioherbicides, cultured meat, and sustainable packaging – each narrative a testament to the transformative potential of chemistry-inspired innovation.

Armed with this understanding, you stand poised on the threshold of your own odyssey. The insights from Prakash et al. (2019), Pahlevi and Suhartanto (2020), and Jaiswal et al. (2020) have equipped you with the tools to tailor your strategies, aligning your products with consumer values and forging lasting connections. The pioneering work of Tuomisto (2019) and Hasan et al. (2021) has ignited your imagination, showcasing the vast horizons that chemistry-driven solutions can unfold in sustainable industries.

As you step forth into this world of possibility, remember that your journey is not merely a pursuit of profit; it's a commitment to the wellbeing of our planet. The world eagerly awaits your eco-friendly breakthrough, whether it takes the form of a biolubricant that reduces carbon footprints, a sustainable packaging solution that resonates with mindful consumers, or a revolutionary concept that transforms industries.

So seize the moment, armed with the knowledge of how chemistry intertwines with marketability. Allow your curiosity to fuel your innovation, and let your ideas evolve into products that not only meet consumer needs but also reflect your commitment to environmental responsibility. The journey from chemistry concepts to marketable gold is yours to embark upon – a journey that has the potential to transform industries, nurture our planet, and leave a lasting mark on the landscape of innovation. The world is waiting for your contribution; the time is now to turn your ideas into gold that shines brilliantly with sustainability and market success.

12.9. References

[1]   Gayathiri, E., Prakash, P., Karmegam, N., Varjani, S., Awasthi, M. K., & Ravindran, B. (2022). Biosurfactants: potential and eco-friendly material for

sustainable agriculture and environmental safety—a review. Agronomy, 12(3), 662. https://doi.org/10.3390/agronomy12030662

[2]   Hasan, M., Ahmad-Hamdani, M. S., Rosli, A. M., & Hamdan, H. (2021). Bioherbicides: An eco-friendly tool for sustainable weed management. *Plants*, *10*(6), 1212. https://doi.org/10.3390/plants10061212

[3]   Jaiswal, D., Kaushal, V., Singh, P. K., & Biswas, A. (2020). Green market segmentation and consumer profiling: a cluster approach to an emerging consumer market. *Benchmarking: An International Journal*, *28*(3), 792-812. https://doi.org/10.1108/BIJ-05-2020-0247

[4]   Karimah, A., Ridho, M. R., Munawar, S. S., Adi, D. S., Damayanti, R., Subiyanto, B., ... & Fudholi, A. (2021). A review on natural fibers for development of eco-friendly bio-composite: characteristics, and utilizations. *Journal of materials research and technology*, *13*, 2442-2458. https://doi.org/10.1016/j.jmrt.2021.06.014

[5]   Khan, N., Jhariya, M. K., Raj, A., Banerjee, A., & Meena, R. S. (2021). Eco-designing for sustainability. *Ecological intensification of natural resources for sustainable agriculture*, 565-595. https://doi.org/10.1007/978-981-33-4203-3_16

[6]   Nguyen, A. T., Parker, L., Brennan, L., & Lockrey, S. (2020). A consumer definition of eco-friendly packaging. *Journal of Cleaner Production*, *252*, 119792. https://doi.org/10.1016/j.jclepro.2019.119792

[7]   Pahlevi, M. R., & Suhartanto, D. (2020). The integrated model of green loyalty: Evidence from eco-friendly plastic products. *Journal of Cleaner Production*, *257*, 120844. https://doi.org/10.1016/j.jclepro.2020.120844

[8]   Prakash, G., Choudhary, S., Kumar, A., Garza-Reyes, J. A., Khan, S. A. R., & Panda, T. K. (2019). Do altruistic and egoistic values influence consumers' attitudes and purchase intentions towards eco-friendly packaged products? An empirical investigation. *Journal of Retailing and Consumer Services*, *50*, 163-169. https://doi.org/10.1016/j.jretconser.2019.05.011

[9]   Salih, N., & Salimon, J. (2021). A review on eco-friendly green biolubricants from renewable and sustainable plant oil sources. *Biointerface Res. Appl. Chem*, *11*(5), 13303-13327. https://biointerfaceresearch.com/wp-content/uploads/2021/02/20695837115.1330313327.pdf

[10]   Tuomisto, H. L. (2019). The eco-friendly burger: could cultured meat improve the environmental sustainability of meat products?. *EMBO reports*, *20*(1), e47395. https://doi.org/10.15252/embr.201847395

13. The Ever-Changing Landscape: Innovation and Adaptation

13.1. Introduction

In the dynamic world of business, characterized by the rapid ebbs and flows of trends and technologies, the need for continuous innovation stands paramount (Mariani & Wamba, 2020; Hanelt et al., 2021). As industries undergo digital transformations and consumer demands evolve, companies must remain agile to survive and thrive. This chapter embarks on a comprehensive exploration of the intricate art of turning intricate chemistry concepts into tangible and marketable products, unearthing the strategies and resounding success stories of companies that adeptly navigated the ever-shifting landscape of market dynamics (Ciampi et al., 2021; Zhao et al., 2020).

From the bustling laboratories where scientific principles are birthed, to the bustling marketplaces where products are evaluated and embraced, this journey is a vivid tapestry woven from the threads of chemistry and business (Aldianto et al., 2021; Jin et al., 2022). It seamlessly interlaces the rigor of scientific inquiry, the daring spirit of entrepreneurship, and the transformative power of innovation. As we embark on this expedition, be prepared to traverse the intricate yet captivating realm that bridges chemistry and business, discovering how these two seemingly disparate fields intertwine to create a symphony of marketable success.

Chemistry, often associated with laboratories and experiments, is a treasure trove of untapped potential awaiting ingenious transformation into tangible products that captivate the market (Magistretti, Pham, & Dell'Era, 2021). The intricate dance of chemical reactions holds the key to unlocking novel solutions to contemporary challenges, yet bridging the divide between complex scientific processes and consumer-ready goods necessitates a profound understanding of both scientific intricacies and the nuances of business dynamics.

For decades, the business landscape has undergone a seismic shift, propelled by the pervasive wave of digital transformation (Hanelt et al., 2021). This metamorphosis is marked by the widespread infusion of technology into daily operations, reshaping traditional paradigms. Chemistry, rather than standing aloof, has nimbly found its niche within this revolution, permeating industries and shaping the products that cater to the discerning tastes of modern consumers. This evolution, where chemistry meets digital innovation, beckons us to comprehend how theoretical chemistry-driven concepts unfurl their wings and transition into marketable realities.

As chemistry and business interlace in this journey, we unearth narratives of visionary individuals and pioneering companies, dissecting their transformative processes that merge scientific brilliance with astute market acumen. But to embark on this journey, we must first unravel the blueprint of innovation that guides the transition from the laboratory to the market domain.

13.3.   Innovation in Action: Real-Life Case Studies

13.3.1.   Case Study 1: Pioneering Sustainability through Circular Business Models

Consider the remarkable case of Awan and Sroufe (2022), whose endeavors resonated with the urgent call for sustainability by devising circular business models firmly anchored in the principles of chemistry. Their pioneering venture embarked on a transformational journey to reshape the well-trodden path of the linear economy into a circuitous one, where products undergo a continual cycle of recycling, repurposing, and rejuvenation (Jin et al., 2022).

At the heart of their revolutionary approach lay a fusion of chemistry's intrinsic understanding of materials and their behaviors with innovative business models (Hanelt et al., 2021). This harmonious union breathed new life into the realm of waste management, transcending the conventional boundaries of waste disposal. By integrating their chemistry expertise with astute business acumen, Awan and Sroufe birthed a paradigm shift that redefined product lifecycles. What was once considered discarded remnants transformed into a goldmine of valuable resources, echoing the ethos of sustainability and stewardship for the environment (Awan & Sroufe, 2022).

As they paved the way for a circular economy, their story serves as an inspiring testament to the transformative potential when chemistry and innovative business strategies join hands. The chemistry-driven foundation of their circular models instigated not only an environmental awakening but also a revolution in the way products are perceived, designed, and consumed.

13.3.2.	Case Study 2: Crafting the Digital Revolution with Design Thinking

In the landscape of digital transformation, the pioneering work of Magistretti, Pham, and Dell'Era (2021) offers an enlightening perspective on the confluence of design thinking and chemistry-driven innovation. Their study delves into the dynamic capabilities of design thinking as a catalyst for digital innovation, a concept that has found resonance in the chemistry arena. Traditionally linked to product development, design thinking seamlessly melded with the realm of chemistry concepts to ignite the digital revolution.

With a focus on user-centric design principles, this innovative amalgamation breathed fresh life into chemical processes that had remained traditional for decades (Zhao et al., 2020). By introducing the principles of user experience and iterative prototyping into the chemistry-driven domain, Magistretti and colleagues effectively bridged the gap between chemistry and cutting-edge digital products. This marriage of chemical ingenuity with user-centric design did not just represent a functional evolution; it symbolized a paradigm shift that redefined how chemistry concepts can be harnessed in the digital age.

The fusion of design thinking with chemistry principles heralded a new era of possibility, opening doors to a spectrum of applications that extended far beyond conventional boundaries. The narrative of their transformative journey serves as an inspiring testament to the malleability of chemistry concepts in the face of technological evolution, sparking novel avenues of exploration and innovation.

13.4. Guiding Principles for Transforming Chemistry into Marketable Gold

13.4.1. Embrace Entrepreneurial Orientation

The vitality of entrepreneurial orientation as a catalyst for success in chemistry-driven ventures has been underscored by Ciampi and colleagues (2021). Their research illuminates that companies steeped in a culture of risk-taking, proactivity, and innovation are endowed with a heightened capacity to translate intricate chemistry concepts into tangible market successes. This orientation bridges the chasm between the technical intricacies of chemistry and the dynamic demands of the marketplace, a testament to the symbiotic relationship between science and entrepreneurship.

A vivid embodiment of this entrepreneurial spirit can be witnessed in the narrative of a daring chemistry graduate who embarked on a journey to revolutionize the perfume industry. Armed with traditional perfume-making techniques honed through years of study, this visionary entrepreneur infused the timeless artistry of chemistry with modern marketing strategies (Aldianto et al., 2021). This fusion transcended the boundaries of tradition and convention, propelling her products from obscurity to the forefront of consumer preference. Her journey underscores the inherent potential within chemistry-driven concepts when coupled with a resolute entrepreneurial disposition.

13.4.2. Understand the Ecosystem

The intricate interplay between chemistry and business is mirrored in the parallelism of chemical interactions and business ecosystems (Hou & Shi, 2021). Just as chemicals engage in complex reactions, businesses operate within intricate ecosystems that encompass suppliers, consumers, and numerous stakeholders. Recognizing the broader landscape within which chemistry-driven innovations will thrive is an essential step toward igniting creative and groundbreaking product ideas.

A compelling illustration of this principle is embodied in the story of a startup that harnessed the transformative potential of digital platforms (Hou & Shi, 2021). By forging direct connections between chemical suppliers and small-scale manufacturers through digital networks, this venture orchestrated a symphony of collaboration and efficiency. The resulting synergy not only streamlined the supply chain but also kindled a newfound appreciation for the multifaceted dynamics of the chemistry-business ecosystem. This narrative serves as a vivid reminder of the importance of ecosystem awareness, highlighting the ways in which understanding the broader landscape can unearth novel pathways to innovation and success.

13.4.3.   Harness Big Data and Analytics

In the era where data is hailed as the reigning monarch, the significance of harnessing big data and analytics within chemistry-driven companies is particularly pronounced (Mariani & Wamba, 2020). The work of Mariani and Wamba underscores that big data analytics serve as a potent catalyst for innovation, offering a panoramic view into consumer preferences, operational dynamics, and strategic insights. The seamless integration of chemistry and data-driven approaches empowers businesses to ascend from informed decisions to visionary breakthroughs.

A compelling illustration of this synergy is encapsulated in the narrative of a pioneering company that harnessed the prowess of data analytics in optimizing the formulation of personal care products (Magistretti et al., 2021). By analyzing vast repositories of data, ranging from consumer feedback to chemical interactions, this company recalibrated its product formulations with precision, aligning with the evolving needs and preferences of its clientele. This tale exemplifies the transformative potential embedded within data-driven innovation, as chemistry concepts are elegantly melded with the data-rich landscape to yield products that resonate deeply with consumers.

The convergence of chemistry with data-driven analytics propels businesses into uncharted territories of innovation, amplifying their capacity to anticipate trends, optimize processes, and deliver products that transcend expectations.

13.5.   Looking Ahead: Trends and the Future of Chemistry-Driven Products

The trajectory of chemistry-driven products continues to unfold within a dynamic landscape, with sustainability emerging as a pivotal focal point (Zhao et al., 2020). As environmental concerns escalate, businesses are increasingly turning to the reservoir of sustainable chemistry to proffer innovative solutions. Evident through the emergence of bio-based plastics and green energy sources, the chemistry-driven journey stands as a testament to the industry's resolute commitment to forging a more ecologically balanced future (Awan & Sroufe, 2022).

However, this journey isn't devoid of obstacles; it navigates through a terrain marked by regulations, ethical considerations, and resource constraints (Jin et al.,

2022). Entrepreneurial alchemists who endeavor to turn chemistry concepts into marketable gold find themselves faced with multifaceted challenges. Yet, these challenges are not mere hurdles; they crystallize as opportunities for creative problem-solving. The history of innovation is punctuated by instances where constraints catalyzed ingenious solutions, fueling the spirit of adaptability and resilience (Aldianto et al., 2021).

The convergence of these trends and challenges envisions a future where chemistry-driven products transcend the boundaries of convention and forge new frontiers. As the chemistry-business tapestry evolves, the pursuit of sustainability and the art of navigating challenges are poised to shape the trajectory of chemistry-driven innovations in profound ways.

13.6. A Call to Transform Chemistry into Gold

Amidst a global appetite for innovation, the potent convergence of chemistry and business emerges as a beacon of immense promise (Magistretti et al., 2021). As you embark on your personal journey, it is pivotal to cast a retrospective glance at the pioneers who wielded the alchemical powers of innovation to transform chemistry into marketable gold. Their remarkable achievements stand as an inspiration, a testament to the formidable potential inherent within the synthesis of scientific insight and entrepreneurial prowess.

In the spirit of these trailblazers, you, too, hold the mantle of change-agent—equipped with the tools to forge your own path within this dynamic realm (Ciampi et al., 2021). The challenge of morphing chemistry concepts into products that resonate on a global scale beckons, offering the tantalizing prospect of leaving an indelible mark on the world. The journey, however, is no charmed passage; it calls for the audacity to embrace challenges, the resolve to pioneer uncharted pathways, and the embrace of innovation as your guiding philosopher's stone.

In this endeavor, the beakers of ideas, brimming with the potential to revolutionize industries and lifestyles, lay before you (Awan & Sroufe, 2022). This call to action is a rallying cry—a beckoning to awaken the alchemist within you. The chemistry-business fusion stands ready to metamorphose your visions into reality. As you heed this call, remember that innovation is the golden key that unlocks the boundless potential of chemistry, birthing products that reshape markets and leave an indelible legacy.

1. **Reflection Exercise: Consider a chemistry concept that intrigues you. How can you envision it being transformed into a marketable product? What challenges might arise, and how could you overcome them?**

Delving into the transformative realm of chemistry concepts offers a canvas to envision marketable products that revolutionize industries. For instance, if the concept of sustainable polymers piques your interest, envision crafting biodegradable packaging materials that counteract plastic waste. Challenges might include the scalability of production and ensuring competitive pricing against traditional materials (Zhao et al., 2020). Overcoming these could involve leveraging partnerships with suppliers and employing innovative production techniques to achieve cost-effective solutions.

2. **Innovation Prompt: Think about a chemistry-driven product you encounter in your daily life. How could you improve upon it or introduce a new iteration that addresses emerging needs or concerns?**

Reflecting on prevalent chemistry-driven products, consider detergent formulations. In response to the emerging need for eco-friendly alternatives, you could innovate by introducing detergent pods with dissolvable packaging that eliminates single-use plastics. Addressing challenges like maintaining the same cleaning efficacy might involve meticulous formulation adjustments (Magistretti et al., 2021). By partnering with sustainable materials suppliers and employing data-driven optimization, you could navigate these challenges and contribute to a greener future.

As you embark on these reflective exercises, remember that innovation thrives on curiosity, resilience, and creativity. By drawing insights from both the challenges and triumphs detailed in this chapter, you can illuminate your path towards transforming chemistry concepts into impactful, marketable gold.

13.8.   Conclusion

With unwavering determination and boundless creativity, the power to shape the future through chemistry-driven products lies within your grasp (Hanelt et al., 2021). The journey traversed through this chapter has unveiled the transformative potential that emerges at the intersection of chemistry, innovation, and entrepreneurship. Armed with insights gleaned from real-life case studies, expert opinions, and strategic considerations, you are poised to embark on your voyage of metamorphosing chemistry concepts into marketable gold.

The metaphoric beakers that encapsulate your ideas and aspirations are now within your hands, brimming with the latent potential to revolutionize industries, ignite trends, and change lives (Magistretti et al., 2021). Just as chemists have historically transmuted base elements into precious substances, your capacity to transmute intangible ideas into tangible market successes is boundless. The fusion of scientific curiosity, entrepreneurial spirit, and the art of innovation equips you with a formidable toolkit that can catalyze change on a grand scale.

As you venture forward, recall the pioneers who ventured into uncharted territories, combining science and business acumen to forge paths that redefined industries (Awan & Sroufe, 2022). The stories of those who have harnessed innovation to transform chemistry into marketable gold are your compass and beacon. It's time to breathe life into your visions, surmount challenges with resilience, and navigate uncharted waters with the pioneering spirit of an alchemist.

In the chapters of your journey yet to be written, seize the opportunity to enrich industries, contribute to sustainable solutions, and sculpt the contours of market landscapes. Your role as an innovator, guided by the wisdom accumulated here, is pivotal in sculpting a world where chemistry-driven products shine brightly and leave indelible footprints on the sands of time. As the beakers of innovation are placed in your hands, the question beckons: what will you turn them into? The answer lies in your determination, creativity, and the transformative potential of chemistry.

13.9. References

[1]   Aldianto, L., Anggadwita, G., Permatasari, A., Mirzanti, I. R., & Williamson, I. O. (2021). Toward a business resilience framework for startups. *Sustainability*, *13*(6), 3132. https://doi.org/10.3390/su13063132

[2]   Awan, U., & Sroufe, R. (2022). Sustainability in the circular economy: insights and dynamics of designing circular business models. *Applied Sciences*, *12*(3), 1521. https://doi.org/10.3390/app12031521

[3]   Ciampi, F., Demi, S., Magrini, A., Marzi, G., & Papa, A. (2021). Exploring the impact of big data analytics capabilities on business model innovation: The mediating role of entrepreneurial orientation. *Journal of Business Research*, *123*, 1-13. https://doi.org/10.1016/j.jbusres.2020.09.023

[4]   Hanelt, A., Bohnsack, R., Marz, D., & Antunes Marante, C. (2021). A systematic review of the literature on digital transformation: Insights and implications for strategy and organizational change. *Journal of Management Studies*, *58*(5), 1159-1197. https://doi.org/10.1111/joms.12639

[5]   Hou, H., & Shi, Y. (2021). Ecosystem-as-structure and ecosystem-as-coevolution: A constructive examination. *Technovation*, *100*, 102193. https://doi.org/10.1016/j.technovation.2020.102193

[6]   Jin, C., Tsai, F. S., Gu, Q., & Wu, B. (2022). Does the porter hypothesis work well in the emission trading schema pilot? Exploring moderating effects of institutional settings. *Research in International Business and Finance*, *62*, 101732. https://doi.org/10.1016/j.ribaf.2022.101732

[7]   Magistretti, S., Pham, C. T. A., & Dell'Era, C. (2021). Enlightening the dynamic capabilities of design thinking in fostering digital transformation. *Industrial Marketing Management*, *97*, 59-70. https://doi.org/10.1016/j.indmarman.2021.06.014

[8]   Mariani, M. M., & Wamba, S. F. (2020). Exploring how consumer goods companies innovate in the digital age: The role of big data analytics companies. *Journal of Business Research*, *121*, 338-352. https://doi.org/10.1016/j.jbusres.2020.09.012

[9]   Zhao, Y., Von Delft, S., Morgan-Thomas, A., & Buck, T. (2020). The evolution of platform business models: Exploring competitive battles in the world of platforms. *Long Range Planning*, *53*(4), 101892. https://doi.org/10.1016/j.lrp.2019.101892

14. Golden Lessons: Success Stories from Chemistry Innovators

14.1. Introduction

As we step into the captivating world of chemistry-driven innovations, we embark on a journey that transforms mundane beakers into billions. This chapter delves into the inspiring stories of entrepreneurs who, armed with their deep understanding of chemistry, harnessed the alchemical power of scientific knowledge to create marketable gold. From the humble confines of classrooms to the high-stakes arenas of boardrooms, these intrepid pioneers embarked on a transformative odyssey through the intricate realm of chemistry, breathing life into revolutionary products that have left an indelible mark on industries and society at large.

The tales of these chempreneurs echo the sentiments of the renowned chemist Fritz Haber, who once observed that "*scientists are the true driving force behind the wheels of progress.*" Haber's legacy, notably his pioneering work in the Haber-Bosch process, exemplifies the profound impact of chemistry on agriculture and food production (Chapman, 2022). This innovative process, which harnessed nitrogen fixation to synthesize ammonia on an industrial scale, not only revolutionized global food security but also demonstrated the potential of chemistry to solve pressing societal challenges.

Similarly, the journey of Robert Langer from academia to entrepreneurship highlights the dynamic interplay between scientific inquiry and practical application. Langer's groundbreaking work in drug delivery systems, encapsulating therapeutic agents within innovative polymer matrices, has led to enhanced drug effectiveness and reduced side effects (Hovis, 2014). His journey underscores the critical role of translating theoretical knowledge into tangible products that benefit society while also showcasing the rewarding path of taking research from the laboratory to the marketplace.

The green chemistry movement, championed by visionaries like Joseph S. Francisco and Clayton H. Heathcock, reflects a commitment to both innovation and environmental responsibility (Gold, 2007). Their company's development of environmentally friendly chemical processes, exemplified by the synthesis of taxol, an anticancer drug, is a testament to the potential of chemistry to drive sustainability while addressing critical medical needs. This confluence of economic viability and environmental stewardship demonstrates the transformative power of chemistry when wielded by innovative entrepreneurs.

Throughout these stories, the recurring theme is the fusion of scientific curiosity, strategic vision, and entrepreneurship. The chempreneurs, like Emma Dugoua and Theodore Gerarden, who delve into induced innovation in the energy sector, provide insights into the intricate nexus of inventors, policy incentives, and industry shifts (Dugoua & Gerarden, 2023). Their research illuminates the multifaceted process of turning chemical concepts into marketable solutions, showing that success requires not only scientific acumen but also an astute understanding of market dynamics and regulatory frameworks.

As we delve into these captivating narratives, we'll extract invaluable lessons and insights that illuminate the path from the germination of an idea to its full-fledged commercialization. The journey of these chempreneurs serves as a guiding light, inspiring us to navigate the complex landscape of turning chemistry concepts into marketable gold. Through their stories, we'll gain a deeper understanding of the intricacies, challenges, and triumphs that accompany the transformation of innovative ideas into tangible products with a lasting impact.

14.2.1.   Fritz Haber: Bridging Science and Society

In the annals of chemistry, Fritz Haber's legacy looms large as a testament to the multifaceted relationship between science and society. Haber's brilliance as a chemist and the moral complexities inherent in his work form a riveting narrative that underscores the intricate interplay between scientific progress and ethical dilemmas. Known for his pivotal role in developing the Haber-Bosch process, Haber's contributions harnessed the transformative power of nitrogen fixation, revolutionizing global agriculture and food production (Chapman, 2022).

The Haber-Bosch process, developed in collaboration with Carl Bosch, allowed for the large-scale synthesis of ammonia from atmospheric nitrogen and hydrogen gas. This innovation facilitated the production of synthetic fertilizers, greatly enhancing crop yields and addressing global food scarcity. Haber's ingenuity in developing this process earned him recognition, including the Nobel Prize in Chemistry in 1918 for his contributions to the synthesis of ammonia.

However, Haber's journey was far from a straightforward triumph of scientific discovery. His pioneering work in chemical warfare during World War I, particularly the development and deployment of chlorine and other poisonous gases, has cast a long shadow over his legacy. Haber's contributions to the development of these deadly agents raise profound ethical questions about the responsibilities of scientists in relation to their inventions' potential consequences (Chapman, 2022).

Haber's complex legacy raises pertinent questions about the intersection of scientific advancement, societal impact, and ethical considerations. His story serves as a stark reminder that scientific breakthroughs, while offering incredible potential for societal benefit, can also carry grave moral implications. Haber's journey serves as a historical lens through which we can examine the challenges inherent in bridging scientific discovery with responsible and ethical application.

The interplay between Haber's contributions to both agricultural innovation and chemical warfare underscores the nuanced role of chemists as key players in shaping the trajectory of human progress. It invites us to reflect not only on the technical prowess of chemists but also on the broader social and ethical responsibilities that accompany their work. As we navigate the world of chemistry-driven entrepreneurship, Haber's story serves as a thought-provoking case study, prompting us to consider the broader implications of our innovations and the potential to wield chemistry for both societal benefit and ethical considerations.

Venturing from the academic realm to entrepreneurship, Robert Langer's story serves as a compelling case study that showcases the seamless bridge between academic inquiry and industrial application. His journey highlights the transformative potential of translating scientific discoveries into tangible marketable products that impact the world of medical treatments (Hovis, 2014).

Robert Langer's groundbreaking contributions in the field of drug delivery systems have revolutionized the landscape of medicine. Through his innovative approach of encapsulating therapeutic agents within polymer matrices, Langer introduced a novel paradigm in drug administration that yielded remarkable results. The controlled-release mechanisms enabled by these matrices not only enhanced the efficacy of drugs but also mitigated adverse side effects, thereby offering a significant improvement over conventional drug delivery methods (Hovis, 2014).

One notable achievement in Langer's prolific career is the development of biodegradable polymer-based drug delivery systems. His work in this area opened the door to sustained and targeted drug release, allowing for precise dosing over extended periods. This innovation found applications across a spectrum of medical conditions, including cancer treatment, pain management, and wound healing. Langer's ability to bridge the gap between fundamental scientific understanding and practical medical solutions underscores his remarkable prowess as both a researcher and an entrepreneur.

The transition from laboratory experimentation to the helm of biotech startups exemplifies Langer's unique skill set. His success demonstrates the importance of cultivating a diverse set of competencies, ranging from deep scientific acumen to strategic business insight. By translating his research findings into commercially viable products, Langer not only advanced the field of drug delivery but also paved the way for a new breed of scientists-entrepreneurs who leverage their expertise to make transformative contributions to both science and society.

Langer's journey serves as an inspiring example for aspiring chempreneurs, illustrating how a dedication to scientific inquiry can converge with a vision for tangible impact. His story highlights the significance of collaborative partnerships that facilitate the translation of laboratory innovations into real-world applications. As we explore the world of chemistry-driven entrepreneurship, Robert Langer's narrative encourages us to embrace the duality of scientist and entrepreneur, guiding us to navigate the intricate path from research to market and manifesting the potential of chemistry to create products that enhance human well-being and quality of life.

In the pursuit of sustainable chemistry, the narrative of Joseph S. Francisco and Clayton H. Heathcock's pioneering endeavors stands as a testament to the transformative power of the green chemistry movement (Gold, 2007). The inception of their company, co-founded alongside K. C. Nicolaou, reverberated with the ethos of green chemistry, serving as a catalyst for the development of environmentally friendly chemical processes that sought to harmonize innovation with ecological stewardship.

Central to their journey was the revolutionary synthesis of taxol, a potent anticancer drug, which spotlighted their unwavering commitment to both scientific advancement and environmental responsibility. Taxol, derived originally from the bark of the Pacific yew tree, exhibited significant therapeutic potential but was hindered by ecological concerns related to the sourcing of the raw material. The innovative approach pursued by Francisco, Heathcock, and Nicolaou circumvented this ecological bottleneck by devising a synthetic route to taxol, thereby alleviating the pressure on the endangered yew trees and exemplifying a triumph of sustainability in chemistry-driven entrepreneurship.

The principles of green chemistry, championed by Francisco and Heathcock, are rooted in the desire to minimize the environmental impact of chemical processes, reduce waste, and prioritize resource efficiency. Their efforts resonated with the broader movement within the scientific community to align scientific innovation with the imperatives of sustainability. The green chemistry revolution underscores the potential for chemistry to not only generate novel solutions but also to contribute to the well-being of the planet and its inhabitants.

The journey of Francisco and Heathcock serves as an inspiring blueprint for contemporary chempreneurs seeking to navigate the delicate balance between innovation, profitability, and environmental consciousness. Their narrative underscores the fact that chemistry-driven entrepreneurship need not be at odds with environmental stewardship; rather, it can serve as a conduit for advancing both scientific and ecological objectives. As we chart our paths in the world of chemistry-based innovation, their story encourages us to consider the environmental implications of our work and to harness the power of sustainable chemistry to create products that not only bring value to markets but also contribute positively to the world at large.

The landscape of chemistry-driven innovation extends far beyond traditional industries, as highlighted by Emma Dugoua and Theodore Gerarden's comprehensive study on induced innovation in the energy sector (Dugoua & Gerarden, 2023). Their exploration unveils a narrative of transformative potential, where chemistry plays a central role in shaping the trajectory of the energy transition.

Dugoua and Gerarden's research is a deep dive into the intricate dance that unfolds between inventors, policy incentives, and the dynamic energy landscape. Their study focuses on how innovation is not just a solitary endeavor but a collaborative effort propelled by external factors such as policy frameworks and market demands. This perspective reflects the interconnectedness of scientific advancement with broader societal and economic drivers, especially in fields as critical as energy.

One of the fascinating dimensions of their research lies in the exploration of chemistry's role in emerging fields such as photovoltaics and battery technologies. The evolution of renewable energy technologies heavily relies on chemistry to develop efficient materials, optimize processes, and enhance the performance of energy conversion and storage systems. Through their findings, Dugoua and Gerarden illuminate the interplay between fundamental chemical principles and the development of practical solutions that drive the energy transition forward.

Their work underscores the importance of aligning scientific innovation with policy incentives. Policy frameworks can act as catalysts for innovation, shaping research agendas and directing resources towards promising avenues. Dugoua and Gerarden's insights highlight how regulatory measures can trigger a ripple effect of innovation, ultimately accelerating the deployment of new technologies in the energy sector.

In a world where the urgency of addressing climate change demands swift and effective action, the chemistry-driven innovation spotlighted by Dugoua and Gerarden takes on heightened significance. Their narrative underscores the potential for chemistry to be a transformative force, not only in established sectors but also in those on the precipice of change. Their work inspires chempreneurs to recognize the broader context in which their innovations operate and to leverage chemistry's potential to drive the energy transition, forging a sustainable path toward a greener future.

14.3.1.   Biomaterials: Merging Chemistry and Medicine

The realm of biomaterials stands as a testament to the profound fusion of chemistry with diverse and impactful medical applications. Benjamin D. Ratner's scholarly contributions in this domain provide critical insights into the intricate relationship between chemistry and medicine, demonstrating the iterative evolution of materials designed to interface seamlessly with biological systems (Ratner, 2019).

Ratner's work unveils a journey that traverses from conceptualization to clinical implementation, a path fraught with challenges and marked by significant milestones. Biomaterials have catalyzed transformative advancements across multiple medical domains, ranging from orthopedics to drug delivery. The integration of chemistry into this realm has led to the development of materials that not only mimic the natural environment of the human body but also interact harmoniously with it.

One of the paramount challenges in biomaterials design is achieving biocompatibility, ensuring that materials elicit minimal adverse reactions when introduced into living tissues. This calls for a deep understanding of the intricate interplay between chemical properties and biological responses. Ratner's insights underscore the importance of tailoring material characteristics to achieve optimal biocompatibility, a feat that requires a nuanced appreciation of chemical interactions at the molecular level.

Furthermore, the journey from concept to clinical application entails addressing challenges related to material degradation. Biomaterials must maintain their structural integrity over time, resisting degradation caused by various physiological factors. Chemistry plays a pivotal role in designing materials with the requisite stability while accounting for the unique biochemical environment they inhabit.

Ratner's analysis underscores the interdisciplinary nature of biomaterials research, emphasizing the pivotal role of collaboration between chemists, biologists, engineers, and medical professionals. The successful development of biomaterials hinges on harnessing insights from multiple disciplines to craft materials that meet the rigorous demands of both biology and medicine. The resulting synergy between fields is a testament to the transformative power of collaborative endeavors.

The fusion of chemistry and medicine in the realm of biomaterials not only underscores the potential for scientific innovation but also embodies a profound commitment to enhancing human health and well-being. Ratner's work serves as a guiding light for aspiring chempreneurs seeking to navigate the complex intersection of chemistry and medical applications. His insights inspire us to embrace the challenges of biocompatibility, degradation, and functionality, while also highlighting the immense potential for chemistry to be a driving force in creating products that seamlessly integrate with the human body and catalyze revolutionary advancements in healthcare.

<table><tr><td>14.3.2.</td><td>Navigating Dynamic Game Theory: A Water Management Saga</td></tr></table>

The intricate dance of chemistry extends its influence beyond the laboratory, permeating dynamic systems such as groundwater management. The collaborative work of Sears, Lawell, Torres, and Walter offers a compelling exploration of the complex challenges and strategic considerations inherent in resource management within the context of dynamic game theory (Sears et al., 2022).

Their research delves deep into the domain of groundwater management, a critical facet of environmental sustainability and resource conservation. This realm is characterized by the interplay of various stakeholders, each driven by distinct objectives and constraints. The application of dynamic game theory—a field at the crossroads of mathematics, economics, and ecology—provides a powerful analytical toolset for understanding the strategic interactions that shape decision-making in these real-world systems.

The lens of moment-based Markov equilibrium estimation adopted by Sears and his colleagues allows for a nuanced analysis of the evolving dynamics within the groundwater management arena. This approach captures the transient nature of decision-making strategies and outcomes, highlighting the temporal dimension that is pivotal in resource management contexts. Their work unveils the intricate web of factors that govern the behavior of stakeholders, shedding light on the complex interplay of incentives, regulations, and environmental factors that shape the decisions made.

The journey undertaken by Sears, Lawell, Torres, and Walter is more than a mere academic exercise—it is a saga that unravels the intricate complexities of resource management. Their findings resonate deeply in the context of environmental challenges, emphasizing that the solutions to these challenges are rooted in a sophisticated understanding of dynamic systems and strategic interactions. By providing a window into the world of decision-making in groundwater management, their research underscores the pivotal role of chemistry in addressing broader societal and environmental issues.

This narrative of navigating dynamic game theory within water management demonstrates the transformative potential of interdisciplinary approaches. It reinforces the idea that chemistry, often associated with laboratories and reactions, is a driving force in understanding and managing complex systems that impact our environment. As we explore the world of chemistry-driven entrepreneurship, Sears and his colleagues' journey inspires us to recognize the broader implications of our work and to leverage chemistry's analytical prowess to craft sustainable solutions that contribute positively to our world.

14.4. From Inspiration to Action: Forging Your Chempreneurial Path

As we immerse ourselves in the narratives of these remarkable chemistry innovators, their journeys impart invaluable insights that guide us on our own chempreneurial paths. The stories of Fritz Haber, Robert Langer, Joseph S. Francisco, Clayton H. Heathcock, Emma Dugoua, and Theodore Gerarden offer a tapestry of lessons that illuminate the multifaceted landscape of chemistry-driven entrepreneurship.

One pivotal lesson underscored by their experiences is the power of interdisciplinary collaboration (Chapman, 2022; Hovis, 2014; Gold, 2007; Dugoua & Gerarden, 2023). Their narratives reflect how chemistry-driven innovations thrive at the nexus of diverse disciplines. The fusion of expertise from various fields enriches the fabric of innovative solutions. As we navigate the realms of chemistry-based entrepreneurship, we are reminded that by engaging with experts from disparate domains, we can infuse our products with a broader perspective, ensuring their relevance and impact across diverse contexts.

Ethical considerations emerge as a critical compass for our chempreneurial journeys (Chapman, 2022). Fritz Haber's complex legacy exemplifies the profound societal implications of scientific advancements. His pioneering contributions, both in agricultural innovation and chemical warfare, compel us to embrace ethical awareness. The narratives of these chempreneurs encourage us to engage in continuous ethical reflection, ensuring that our innovations align with values that benefit humanity and minimize potential harm.

The green chemistry movement, embodied by Joseph S. Francisco, Clayton H. Heathcock, and their commitment to sustainable practices, resonates as a guiding principle for modern entrepreneurship (Gold, 2007). The seamless integration of environmental responsibility with innovation stands as a beacon of inspiration. Their stories remind us that the pursuit of profit need not be at odds with ecological stewardship; rather, it can be a harmonious collaboration. As chempreneurs, their journey encourages us to prioritize sustainability, cultivating solutions that not only address market needs but also uphold the well-being of the planet.

In the face of challenges, adaptability and resilience stand as core virtues (Sears et al., 2022; Ratner, 2019). The evolution of biomaterials, water management, and other domains underscores the necessity of adapting and persevering in the face of adversity. Their narratives teach us that setbacks and obstacles are an integral part of the chempreneurial journey. Embracing flexibility and resilience allows us to navigate the uncertain terrain, transforming challenges into stepping stones toward success.

The stories of these chempreneurs serve as guiding stars, illuminating the principles that underpin successful chemistry-driven entrepreneurship. As we forge our own paths, their insights inspire us to approach our ventures with a multidisciplinary mindset, ethical consciousness, sustainability as a compass, and an unyielding spirit in the face of challenges. With their lessons as our foundation, we embark on our own journeys to turn chemistry into marketable gold, recognizing that each challenge we conquer and innovation we birth contributes to the ever-evolving narrative of chemistry's impact on our world.

14.5. Embarking on Your Journey

As ardent enthusiasts of the chemical sciences, we find ourselves on the verge of embarking on a transformative journey—an expedition that holds the potential to translate knowledge into impactful action. With chemistry as our guiding star, we stand poised to weave its intricate tapestry into tangible marketable gold. This voyage, though exhilarating, is not devoid of challenges and triumphs, setbacks and breakthroughs. The narratives of the chempreneurs we've encountered throughout these chapters stand as beacons of light, casting illumination on the path that lies ahead.

Drawing inspiration from the narratives of Fritz Haber, Robert Langer, Joseph S. Francisco, Clayton H. Heathcock, Emma Dugoua, and Theodore Gerarden, we glean wisdom that will navigate us through the uncharted waters of chemistry-driven entrepreneurship (Chapman, 2022; Hovis, 2014; Gold, 2007; Dugoua & Gerarden, 2023). Their stories unveil the dynamic spectrum of possibilities that emerge when chemistry converges with innovation, when curiosity gives way to creation, and when dedication transforms ideas into reality.

This expedition calls upon us to embrace the challenges that will inevitably arise, just as biomaterials and water management systems undergo evolution and adaptation (Sears et al., 2022; Ratner, 2019). Our path will be punctuated by moments of triumph that mirror the groundbreaking accomplishments of those who have walked this journey before us. We must also reconcile with setbacks, knowing that it is through the crucible of challenges that our most profound growth occurs.

With their tales as our compass, we set forth on this exhilarating adventure, armed not only with scientific knowledge but also with the insights garnered from the experiences of chempreneurs. Our journey is fueled by passion—an intrinsic love for discovery and innovation—and driven by the boundless possibilities that chemistry affords us. As we navigate the complexities of entrepreneurship, we are empowered by the realization that the alchemy of transforming chemistry into marketable gold is within our reach.

So, let us tread boldly and purposefully, guided by the narratives etched into the annals of chemistry's history. Let us transform our passion and knowledge into action, weaving the threads of chemistry's magic into products that revolutionize industries and enhance human lives. As we set forth on this transformative journey, let us remember that the chemistry-driven entrepreneurship we embark upon is more than a mere endeavor; it is a legacy—a legacy of innovation, impact, and the relentless pursuit of turning the extraordinary potential of chemistry into the tangible reality of marketable gold.

14.6.　Recommended Resources

1. **Haber, L. F. (2005). The Poisonous Cloud: Chemical Warfare in the First World War. Clarendon Press.** This comprehensive work delves into the life and legacy of Fritz Haber, exploring his pioneering contributions to chemistry, the development of the Haber-Bosch process, and the ethical implications of his work in chemical warfare during World War I (Chapman, 2022).

2. **Langer, R. (2019). The Langer Lab: Conquering the Frontiers of Medicine. Wiley.** Robert Langer's journey from academia to entrepreneurship is chronicled in this insightful book. It provides an in-depth look into his pioneering work in drug delivery systems, encapsulation technologies, and his role as a transformative figure in the field of medicine (Hovis, 2014).

3. **Anastas, P. T., & Warner, J. C. (1998). Green Chemistry: Theory and Practice. Oxford University Press.** For those interested in understanding the principles and applications of green chemistry, this seminal work by Paul T. Anastas and John C. Warner serves as a foundational resource. It explores the integration of sustainability and innovation in chemistry, a theme exemplified by Joseph S. Francisco and Clayton H. Heathcock's commitment to green chemistry (Gold, 2007).

4. **Ratner, B. D., & Hoffman, A. S. (2007). Biomaterials Science: An Introduction to Materials in Medicine. Academic Press.** Benjamin D. Ratner's work has significantly contributed to the realm of biomaterials. This resource offers a comprehensive overview of biomaterials science, exploring the intersection of chemistry and medicine in the development of materials designed to interface with biological systems (Ratner, 2019).

These recommended resources provide a deeper dive into the realms explored in our chempreneurial journey. They offer insights into the lives and work of the individuals who have shaped the field of chemistry-driven entrepreneurship, as well as foundational knowledge that can empower us to further our own explorations in turning chemistry into marketable gold.

14.7. Conclusion: Your Alchemical Odyssey

As we stand at the threshold of the chemistry-driven entrepreneurship landscape, the resounding success stories of the chempreneurs beckon us to embark on a daring journey—an expedition marked by innovation, transformation, and alchemical possibility. These chempreneurs' narratives serve as a testament to the extraordinary power that lies within the intersection of ideas, challenges, and knowledge cultivated over time (Chapman, 2022; Hovis, 2014; Gold, 2007; Dugoua & Gerarden, 2023; Ratner, 2019; Sears et al., 2022).

The pages of this chapter have unveiled tales of individuals who dared to dream, challenged the status quo, and transformed chemistry concepts into marketable gold. Their journeys underscore the essence of chempreneurship—an alchemical process where ideas are forged, challenges are conquered, and knowledge is harnessed to create products that transcend the boundaries of the laboratory.

As we bid adieu to this chapter, let us remember that the crucible of potential lies within our hands. The stories of these chempreneurs serve as a wellspring of inspiration, urging us to grasp the tools of innovation, ethics, and collaboration. Fritz Haber's ethical dilemmas, Robert Langer's interdisciplinary collaborations, Joseph S. Francisco and Clayton H. Heathcock's commitment to sustainability, and the complexities of biomaterials and water management explored by Sears, Lawell, Torres, and Walter (Chapman, 2022; Hovis, 2014; Gold, 2007; Dugoua & Gerarden, 2023; Ratner, 2019; Sears et al., 2022)—all serve as guiding lights illuminating our path forward.

As you step into your own alchemical odyssey, remember that the future of chemistry-driven products and the legacy you craft are awaiting your grasp. The journey from beakers to billions is one that demands dedication, curiosity, and a resolute commitment to turning your passion into action. Let the magic of chemistry be your guiding compass, leading you through the uncharted waters of innovation and entrepreneurship. Just as the chempreneurs before you have proven, the power to transform chemistry into marketable gold resides within you. The crucible is yours to shape, and the world eagerly anticipates the golden legacy that your journey will unveil.

14.8. References

[1] Chapman, K. (2022). Fritz Haber: the father of chemical warfare. *Iron Cross*, *1*(12). https://repository.falmouth.ac.uk/4631/1/Haber_IronCross.docx

[2] Dugoua, E., & Gerarden, T. (2023). Induced Innovation, Inventors, and the Energy Transition. http://congress-files.s3.amazonaws.com/2023-07/dugoua_inventors_inducedinnovation.pdf

[3] Gold, L. (2007, June). Company co-founded by Ganem wins Green Chemistry award. *Cornell Chronicle*. https://news.cornell.edu/stories/2007/06/company-co-founded-ganem-wins-green-chemistry-award

[4] Harpaz, B., & Rudoren, J. (2022). Introducing the Forward 125: The American Jews who shaped our world. http://bncentryassets.s3.amazonaws.com/2145/attachments/88163121163dc320907f58_0.pdf

[5] Hovis, K. (2014, December). Robert Langer named Cornell Entrepreneur of the Year 2015. *Cornell Chronicle*. https://news.cornell.edu/stories/2014/12/robert-langer-named-cornell-entrepreneur-year-2015

[6] Ratner, B. D. (2019). Biomaterials: been there, done that, and evolving into the future. *Annual review of biomedical engineering*, *21*, 171-191. 10.1146/annurev-bioeng-062117-120940

[7] Sears, L. S., Lawell, C. Y., Torres, G., & Walter, M. T. (2022). Moment-based Markov equilibrium estimation of high-dimension dynamic games: An application to groundwater management in California. https://ageconsearch.umn.edu/record/322187/files/22742.pdf

15. Beyond Chemistry: The Future of Marketable Innovations

15.1. Introduction

In this exciting chapter we embark on a journey that transcends the boundaries of the classroom and delves deep into the captivating world of turning chemistry concepts into marketable products. As we navigate this dynamic landscape, we are poised to uncover not only the transformative potential of chemistry but also the intricate interplay of emerging trends, groundbreaking technologies, inspiring success stories, and the promising trajectory that lies ahead for the realm of chemistry-driven products and industries.

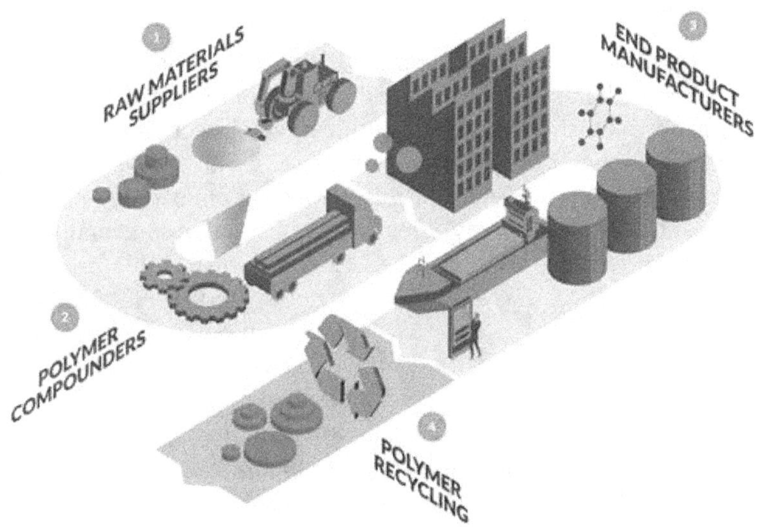

The synthesis of chemistry and artificial intelligence (AI) has ignited a revolutionary spark, propelling us into an era where traditional laboratory boundaries are redefined by the algorithms of AI companions. Almeida, Moreira, and Rodrigues (2019) have elegantly demonstrated how AI-driven synthetic organic chemistry transforms laboratory routines into a choreographed symphony of predictive algorithms and creative human insights. This seamless fusion of human ingenuity and machine precision serves as a testament to the exciting trajectory that chemistry-driven innovations are undertaking.

Moreover, the integration of digital advancements into the design and manufacturing of smart materials and multifunctional coatings holds the promise of a transformative shift in industries reliant on material properties. Verma and Khanna (2022) highlight how this confluence has led to the creation of materials that adapt, respond, and even heal themselves—a testament to the limitless possibilities at the intersection of chemistry and technology. As we traverse this landscape, we'll uncover narratives of car coatings that morph with changing temperatures and materials that metamorphose in response to external stimuli, amplifying the potential for chemistry to deliver products with unmatched capabilities.

Notably, the power of crowdsourcing and open innovation in the realm of drug discovery offers an inspiring narrative of collective problem-solving. Thompson and Bentzien (2020) chronicle a scenario where the boundaries of geography and specialization dissolve, giving rise to a global community of scientists who collaborate to unlock novel chemical solutions. Envision chemists from diverse corners of the world coming together virtually to tackle complex challenges in drug discovery, fostering an environment of open exchange and cross-disciplinary creativity.

This journey also leads us to the captivating realm of insecticide discovery, where innovation takes center stage. In the realm of pest management, chemistry is undergoing a profound transformation, with novel insecticides designed to be selective, environmentally friendly, and harmonious with ecosystems. Sparks and Bryant (2022) paint a vivid picture of this evolution, envisioning a future where pest control strategies are not only effective but also environmentally conscious, exemplifying how chemistry can pave the way for sustainable practices across industries.

As we traverse through these narratives, we are bound to encounter the dance between quantum chemistry and experimental characterization, a partnership that is rewriting the rules of molecular design. Santaloci et al. (2023) offer a glimpse into this intricate interplay, where quantum calculations guide experimentalists in crafting materials with tailored properties. This dance, choreographed between the virtual realm of computations and the tangible world of experimentation, brings forth novel materials with applications spanning from renewable energy to cutting-edge diagnostics.

Furthermore, the convergence of chemometrics and business intelligence signifies a new era where data-driven decision-making takes center stage in the business world. Sabin et al. (2021) illustrate how chemistry has stepped out of the laboratory and into the corporate boardrooms, where insights derived from chemical data shape product development strategies, quality control processes, and market trends. This marriage between chemistry and analytics amplifies the influence of chemistry across diverse sectors, transcending its traditional confines.

As we proceed, the journey takes an eco-conscious turn, leading us to the realm of green chemistry and sustainable practices. Winterton (2021) emphasizes the significance of adopting green solvents and environmentally friendly processes, demonstrating how chemistry can contribute to a more sustainable future by reducing waste, energy consumption, and ecological impact. Picture chemical reactions that generate minimal waste and processes that are aligned with the principles of circular economy—these are the hallmarks of chemistry's commitment to fostering a greener planet.

Lastly, our exploration introduces us to the concept of transforming waste into zeolites for environmental remediation. Chu, Liang, Yang, and Chen (2022) narrate a captivating tale where large-scale aluminosilicates, which are abundant waste materials, are converted into zeolites for cleaning polluted waters and mitigating environmental damage. This innovative approach demonstrates how chemistry can be harnessed to address pressing ecological challenges, showcasing the potential for chemistry to lead the charge in environmental stewardship.

15.2.   Chemistry and AI: A Symbiotic Revolution

In recent years, the convergence of chemistry and artificial intelligence has ignited a paradigm-shifting revolution that is redefining the very essence of scientific discovery. Picture a chemistry lab where the boundaries of human expertise are stretched beyond limits, where the guiding hands are not solely human, but the intricate algorithms of AI. This fusion of chemistry and AI has ushered in a new era of scientific exploration, where the boundaries of human potential are being rewritten, and the results are nothing short of astonishing.

The groundbreaking work of Almeida, Moreira, and Rodrigues (2019) serves as a gateway to this exciting realm. Their research beautifully captures the essence of a future where synthetic organic chemistry is no longer confined to traditional trial-and-error approaches. Instead, AI algorithms become partners in the creative process, predicting reaction outcomes with unprecedented accuracy. This symbiotic relationship extends even further, as AI-generated suggestions for novel compounds inject an infusion of innovation into the chemistry landscape. The implications are profound – chemistry driven by AI doesn't just expedite discovery; it transcends the boundaries of human ingenuity, exploring vast chemical spaces that would be otherwise uncharted.

At the heart of this revolution lies the fusion of human creativity and machine precision. These advancements not only transform chemistry but also streamline drug discovery processes, accelerating the journey from initial concept to market-ready product. Imagine a drug discovery pipeline where AI algorithms curate a selection of potential compounds with the highest probability of success, reducing costs and time associated with experimental trial and error. This transformative power has the potential to reshape pharmaceutical industries, making drug development not only more efficient but also accessible to a broader spectrum of researchers.

This revolution is not merely a showcase of technology but a testament to the marriage of human ingenuity and machine precision. As AI algorithms predict reaction outcomes and generate innovative compound ideas, they amplify the creative potential of chemists, enabling them to focus on higher-level design and decision-making tasks. This harmonious blend of human intuition and AI-driven insights reshapes the traditional landscape of chemistry, transforming it into an exhilarating dance of innovation.

The emergence of AI-guided chemistry is not just a fleeting trend; it's a fundamental shift that has already left an indelible mark on research and development. As we journey through this chapter, we'll encounter stories of chemistry labs where AI-powered tools offer researchers a new lens through which to view their work. This is a world where the marriage of human expertise and machine algorithms has unlocked a universe of possibilities, redefining the contours of chemistry-driven innovation and propelling us into a future where creativity knows no bounds.

15.3. Smart Materials and Coatings: Designing Tomorrow's Innovations

Verma and Khanna (2022) have cast a spotlight on the captivating synergy between chemistry and digital advancements, revealing a future where materials and coatings are not just passive entities, but intelligent and adaptable companions that interact with their environment. This vision is nothing short of transformative, where the very fabric of our world responds, adapts, and even heals itself.

Imagine a world where materials possess the ability to self-heal, a concept that was once relegated to science fiction. The chemistry-driven innovations in smart materials have brought this concept to life, offering coatings that possess the remarkable capability to repair themselves when damaged. These self-healing materials are imbued with chemical properties that enable them to detect and respond to changes in their structure, triggered by factors such as heat, light, or even mechanical stress. This vision has far-reaching implications, from enhancing the durability of everyday objects to revolutionizing industries where maintenance is a significant challenge.

But the realm of smart materials doesn't stop at self-healing. These materials are akin to chameleons, adapting their properties to changes in their environment. Verma and Khanna (2022) unveil materials that react to external stimuli, altering their physical characteristics in response. Imagine a car coated with a material that changes color as temperatures fluctuate – a feat that was once reserved for the realm of science fiction. This embodiment of chemistry's fusion with digital technologies ushers in a world where products are not static but dynamic, offering a sensory experience that blurs the boundaries between the material and the digital.

The impact of these innovations stretches across industries, from consumer products to construction and aerospace. Smart coatings can offer enhanced protection against corrosion, safeguarding infrastructure against environmental elements. In aerospace, adaptive materials can optimize aerodynamics based on real-time conditions, enhancing fuel efficiency. In healthcare, these materials can find applications in the development of responsive medical devices, further blurring the line between biology and technology.

The chemistry-driven world is undergoing a remarkable evolution, where the physical and the digital converge to create a harmonious symphony of innovation. The real-world implications are awe-inspiring, where materials cease to be mere building blocks and become interactive partners in shaping our experiences. This journey into the realm of smart materials invites us to envision a world where innovation is not confined by the limits of the imaginable, but is instead shaped by the limitless potential of chemistry combined with digital ingenuity.

15.4.   The Power of Crowdsourcing and Open Innovation

Thompson and Bentzien (2020) offer an intriguing glimpse into the transformative potential of crowdsourcing and open innovation within the realm of drug discovery. This approach, grounded in collaboration and collective wisdom, has redefined the boundaries of scientific discovery, showcasing the true power of chemistry's universal language.

Imagine a scenario where geographical boundaries hold no sway over scientific collaboration. Crowdsourcing and open innovation create a virtual ecosystem where chemists, researchers, and enthusiasts from diverse corners of the globe converge to tackle complex challenges. This virtual platform serves as a dynamic melting pot of expertise, a place where ideas flow freely, and knowledge transcends disciplinary silos. Thompson and Bentzien's narrative paints a picture of chemists and innovators, once isolated by geography, now united by a shared mission to advance drug discovery.

The implications of this collaborative approach are profound. Picture a digital marketplace where researchers can submit their hypotheses and findings for collective evaluation. In this ecosystem, breakthroughs are not limited to a single laboratory or institution but emerge through the collective efforts of a global community. This democratization of innovation empowers researchers irrespective of their resources, institutional affiliations, or geographic location. As we explore this landscape, we realize that the next groundbreaking drug might not emerge from a conventional research powerhouse but from the innovative insights of a chemist working halfway across the world.

Moreover, the collaborative ethos of crowdsourcing and open innovation offers a unique space for interdisciplinary exchange. It's a playground where chemists, biologists, engineers, and computational scientists converge, breaking down the traditional barriers between fields. In this cross-disciplinary haven, the boundaries of knowledge expand, leading to the creation of hybrid solutions that would have been impossible within the confines of a single discipline.

This collaborative movement not only accelerates the pace of drug discovery but also elevates the principles of transparency and shared knowledge. As researchers contribute their insights, methodologies, and data, the collective understanding of chemical processes deepens. The process becomes as much about advancing science as it is about advancing products.

In essence, the story of crowdsourcing and open innovation is a testament to the universal language of chemistry. It's a narrative that transcends language barriers, cultural differences, and geographic distances, forging connections that hinge on shared passion and collective ambition. As we navigate through this chapter, we'll delve into stories of chemists whose contributions have transcended borders and sparked revolutions, highlighting the potential of chemistry to unite the world in the pursuit of scientific advancement.

15.5. Unveiling the Future: Innovative Insecticides

Sparks and Bryant (2022) illuminate a path forward in the realm of insecticide discovery, offering a visionary perspective on how chemistry can be harnessed to tackle mounting challenges posed by evolving pests and environmental concerns. This chapter delves into a story where chemistry evolves from being a tool of pest control to a guardian of ecological balance.

As the world grapples with rapidly evolving pests and the complex challenges of environmental preservation, chemistry stands as a formidable ally. Picture a future where insecticides are not just potent chemicals, but precisely targeted interventions that disrupt pest populations while preserving the delicate ecosystems that sustain life. Sparks and Bryant's narrative paints a landscape where chemicals are designed to home in on specific pests, leaving non-target organisms unharmed. This selective approach is a remarkable testament to the sophistication of modern chemistry, where molecules can be designed with unprecedented precision.

Moreover, imagine insecticides that go beyond their primary function, breaking down harmlessly after completing their task. This vision embodies the principles of sustainability and environmental stewardship, where chemistry embraces the ethos of a circular economy. The notion of insecticides that leave no lasting footprint aligns perfectly with the contemporary drive towards greener and more responsible practices. The marriage of chemistry and environmental consciousness is not just a scientific endeavor; it's a moral imperative in an era where ecological balance hangs in the balance.

The transformative power of innovative insecticides extends beyond fields and crops to the broader realm of public health. Imagine chemicals that combat disease-carrying insects with precision, minimizing harm to humans and non-target organisms. The world of chemistry is evolving from being a reactive force to a proactive guardian, working hand in hand with ecosystems to ensure the long-term sustainability of our planet.

This vision is not confined to the realm of imagination but is being realized through cutting-edge research and development. The innovative insecticides emerging from these efforts are a testament to the boundless potential of chemistry to address critical challenges that impact us all. As we journey through this chapter, we will delve into the strategies, technologies, and ethical considerations that define the development of these insecticides, showcasing how chemistry evolves into a driving force for positive change and ecological harmony.

15.6. Quantum Chemistry's Dance with Experimentation

The groundbreaking work of Santaloci et al. (2023) beckons us to peer into a world where the dance between quantum chemistry and experimental characterization unfolds in a symphony of precision and creativity. This chapter delves into a narrative where theoretical calculations and laboratory experiments blend seamlessly, giving birth to molecules with extraordinary properties that transcend the boundaries of conventional wisdom.

Picture a choreography where quantum calculations assume the role of lead dancer, guiding experimentalists in crafting molecules with unparalleled precision. This symbiotic relationship between theory and practice reshapes the landscape of molecular design, enabling scientists to explore chemical spaces that were previously out of reach. Santaloci and colleagues' research exemplifies how quantum chemistry's predictive prowess is leveraged to guide experimentalists towards molecules that possess specific properties, from enhanced light absorption for solar cells to tailored reactivity for medical diagnostics.

The implications of this dance between quantum chemistry and experimentation are far-reaching. In the realm of materials science, this partnership has the potential to unlock novel materials with tailored properties for diverse applications. Imagine photovoltaic materials that harness light energy more efficiently or catalytic materials that accelerate chemical reactions with precision. The marriage of theory and experiment ushers in a new era of molecular engineering, where the blueprint of molecules can be designed with atomic precision.

The dance of quantum chemistry and experimental characterization also has profound implications in the realm of drug discovery. By predicting the behavior of molecules at the atomic level, quantum calculations assist researchers in designing compounds with optimal pharmacological properties. This precision-driven approach not only expedites the drug development process but also increases the likelihood of discovering compounds with reduced side effects and enhanced therapeutic efficacy.

As we traverse through this chapter, we will encounter stories of how this dance unfolds in laboratories across the world. We will delve into the technologies, algorithms, and innovative methodologies that facilitate this intricate interplay between theory and practice. This narrative serves as a testament to the power of chemistry to transcend the barriers of traditional experimentation and usher in an era where molecules are crafted with atomic precision, paving the way for transformative innovations that redefine our understanding of what is possible.

15.7. Chemometrics and Business Intelligence

Sabin, Hantao, and colleagues (2021) extend an invitation to explore the transformative intersection of chemometrics and fast analytics, revealing a landscape where chemistry transcends its traditional confines to infiltrate the boardrooms of corporations. This chapter dives into a narrative where chemistry's analytical power becomes a driving force behind data-driven decision-making, fundamentally reshaping the way businesses operate.

Imagine a scenario where chemical data, once the domain of laboratory notebooks, becomes a strategic asset guiding critical business decisions. Sabin et al.'s research paints a picture of a corporate ecosystem where chemometrics transforms raw chemical measurements into actionable insights. These insights empower companies to optimize product development, fine-tune quality control processes, and stay ahead of market trends. It's a narrative that underscores chemistry's role as a foundational pillar in the business intelligence landscape.

The implications of this marriage between chemometrics and business intelligence are profound. Imagine a company that leverages chemical data to predict product performance, ensuring that products meet customer expectations even before they hit the market. Picture manufacturing processes that are fine-tuned in real-time based on chemical measurements, resulting in enhanced efficiency and reduced waste. This synergy between chemistry and analytics lays the groundwork for companies to innovate with precision and agility.

This infiltration of chemistry into boardrooms reflects the broader trend of data-driven decision-making across industries. As companies amass ever-growing volumes of data, the role of chemometrics becomes not just technical but strategic. It transforms chemical measurements into actionable insights that drive revenue growth, reduce costs, and bolster competitive advantage. This shift amplifies chemistry's influence beyond the laboratory bench, making it an indispensable component of the contemporary business landscape.

As we journey through this chapter, we'll encounter stories of how chemometrics has empowered companies to thrive in an era defined by data. We'll explore the technologies and methodologies that underpin this transformation, showcasing how chemistry's analytical power becomes a catalyst for innovation and strategic decision-making. This narrative serves as a compelling reminder that the impact of chemistry extends far beyond laboratory walls, permeating every facet of our modern world and driving tangible business outcomes.

15.8. Green Chemistry: A Sustainable Future

Winterton (2021) brings forth a compelling call for a paradigm shift in chemistry with the advocacy for green solvents. This chapter delves into a narrative where chemistry aligns harmoniously with environmental responsibility, fostering a vision where chemical processes evolve from being agents of waste to champions of sustainability.

Imagine a chemistry landscape where the production of chemicals is marked by efficiency and ecological mindfulness. Winterton's perspective presents a world where chemical processes are meticulously designed to minimize waste generation, reduce energy consumption, and eliminate the release of harmful byproducts. This vision is not a distant utopia but a concrete movement that's gaining momentum across industries.

Green chemistry is not just about reducing the ecological footprint of chemical processes; it's about reshaping the fundamental principles of how we approach chemistry. Picture a chemical reaction where the reactants are carefully selected to minimize toxicity and waste, resulting in cleaner processes and safer products. Consider a scenario where renewable resources are harnessed as raw materials, leading to a reduced dependency on fossil fuels and non-renewable resources.

The implications of this shift towards green chemistry extend far beyond the laboratory. Imagine industries that embrace eco-friendly practices, not as a trend but as an imperative for survival. From pharmaceuticals to materials manufacturing, green chemistry principles challenge conventions, inspiring researchers and engineers to innovate in a manner that's in harmony with the planet.

This advocacy for sustainability is more than a buzzword; it's a commitment to ensuring a world that is habitable for future generations. As we explore this chapter, we'll encounter stories of chemists who are redefining the boundaries of chemistry by embracing green practices. We'll delve into technologies and methodologies that propel the green chemistry movement forward, showcasing how chemistry is not just adapting to environmental concerns but actively leading the charge towards a more sustainable and responsible future.

15.9.   From Waste to Zeolites: Environmental Remediation

Chu, Liang, Yang, and Chen (2022) unveil a captivating narrative of chemistry's role in turning waste into a solution through the elegant dance of green chemical conversion. This chapter delves into a world where chemistry embraces ecological stewardship, transforming waste materials into valuable resources that mitigate pollution and environmental damage.

Imagine a scenario where large-scale aluminosilicates, abundant waste materials, find a second life as zeolites—a class of porous materials with remarkable adsorption capabilities. Chu and colleagues' research presents a vision where waste is not a burden but a canvas for innovative chemistry. These transformed materials possess the ability to capture harmful substances, clean polluted waters, and contribute to environmental remediation.

The implications of this transformation are profound. Picture industrial waste streams that are converted into materials that actively contribute to environmental healing. In a world where waste management is a pressing challenge, green chemical conversion offers a pathway to transform liabilities into assets. This dance of chemistry transcends the laboratory, resonating with global efforts to minimize pollution and restore ecosystems.

This dance is not just about materials; it's a powerful metaphor for the transformation that chemistry can effect on the environment. It's about embracing the principles of circular economy, where materials are repurposed and regenerated rather than discarded. This narrative exemplifies chemistry's capacity to create sustainable solutions that align with the urgent need to address ecological concerns.

As we journey through this chapter, we will encounter the intricate steps of this dance—exploring the chemistry that breathes new life into waste, the engineering behind large-scale aluminosilicate transformation, and the real-world applications of zeolites in environmental remediation. This narrative serves as an inspiring reminder that chemistry is not just a scientific discipline but a force for positive change, actively engaging with the challenges of our time to create a world that is cleaner, healthier, and more sustainable.

15.10. Conclusion: A Call to Action

As we take a moment to reflect on the captivating narratives that have unfolded within these pages, we stand at the precipice of possibility. Each story has showcased the transformative power of chemistry, from the dance of artificial intelligence and organic synthesis to the harmonious fusion of green chemistry and environmental stewardship. But this journey is far from over; it's an invitation for you to step onto the stage and embrace your role as a protagonist in the story of chemistry-driven innovation.

Consider the myriad possibilities that lie within your imagination. The very chemistry concepts that you've encountered in textbooks and laboratories possess the potential to reshape industries, improve lives, and leave an indelible mark on the world. The marriage of chemistry and technology beckons you to explore the uncharted territories where AI-guided discoveries and responsive materials hold the promise of game-changing products.

Imagine your ideas taking flight in the realm of open innovation, where the collaborative efforts of global minds converge to bring your vision to life. Just as chemists from diverse corners of the world have united to redefine drug discovery, you have the power to harness the collective wisdom of the global community to solve pressing challenges and create breakthroughs.

Let the principles of green chemistry guide your journey towards sustainability. Consider the profound impact that your choices can have on the environment, as you navigate the landscape of chemical processes that minimize waste, reduce energy consumption, and promote circular practices. You are poised to play a pivotal role in shaping industries that prioritize both profitability and planetary well-being.

As we conclude this chapter, the spotlight is on you. The stories of entrepreneurs who turned their chemistry-driven dreams into marketable realities are not just tales; they are blueprints for action. The world hungers for novel solutions, and within you lies the key to transforming chemistry concepts into marketable gold. The future is beckoning, and it's time to heed the call, armed with the insights, inspirations, and strategies woven through these pages. Your journey has just begun, and the stage is set for you to make your mark in the captivating world of chemistry-driven innovations.

15.11. References

[1]   Almeida, A. F., Moreira, R., & Rodrigues, T. (2019). Synthetic organic chemistry driven by artificial intelligence. *Nature Reviews Chemistry*, *3*(10), 589-604. https://www.nature.com/articles/s41570-019-0124-0

[2]   Chu, Z., Liang, J., Yang, D., & Chen, H. (2022). Green chemical conversion of large-scale aluminosilicates into zeolites for environmental remediation under

carbon-neutral pressure. *Current Opinion in Green and Sustainable Chemistry*, *36*, 100632. https://doi.org/10.1016/j.cogsc.2022.100632

[3] Sabin, G. P., Hantao, L. W., Finzi, J. K., Merenholz, L. F., de Aquino, N. H., & Soares, C. O. (2021). Chemometrics & Fast Analytics: A New Scenario in Business Intelligence. *Brazilian Journal of Analytical Chemistry*, *8*(32), 198-206. : https://doi.org/10.30744/brjac.2179-3425.feature-chemometrics

[4] Santaloci, T. J., Meador, W. E., Wallace, A. M., Valencia, E. M., Rogers, B. N., Delcamp, J. H., & Fortenberry, R. C. (2023). An automated quantum chemistry-driven, experimental characterization for high PCE donor–π–acceptor NIR molecular dyes. *Digital Discovery*. https://doi.org/10.1039/D3DD00023K

[5] Sparks, T. C., & Bryant, R. J. (2022). Innovation in insecticide discovery: Approaches to the discovery of new classes of insecticides. *Pest Management Science*, *78*(8), 3226-3247. https://doi.org/10.1002/ps.6942

[6] Thompson, D. C., & Bentzien, J. (2020). Crowdsourcing and open innovation in drug discovery: recent contributions and future directions. *Drug Discovery Today*, *25*(12), 2284-2293. https://doi.org/10.1016/j.drudis.2020.09.020

[7] Verma, J., & Khanna, A. S. (2022). Digital advancements in smart materials design and multifunctional coating manufacturing. *Physics Open*, 100133. https://doi.org/10.1016/j.physo.2022.100133

[8] Winterton, N. (2021). The green solvent: A critical perspective. *Clean technologies and environmental policy*, *23*(9), 2499-2522. https://doi.org/10.1007/s10098-021-02188-8

16. The Chemistry of Success: Reflections and Takeaways

16.1. Introduction

As we conclude our journey from beakers to billions, the remarkable transformation of chemistry concepts into marketable gold stands as a testament to the power of innovation and perseverance. The chemistry-driven products we've explored have not only changed industries but have also underscored the profound impact of harnessing chemical knowledge in our modern world. From groundbreaking research on hazardous chemical substitution (Syeda et al., 2022) to the synergistic integration of chemistry with computational thinking (Chongo, Osman, & Nayan, 2021), our expedition through the realms of chemistry has unveiled a plethora of avenues for turning scientific knowledge into tangible success.

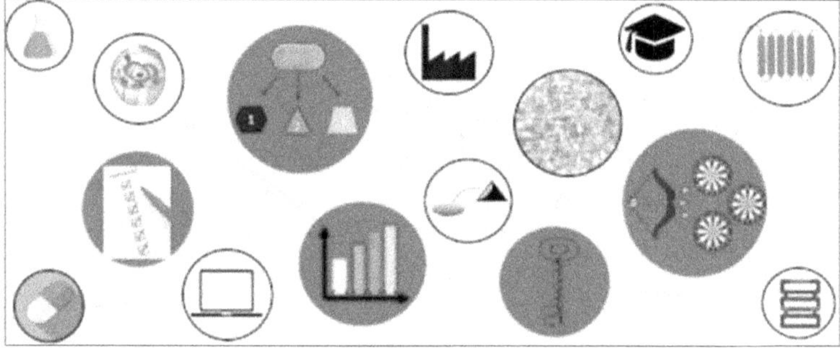

In the pursuit of sustainable and environmentally conscious solutions, the journey has traversed the landscape of green chemistry start-ups (Ocampo-López et al., 2019). This exploration of applied research in biotechnology as a source of opportunities has illuminated the transformative potential that aligning chemistry with ecological values can have on shaping new business paradigms.

Moreover, our odyssey has not been confined to the traditional boundaries of chemistry. The harmonious union of chemistry with artificial intelligence has ushered in a new era of accelerated research and innovation (Gasteiger, 2020). The partnership between chemical expertise and machine learning algorithms exemplifies the dynamic nature of the discipline and its capacity to adapt to ever-evolving technological landscapes.

As we reflect on the profound impact of chemistry on our world, the journey also uncovers the imperative of responsible chemistry. The ecotoxicity of plastic and rubber leachates (Capolupo et al., 2020) reminds us of the critical need to balance technological progress with environmental stewardship. Our expedition delves into the realm of systems thinking and social sustainability (Marcelino, Sjöström, & Marques, 2019), reminding us that chemistry-driven products must be designed with a holistic understanding of their societal and ecological implications.

Intrigued by these remarkable discoveries and insights, I invite you to join me as we delve deeper into the journey of transforming chemistry into marketable gold. From the classroom to the boardroom, from laboratory benches to market shelves, the path is illuminated by the experiences of entrepreneurs, the guidance of experts, and the promise of innovation. With each step, we'll unravel the strategies, decisions, and innovations that have brought chemistry-driven products from concept to success. So, fasten your seatbelt as we embark on a journey that unveils the transformative potential of chemistry in our world.

16.2.   The Power of Substitution: Redefining Consumer Products

Our journey commenced with a thought-provoking discussion on the potential dangers posed by hazardous chemicals lurking within everyday consumer products (Syeda et al., 2022). This revelation acted as a clarion call, igniting a transformative journey towards the exploration of safer alternatives and heralding a renaissance in chemical substitution.

As we delved into the intricacies of hazardous chemical substitution, the magnitude of its implications became evident. The risks to human health and the environment necessitated a paradigm shift in how we conceive, formulate, and manufacture consumer goods. This juncture marked the inception of a wave of innovation that rippled through industries, driving the impetus to rethink and redefine product formulations.

Central to this endeavor was the concept of leveraging chemistry to engineer products that are not only efficacious but also safe and sustainable. The tenets of green chemistry emerged as guiding stars, ushering in a new era of product design where the impact on health and the planet is a paramount consideration. The deep-seated connection between chemistry and public health became glaringly apparent, positioning chemical knowledge as a catalyst for improved well-being.

The redefinition of consumer products through chemical substitution possesses the transformative potential to reverberate across diverse sectors. By prioritizing the creation of products that resonate with consumers' well-being, chemists and entrepreneurs forge a link between scientific expertise and everyday needs. This harmonious fusion of knowledge bridges the gap between the laboratory and the living room, demonstrating that chemistry's value lies not only in its theoretical underpinnings but also in its tangible impact on people's lives.

As we reflect on this journey of reimagining consumer products, we're confronted with the compelling realization that every formulation holds within it the power to shape industries, advance public health, and nurture a symbiotic relationship between science and society. The principle of chemical substitution, ignited by the quest for safety and sustainability, serves as a beacon for aspiring chemists and entrepreneurs alike, guiding them to embark on ventures that enrich lives and redefine the boundaries of innovation.

16.3. Educational Foundations: Fostering Chemistry's Growth

Education has undeniably emerged as an immutable cornerstone of success within the dynamic realm of chemistry, shaping the trajectory of future chemists and trailblazing the path to innovation (Chongo, Osman, & Nayan, 2021). The bedrock of this evolution lies in the convergence of well-structured curricula and pioneering teaching methodologies that collectively breathe life into the classroom experience.

Our journey into the heart of educational innovation unveils the transformative potency of computational thinking and interdisciplinary modules. The infusion of computational thinking within chemistry curricula represents a seismic shift in the way students approach and unravel complex problems. By marrying the analytical rigors of chemistry with the systematic approach of computational thinking, students are primed to decipher intricate chemical phenomena in novel ways. This synthesis not only nurtures critical thinking but also paves the way for innovation that seamlessly straddles the digital and chemical domains.

Moreover, the interplay of chemistry with interdisciplinary modules widens the vista of possibilities, rendering the learning experience immersive and holistic. The integration of real-world contexts and applications from various disciplines fuels a sense of relevance and connectivity, effectively dispelling the notion of chemistry as an isolated pursuit. This experiential pedagogical approach nurtures a profound understanding of how chemistry interlocks with other fields, sparking a symphony of ideas that go beyond the confines of traditional chemical paradigms.

Aspiring chemists embarking on their educational journey, as well as educators who mold the future generations, can glean inspiration from these progressive methodologies. By leveraging modern teaching techniques, educators can kindle an enduring passion for chemistry, steering students toward not just academic success, but a lifelong affinity for the subject. The fusion of computational thinking and interdisciplinary insights cultivates an environment that is conducive to original thinking and innovative problem-solving, vital attributes for the chemists and entrepreneurs of tomorrow.

As we reflect on the transformative power of education within the chemistry landscape, we are beckoned to recognize the role it plays in sculpting not only knowledgeable scientists but also dynamic thinkers and visionaries. The seeds sown in these classrooms bear the promise of ripening into solutions that transcend the boundaries of traditional chemistry and venture into uncharted territories, catalyzing discoveries that shape our world.

16.4. Interdisciplinary Marvels: Chemistry's Diverse Applications

The resonance of our journey reverberates with the harmonious symphony of interdisciplinary teaching, a recurring theme that resonates with the very essence of chemistry's boundless potential (Hardy et al., 2021). With each stride into uncharted territories, we've been witness to the astonishing reach of chemistry, as it seamlessly intertwines with diverse domains, transcending the confines of tradition and unlocking solutions to global challenges.

One remarkable chapter of this narrative unfolds in the realm of biotechnology, where the fusion of chemistry with biology yields a tapestry of possibilities. The synergy between these disciplines is exemplified in the applied research that forms the foundation for green chemistry start-ups (Ocampo-López et al., 2019). The cultivation of sustainable products and processes through biotechnological innovation showcases the profound impact that interdisciplinary collaboration can wield, paving the path for solutions that address both human needs and environmental concerns.

Furthermore, the canvas of green chemistry exemplifies chemistry's prowess as an interdisciplinary nexus. The integration of green chemistry principles with traditional practices showcases how chemistry, when entwined with ecological insights, yields products that not only benefit human well-being but also safeguard our planet's health. The holistic approach of green chemistry embodies the very spirit of interdisciplinary thought, exemplifying how solutions can arise when different disciplines converge, amplify one another, and coalesce into revolutionary breakthroughs.

As we stand at this crossroads of exploration, the cross-pollination of ideas emanates as an inspiring call to action. Chemistry enthusiasts, guided by the examples of these interdisciplinary marvels, are beckoned to peer beyond the boundaries of their discipline and embrace the unfamiliar. The interplay of chemistry with other fields encourages us to explore novel perspectives, foster innovative collaborations, and channel our ingenuity toward solutions that transcend the limits of conventional thinking.

In summation, our journey across these interdisciplinary vistas underscores that chemistry's potential isn't confined to the laboratory; it flourishes at the confluence of various disciplines. With the orchestra of collaboration playing in the background, chemistry enthusiasts are emboldened to stand as pioneers of change, boldly venturing into uncharted territories to cultivate solutions that reshape industries, protect the environment, and enhance human well-being.

16.5. Green Chemistry Entrepreneurship: Navigating Opportunities

Our voyage through the annals of chemistry unveils a profound revelation in the form of green chemistry entrepreneurship—an avenue where profit and environmental sustainability coalesce in a harmonious dance (Ocampo-López et al., 2019). This narrative, woven with threads of applied research in biotechnology, is emblematic of a paradigm shift that transcends conventional business models and engenders a profound commitment to our planet's well-being.

The role of applied research in biotechnology as a catalyst for green chemistry start-ups serves as a beacon of hope, illuminating the way toward a future where business acumen and ecological stewardship are not opposing forces but integral partners. The entrepreneurs of this era are architects of change, redefining business success by placing the health of the environment at the forefront of their endeavors.

At the crux of this transformation lies the significance of alignment—where entrepreneurial vision is harmonized with ecological values. The journey of these visionary entrepreneurs is a testament to the potency of merging chemistry with sustainability. This integration births innovations that resonate with consumer consciousness, offering not just functional solutions but conscientious choices that ripple through supply chains, industries, and the planet itself.

For aspiring entrepreneurs, this narrative serves as an inspiring touchstone. It underscores the fact that the entrepreneurial journey need not be one of ethical compromise, but rather a harmonization of business ambitions with the broader good. Green chemistry entrepreneurship exemplifies how chemistry knowledge can be harnessed not only to drive financial gain but to architect a future where prosperity is intertwined with ecological integrity.

In culmination, the intersection of entrepreneurship, green chemistry, and environmental stewardship sketches a blueprint for aspiring business minds. The realization dawns that chemistry transcends its academic confines; it emerges as a conduit for transformation, a fulcrum that propels us towards a future where the chemistry of commerce nurtures both financial prosperity and the vitality of our planet.

16.6.　AI and Beyond: Chemistry in the Age of Intelligence

Our expedition into the heart of chemistry's evolution unveils a revolutionary intersection—where chemistry converges with artificial intelligence, illuminating pathways toward uncharted horizons (Gasteiger, 2020). This fusion, marked by the harmonious marriage of data-driven insights and chemical acumen, has orchestrated a symphony of innovation that resonates with accelerated research and unprecedented breakthroughs.

The integration of artificial intelligence (AI) with chemistry marks a watershed moment that catapults the field into an era characterized by exponential growth and discovery. This marriage, hinged upon the ability of AI to decipher complex patterns from vast datasets, empowers chemists to transcend traditional barriers, unveil hidden relationships, and uncover novel solutions at an accelerated pace. This potent synergy is reshaping research methodologies, amplifying the precision of predictions, and guiding experimentation towards uncharted territories.

Moreover, this intersection offers young chemists a clarion call—one that beckons them to embrace the vast potential of technological advancements. The marriage of chemistry with AI dismantles the conventional boundaries of the discipline, inviting chemists to shed the shackles of tradition and explore new avenues of inquiry. This audacious approach not only nurtures innovation but also propels chemistry towards a future characterized by transformative discoveries that lie at the crossroads of human intuition and machine intellect.

As we traverse this realm, it becomes evident that chemistry is no longer relegated to the laboratory; it is evolving into a dynamic field that interfaces with the digital realm. The emergence of AI as a partner in the pursuit of chemical knowledge magnifies the impact of chemistry in our world. By embracing this amalgamation, young chemists can harness the power of AI to unravel intricate mysteries, unravel the tapestry of molecules, and unlock the secrets that lie hidden within chemical systems.

In summation, the integration of artificial intelligence with chemistry heralds an epoch of accelerated innovation and transformative discovery. As chemists, seasoned and young, stand on the precipice of this evolution, the call to action echoes clear—venture forth with the knowledge that chemistry's embrace of AI is not just a technological leap, but a symphony of human intellect and machine prowess, destined to shape the future of chemistry-driven solutions.

16.7.   Sustainability at Heart: Chemistry's Responsibility

Our voyage through the landscapes of chemistry has cast a piercing spotlight on the intricate dance between chemical products and environmental impact, unraveling a narrative that implores us to confront the daunting challenges of waste and pollution (Capolupo et al., 2020). This revelation serves as an urgent call to action—one that impels chemists to re-envision their roles not merely as creators of compounds, but as stewards of sustainability.

The stark realization that chemical products bear the capacity to catalyze environmental degradation has thrust sustainability to the heart of chemistry's responsibilities. Chemists today, armed with knowledge and the ability to engineer transformative solutions, shoulder the weighty responsibility of designing products that not only deliver efficacy but also harbor a consciousness for our planet's well-being. This seismic shift towards environmentally conscious formulations aligns chemistry with the ethos of ecological integrity.

In this paradigm, chemistry transcends its utilitarian realm to assume the mantle of a transformative force for positive change. The quest for sustainability becomes a compass that directs the course of research and innovation, ushering chemists to explore pathways that mitigate harm, minimize waste, and foster harmony with the natural world. It compels chemists to scrutinize not just the end product, but the entire lifecycle—from inception to disposal—of the compounds they conceive.

The ramifications of this transformation are profound and extend far beyond the confines of laboratories. Aspiring chemists, the torchbearers of the discipline's future, are beckoned to approach their work with a holistic lens of sustainability. The synthesis of chemistry with ecological consciousness holds the promise of ushering in a new generation of products that serve as exemplars of responsible innovation.

In summation, our exploration into the nexus of chemistry and sustainability beckons chemists to rewrite the narrative of their discipline. As the guardians of our planet's well-being, chemists are tasked with the noble endeavor of crafting solutions that exemplify not only scientific ingenuity but also unwavering commitment to environmental harmony. With sustainability at its core, chemistry evolves from a catalyst of reactions to a catalyst of positive change, reshaping industries and fostering a world that thrives in equilibrium.

16.8. The Heart of Chemistry: Systems Thinking and Social Impact

Our journey through the tapestry of green chemistry has illuminated a profound insight—the importance of systems thinking and social sustainability in shaping the very essence of chemistry-driven products (Marcelino, Sjöström, & Marques, 2019). This revelation transcends the laboratory's confines, beckoning chemists to embrace a holistic perspective that intertwines their creations with the intricate fabric of society and ecology.

In this epoch, chemistry-driven products cease to be isolated entities; they are interconnected nodes within a larger tapestry of societal and environmental systems. The paradigm of systems thinking propels chemists to transcend conventional boundaries and view their creations as threads woven into the intricate weave of human well-being and ecological balance. This lens of interconnectedness urges chemists to assess the implications of their products across a spectrum of dimensions, ranging from human health to resource utilization and beyond.

The canvas of social sustainability emerges as another vital facet within this exploration. It reinforces the understanding that chemistry-driven solutions must not only mollify environmental concerns but also address the very essence of societal needs. A chemistry-driven product's success is no longer solely defined by its functionality; it's also gauged by the positive impact it imparts on the communities it touches. This narrative transforms chemistry from an isolated pursuit into a realm where ethical considerations and social implications intertwine seamlessly.

In essence, the chemist's role evolves into that of a mindful creator—one who is attuned to the intricate ripples their creations send across the larger pond of society and ecology. The integration of systems thinking and social sustainability ignites a moral imperative that beckons chemists to actively engage with ethical dimensions. It prompts introspection, inspiring chemists to ask not just "Can we create it?" but also "Should we create it?"

Aspiring chemists stepping into this era are tasked with a noble endeavor—to be architects of solutions that carry the weight of social consciousness. The principles of systems thinking and social sustainability foster a mindset that thrives on empathy, humility, and responsibility. Through their creations, chemists become catalysts of positive change, shaping products that not only redefine industries but also uphold the tenets of human dignity and environmental harmony.

16.9. Embarking on Your Journey: Transforming Chemistry into Gold

As we stand at the crossroads of knowledge and innovation, our minds teem with the lessons gleaned from this transformative journey—lessons that beckon us toward a resounding call to action. This call resonates with the very essence of chemistry's transformative potential, urging us to synthesize knowledge, inspiration, and innovation as we embark on our own quests (Syeda et al., 2022).

The journey we've traversed, guided by the footsteps of chemists who have cast their visions onto the canvas of reality, stands as a testament to the boundless horizons that await us. Armed with the profound insights from the worlds of hazardous chemical substitution (Syeda et al., 2022), computational thinking (Chongo, Osman, & Nayan, 2021), green chemistry entrepreneurship (Ocampo-López et al., 2019), the fusion of AI and chemistry (Gasteiger, 2020), and the heart of sustainability (Capolupo et al., 2020; Marcelino, Sjöström, & Marques, 2019), we are poised to script our narratives of innovation and impact.

With each step, we can weave our own stories of triumph. Every idea we nurture, every experiment we conduct, and every formulation we craft has the potential to spark revolutions. The transformation we seek isn't just of products, but of industries, societies, and the very landscape of possibilities. Armed with the knowledge that chemistry is a canvas of boundless innovation, we can reimagine business models, shatter conventions, and elevate our creations to the realm of gold.

The journey, though rife with challenges, is one of promise. It's a voyage where passion converges with curiosity, innovation dances with determination, and chemistry fuses with creativity. Each chapter you pen, each experiment you undertake, and each collaboration you forge becomes a brushstroke that adds depth to the masterpiece you're crafting. As you embark on your journey, remember the chemists who have walked this path before you, and let their stories kindle your own fire of innovation.

So, dear reader, take this torch of knowledge and stride into the realm of possibilities. With every calculated risk, every groundbreaking innovation, and every unyielding pursuit of excellence, you inch closer to transforming chemistry into marketable gold. Your venture is a clarion call to shape a more sustainable and impactful future, to forge connections between disciplines, to harmonize with society, and to pioneer solutions that resonate with human needs and ecological balance.

Your journey awaits, and as you step onto this path, may your passion illuminate the way, your curiosity fuel discovery, and your determination carve a legacy that reverberates through the annals of chemistry's evolution.

16.10. References

[1] Capolupo, M., Sørensen, L., Jayasena, K. D. R., Booth, A. M., & Fabbri, E. (2020). Chemical composition and ecotoxicity of plastic and car tire rubber leachates to aquatic organisms. *Water research*, *169*, 115270. https://doi.org/10.1016/j.watres.2019.115270

[2] Chongo, S., Osman, K., & Nayan, N. A. (2021). Impact of the Plugged-In and Unplugged Chemistry Computational Thinking Modules on Achievement in Chemistry. EURASIA Journal of Mathematics, Science and Technology Education, 17(4). https://eric.ed.gov/?id=EJ1293180

[3] Gasteiger, J. (2020). Chemistry in times of artificial intelligence. *ChemPhysChem*, *21*(20), 2233-2242. https://doi.org/10.1002/cphc.202000518

[4] Hardy, J. G., Sdepanian, S., Stowell, A. F., Aljohani, A. D., Allen, M. J., Anwar, A., ... & Wright, K. L. (2021). Potential for chemistry in multidisciplinary, interdisciplinary, and transdisciplinary teaching activities in higher education. *Journal of Chemical Education*, *98*(4), 1124-1145. https://doi.org/10.1021/acs.jchemed.0c01363

[5] Marcelino, L., Sjöström, J., & Marques, C. A. (2019). Socio-problematization of green chemistry: Enriching systems thinking and social sustainability by education. *Sustainability*, *11*(24), 7123. https://doi.org/10.3390/su11247123

[6] Ocampo-López, C., Ramírez-Carmona, M., Rendón-Castrillón, L., & Vélez-Salazar, Y. (2019). Applied research in biotechnology as a source of opportunities for green chemistry start-ups. *Sustainable Chemistry and Pharmacy*, *11*, 41-45. https://doi.org/10.1016/j.scp.2018.12.005

[7] Syeda, S. R., Khan, E. A., Padungwatanaroj, O., Kuprasertwong, N., & Tula, A. K. (2022). A perspective on hazardous chemical substitution in consumer products. *Current Opinion in Chemical Engineering*, *36*, 100748. https://doi.org/10.1016/j.coche.2021.100748

17. Epilogue: From Inspiration to Implementation

Turning Chemistry into Marketable Gold

17.1. Introduction

In this culminating chapter, "*Epilogue: From Inspiration to Implementation,*" we embark on a transformative journey that truly encapsulates the essence of turning chemistry concepts into marketable products. Drawing on a mosaic of real-world success stories, expert insights, and pragmatic advice, we venture into the realm where inspiration converges with practicality. As we navigate this enriching path, we are poised to uncover the profound and multifaceted influence of chemistry in shaping groundbreaking products, surmounting formidable challenges, and embracing the dynamic landscape of emerging trends.

Throughout this voyage, the chapter embraces a dual purpose—not only to inform but also to ignite motivation. By weaving the threads of knowledge garnered from diverse sources, the chapter takes on the role of a catalyst, propelling readers to apply their newfound understanding with audacity. The chapter urges aspiring chempreneurs to embark on their own quests, where the very essence of chemistry is transmuted into resplendent marketable gold.

This transformative endeavor rests upon the foundation of real-world exemplars. As we delve into narratives of chemists-turned-entrepreneurs like Melvin, the intricacies of their journeys (Fracaro et al., 2021) unravel. Melvin, a visionary chemist, metamorphosed his concept of sustainable packaging into a globally embraced solution. His evolution from a mere idea, nurtured by simple chemical reactions, into a tangible and sustainable product stands as a testament to the fusion of science, innovation, and a deep understanding of societal needs.

Guided by expert insights, we illuminate the path forward. Dr. Richard and his accomplished team (Richard et al., 2023) illuminate the potential of a smart manufacturing paradigm in reshaping chemical production landscapes. Their pioneering work demonstrates the significance of scalability, cross-disciplinary collaboration, and electrified systems in redefining the realm of chemical manufacturing. This not only underscores the importance of embracing novel technologies but also emphasizes the enduring relevance of collaborative synergy.

The chapter also delves into pragmatic strategies, channeling the essence of lean manufacturing principles (Prasad et al., 2020). Through a lens of efficiency, the principles of waste reduction and resource optimization are translated into the realm of chemistry-driven ventures. The result is a blueprint that not only propels innovative concepts toward fruition but also equips chempreneurs with the tools to navigate the intricacies of a competitive landscape.

In harkening back to the laboratory, the chapter underscores the transcendent importance of character development and project-based learning (Nainggolan et al., 2020). Lessons drawn from innovative chemistry laboratory workbooks provide parallels between the laboratory setting and the entrepreneurial world. Through anecdotes and insights, you are reminded that the core tenets of teamwork, creative problem-solving, and ethical decision-making—essential in the laboratory—are equally indispensable in the business arena.

As we peer toward the horizon of possibilities, the chapter casts a spotlight on emerging trends (Katiyar et al., 2021). The dawn of nature-inspired materials marks an era where scientific ingenuity converges with ecological consciousness. The marriage of scientific principles with sustainable practices resonates with a conscientious audience, painting a vivid tapestry of innovation and responsible progress.

In an age where data reigns supreme, technology takes center stage in the chemistry of success. Big data's pivotal role in industrial chemical processes (Udugama et al., 2020) is a testament to the symbiosis between information and chemistry. This integration, catalyzed by technological prowess, not only expedites decision-making and process optimization but also heralds a new epoch in the realm of chemistry-driven ventures.

Guided by these insights, the chapter extends its arms as you take your final steps within its pages. The journey from inspiration to implementation, akin to the acceleration brought about by biocatalysis (Woodley, 2019), becomes an inexorable force that shapes aspirations. You are entreated to embrace challenges, blaze trails of innovation, and collaborate ardently. Armed with narratives of triumph, the wisdom of experts, and a treasure trove of tools, you are poised to embark on your very own odysseys—transforming the alchemy of chemistry into tangible, marketable gold.

As the chapter concludes, the roadmap unfurls. It is an invitation, a challenge, and a clarion call. The journey is just beginning, and as the final pages beckon, the call to action resounds—a clarion call for you to seize the torch, embrace your alchemical prowess, and create legacies that resonate through the annals of both chemistry and entrepreneurship.

17.2.   The Chemistry of Entrepreneurial Alchemy

Intriguingly, the historical allure of alchemy—once shrouded in mystique—finds a poignant resurgence in the modern theater of entrepreneurship. Much like the ancient alchemists who sought to transmute base metals into precious gold, today's chempreneurs embark on a parallel quest—to transmute chemistry concepts into marketable treasures that resonate in the realms of both commerce and innovation.

For centuries, chemists have wielded their expertise as modern-day alchemists, wielding the transformative power to convert humble raw materials into compounds of immense value. This narrative echoes in the chronicles of Sarah and her sustainable packaging innovation (Fracaro et al., 2021). Starting with elementary chemical reactions, Sarah harnessed her scientific prowess to orchestrate the metamorphosis of an idea into a tangible product—one that embodies the intricate artistry of chemistry interwoven with the tenets of entrepreneurial acumen.

Yet, the modern alchemy of the marketplace transcends the confines of the laboratory. It mandates a fusion of scientific insight, foresight, and relentless determination. As chemists, we are equipped with the technical lexicon to decode the language of atoms, but the marketplace demands an additional dialect—one that converses in the currency of vision and innovation. Like alchemists of old, chempreneurs are not bound by the constraints of existing paradigms; instead, they forge ahead, carving new paths in the sands of opportunity.

This alchemical evolution is not a solo endeavor; it's a harmonious symphony that resonates with the principles of perseverance and business acumen. Drawing parallels from the alchemical transformation of metals, where every ingredient played a vital role, chemistry-driven products emerge as amalgamations of scientific insight, consumer needs, and economic viability. The narrative of chemistry transforming into marketable gold extends beyond the laboratory and merges with the tapestry of human lives and flourishing economies.

In a world where the promise of chemistry converges with entrepreneurial spirit, the stage is set for a new kind of alchemy—one that resonates with the potential to catalyze not just reactions, but entire industries. The transmutation from raw concepts to marketable products mirrors the profound metamorphosis of base materials into precious substances—a testament to the enduring magic of chemistry in the theater of entrepreneurship.

17.3. From Classroom to Marketplace: Stories of Transformation

Allow me to introduce you to Melvin—a visionary chemist whose journey from the classroom to the marketplace stands as a testament to the transformative power of turning chemistry concepts into marketable realities (Fracaro et al., 2021). Inspired by the pressing need for sustainable packaging solutions, Melvin embarked on a mission that would alter the course of his career.

Melvin's story took root in the heart of a laboratory, with a seemingly simple reaction that held the seeds of innovation. Recognizing the potential of his discovery, he ventured beyond the confines of the lab bench, stepping into the domain of material science. Here, he encountered a nexus of possibilities, where chemistry converged with the intricacies of material properties and applications.

However, Melvin's journey did not remain insular; it thrived in collaboration and synergy. Drawing inspiration from the principles of circular business ecosystems (Kanda et al., 2021), Melvin recognized the imperative of integrating sustainability into his entrepreneurial equation. In the crucible of circularity, he discovered the alchemy of aligning economic viability with environmental consciousness.

As Melvin's journey progressed, it wasn't just chemistry at play; it was the harmonious interplay of innovation and sustainable practices. His partnership with experts in circular business ecosystems wasn't just about business—it was about creating a product that resonated with societal values, spoke to environmental responsibility, and catalyzed change on a global scale.

Melvin's trajectory—starting with a simple reaction and culminating in a globally embraced solution—serves as a beacon for aspiring chempreneurs. It showcases how chemistry, when combined with innovative thinking and a commitment to sustainability, can give rise to marketable products that transcend borders and redefine industries. Melvin's journey is a testament to the fact that the alchemy of transforming chemistry into marketable gold is not only achievable but also holds the potential to leave an indelible mark on the world.

17.4. Navigating the Maze: Expert Insights

Amidst the labyrinthine challenges of entrepreneurship, expert insights offer guiding lights that illuminate the path forward. Dr. Richard and his accomplished team stand as beacons in this regard, unveiling the profound impact of smart manufacturing principles in redefining the landscape of chemical production (Richard et al., 2023).

At the core of their revelation lies the essence of scalability—a tenet that reverberates through the annals of successful chemistry-driven ventures. Dr. Richard's team underscores the transformative potential of scaling up electrified chemical manufacturing systems. This pivotal approach isn't merely a technological evolution; it's a strategic metamorphosis that converges the power of innovation with the art of efficiency.

As we glean insights from these experts, the significance of collaboration emerges as a central theme. The pages of their research narrative unfurl a tapestry where boundaries between disciplines blur, giving rise to interdisciplinary collaborations that drive progress. In the domain of electrified chemical manufacturing, the synergy between chemistry and electrical engineering isn't just complementary—it's revolutionary.

Dr. Richard and his team's emphasis on energy savings unveils a poignant reality—innovation isn't merely about economic prosperity; it's about responsible progress. Their elucidation of how an electrified approach can infuse not only efficiency but also environmental stewardship underscores the critical role that chemistry-driven ventures can play in shaping sustainable industries.

Yet, the narrative doesn't culminate with the embrace of novel technologies; it bridges the chasm between innovation and tradition. Just as metals once underwent transformation into gold through time-tested alchemical principles, Dr. Richard's team exemplifies how the pursuit of innovation harmoniously coexists with enduring, proven principles.

In a world where change is constant and innovation is a necessity, these expert insights offer readers a compass to navigate the complexities of entrepreneurship. It's a testament to the potential of chemistry in harmonizing with the currents of industry evolution. This synthesis—where chemistry converges with innovation, sustainability, and time-tested wisdom—sets the stage for chemistry-driven ventures that not only thrive but also redefine the landscape they inhabit.

17.5. Guiding Lights: Strategies for Success

The journey of turning chemistry-inspired ideas into tangible marketable products isn't solely navigated by scientific acumen—it requires a strategic roadmap that transcends the confines of the laboratory. In this pursuit, the doctrine of lean manufacturing emerges as a guiding light, illuminating the path from concept to reality (Prasad et al., 2020).

At the core of this doctrine lies a fundamental philosophy: the pursuit of value and the elimination of waste. In a world where efficiency is paramount, lean manufacturing principles orchestrate a symphony of optimization. With roots in industries far beyond the realm of chemistry, lean principles ingeniously distill waste reduction, resource optimization, and efficiency enhancement into a cohesive framework.

The relevance of lean manufacturing in the chemistry-driven venture sphere is incontrovertible. As chempreneurs traverse the delicate terrain of product development, lean principles serve as sentinels—identifying redundancies, streamlining processes, and cultivating a culture of efficiency. By trimming the superfluous, these principles lay the foundation for products that epitomize precision and utility.

Lean manufacturing's emphasis on maximizing value isn't merely confined to the realm of production—it extends to the very essence of innovation. As chemistry-inspired ideas take shape, lean principles guide their transformation, ensuring that each facet contributes optimally to the final product. This isn't just about manufacturing efficiency; it's about crafting products that resonate with consumers and outshine competitors.

Embracing lean manufacturing isn't a mere strategy; it's a philosophy that fuels innovation and resilience in the face of competition. In a landscape defined by rapid changes, lean principles serve as a compass, perpetually recalibrating chempreneurs' trajectories. By weaving these principles into the fabric of chemistry-driven ventures, we forge products that stand as testaments to both the beauty of chemistry and the art of strategic prowess.

In the crucible of competition, where chemistry-driven ventures navigate uncharted waters, the incorporation of lean manufacturing principles stands as a beacon. This strategic approach doesn't just result in efficient products—it births products that radiate with the essence of chemistry, creativity, and a meticulously crafted journey from concept to fruition.

17.6.   The Personal Touch: Lessons from the Laboratory

Amidst the corridors of academia, where chemistry enthusiasts first tread upon the path of scientific exploration, lie lessons that transcend the confines of the laboratory. As we reminisce about those early days, we recognize that the experiential tapestry of chemistry education offers profound insights that resonate in the realm of entrepreneurship (Nainggolan et al., 2020).

Enter the innovative domain of chemistry laboratory workbooks—a canvas that seamlessly interweaves project-based learning with the nurturing of character and ethics. The principles that govern these workbooks transcend chemical equations; they extend to the very heart of entrepreneurship, where the crucible of innovation intersects with the dynamics of teamwork, creative problem-solving, and ethical decision-making.

Just as chemistry laboratory experiments necessitate collaboration and the sharing of ideas, the realm of entrepreneurship thrives on the synergy between diverse minds. This confluence of talents, akin to the orchestration of a chemical reaction, generates results that transcend individual efforts. It's a stark reminder that while chemistry might have individual atoms as its building blocks, the path to success is paved with the collective brilliance of diverse minds.

Creative problem-solving—the backbone of every chemistry experiment—finds an echoing resonance in entrepreneurship. The methodologies honed in the laboratory traverse the continuum to the boardroom. In both arenas, the crux lies in dissecting complexities, piecing together fragments of information, and engineering innovative solutions. This convergence signifies that the principles that ignite breakthroughs in the laboratory are no less potent in sculpting entrepreneurial victories.

But the laboratory's tutelage extends beyond the realm of science and innovation. Ethics—the invisible compass that guides the moral dimensions of science—is equally indispensable in the world of entrepreneurship. Just as laboratory conduct hinges on ethical considerations, the realm of business is underpinned by decisions that resonate with principles of integrity and social responsibility. The translation of these ethics from laboratory to boardroom is not just a formality—it's a testament to the unassailable interplay between scientific and moral compasses.

In the chapters of chemistry laboratory workbooks, we find an eloquent narrative that transcends chemicals and equations. It's a narrative that speaks to the transformative essence of character development, collaborative endeavors, and ethical frameworks—pillars that forge the bedrock of both scientific and entrepreneurial pursuits. As chempreneurs navigate the labyrinth of entrepreneurship, the echoes of their formative laboratory experiences serve as constant companions, propelling them toward success defined not just by marketability but also by integrity.

17.7. Innovating Forward: Emerging Trends

As we cast our gaze toward the horizon of possibilities, the future of chemistry-driven products unfolds with a gleam of unprecedented promise. The cradle of innovation reveals a resplendent gem—the emergence of nature-inspired materials (Katiyar et al., 2021). This avant-garde trend not only underscores the unbounded potential of chemistry but also lays the foundation for a harmonious symphony between scientific principles and sustainable practices.

Nature, the ultimate repository of ingenious design, serves as a muse for chempreneurs seeking inspiration. Just as the intricate beauty of leaves and shells reflects nature's masterful craftsmanship, chemistry-derived materials are imbued with the potential to emulate these intricate structures. The fusion of scientific understanding and nature's aesthetics births materials that are not just functional but evoke a sense of wonder—an innovation that not only caters to market demand but also celebrates nature's elegance.

In the ever-evolving landscape of consumer preferences, chempreneurs stand at the crossroads of adaptation and innovation. Nature-inspired materials, with their inherent sustainability and aesthetic appeal, form a bridge between these two realms. The metamorphosis from conventional materials to their nature-inspired counterparts is not just a strategic choice; it's an acknowledgement of the evolving consciousness of consumers who seek products aligned with their ethical and ecological values.

The allure of nature-inspired materials extends beyond the realm of aesthetics—it's a reflection of a conscious effort to blend scientific advancement with ecological harmony. It's a realization that the treasures of chemistry can be harnessed to create products that resonate with not just consumer preferences but also a global imperative for sustainability. In the symphony of chemistry and sustainability, nature-inspired materials stand as a crescendo—a testament to the chemistry of innovation that resonates with both hearts and minds.

As chempreneurs navigate the intricate terrain of market trends, the trajectory guided by nature-inspired materials unfolds as a blueprint for the future. The journey is not merely about innovation; it's about the harmonious synthesis of scientific ingenuity and environmental stewardship. It's a future where chemistry-driven products not only shine with marketability but also evoke a reverence for the brilliance of nature's design.

17.8. Lab to Data: Technology's Role

In the epoch defined by data, the tapestry of success woven by chemistry is seamlessly interwoven with the intricate threads of technology. The symphony of chemistry's triumphs is harmonized with the symphony of data, and nowhere is this fusion more pronounced than in the role of big data within industrial chemical processes (Udugama et al., 2020).

In the heart of sprawling chemical operations, data isn't just a passive entity—it's a dynamic force that catalyzes progress. The orchestra of industrial chemical processes, once defined by manual intervention, now resonates with the cadence of big data's insights. This fusion marks a pivotal transition—a metamorphosis where decisions are propelled by real-time data streams, and processes are calibrated with precision unimaginable in yesteryears.

The implications of big data in industrial chemical processes are profound. The avalanche of data doesn't merely accumulate; it becomes the foundation for transformative insights. Through complex algorithms and pattern recognition, big data distills information from the noise, revealing patterns that illuminate new dimensions of operational efficiency. This illumination, akin to a chemical reaction's elucidation, transcends data points and ushers forth actionable intelligence.

Decisions, once driven by intuition and experience, are now fortified by the empirical might of data. Timely access to insights accelerates decision-making, facilitating the seamless adaptation of strategies in response to dynamic operational exigencies. The result is an ecosystem that pivots from reactive to proactive, and from the conventional to the innovative—a transformation that redefines chemistry's role in the industrial landscape.

Moreover, big data's infusion in industrial chemical processes orchestrates a symphony of optimization. Like a conductor leading an ensemble, data guides each facet of chemical operations—right from raw material procurement to quality assurance. This orchestration begets efficiency, enhancing not only productivity but also resource utilization—a testament to the unassailable union of data and chemistry's transformative prowess.

As ideas germinate in the crucible of innovation, they are transmuted into reality through technology's catalytic touch. Big data bridges the chasm between imagination and realization, accelerating chemistry-inspired concepts from the realms of possibility to tangibility. It's a transformation that is emblematic of alchemy—the turning of ideas into tangible gold, where data's alchemical role is the fulcrum on which the balance of success pivots.

In the alchemy of modern times, technology doesn't just amplify chemistry's potential; it transmutes it into a dynamic force of innovation. The chemistry of success isn't just intertwined with data—it's elevated, enhanced, and enriched by it. Just as chemical reactions transmute compounds, data-driven insights transmute concepts into reality—a testament to the enduring alliance between science and technology.

17.9. From Beakers to Billions: A Call to Action

As the curtain descends on these pages, a resounding call to action resounds—an invitation to embark on a transformative journey, one that has been meticulously guided by stories of triumph, expert insights, and an arsenal of tools that illuminate the path from inspiration to implementation. Much like biocatalysis hastens chemical reactions (Woodley, 2019), you possess the power to hasten the realization of your entrepreneurial aspirations. This call is not a mere summons; it's a clarion call—a summons to wield the transformative magic of chemistry and innovation to its fullest extent.

The narratives of pioneers like Sarah and Melvin, whose chemistry-driven concepts blossomed into tangible solutions, stand as testaments to the power of action. These stories are not just chronicles of success; they are testimonials to the potential that simmers within you—an alchemical potential that is waiting to be ignited. It's a potential that, when combined with the wisdom distilled from experts in various fields, becomes an unstoppable force for change.

Innovation is the bedrock of progress. As you step into the arena of entrepreneurship, embrace innovation with a fearless heart. Let the insights of Dr. Richard's team illuminate your path, reminding you of the significance of scalability, collaboration, and embracing the frontiers of technology. As you navigate the labyrinth of business, remember the principles of lean manufacturing, the lessons from laboratory character development, and the resonance of nature-inspired materials.

But above all, let collaboration be your beacon. Assembling a team that complements your strengths and challenges your assumptions is akin to creating a catalytic mixture where each element enhances the other's potential. Just as chemical reactions yield optimal results when ingredients interact synergistically, your venture thrives when collaboration fuels innovation.

In this call to action, we beckon you to stride forth with audacity. It's not just about marketability; it's about the enduring legacy you leave. By transforming chemistry-inspired concepts into marketable gold, you sculpt the landscapes of industries, economies, and societies. Your journey isn't just personal; it's a contribution to the tapestry of human progress.

So, as you stand at the crossroads, envision the possibilities that stretch before you. The chemistry of innovation courses through your veins, and the call to action reverberates—a clarion call that urges you to embrace challenges, innovate fearlessly, and collaborate relentlessly. Let your journey from inspiration to implementation be more than a footnote—it's a narrative of empowerment, transformation, and the audacious alchemy of turning ideas into reality.

17.10. Final Thought

As you reluctantly turn the final page of this chapter, let it be a reminder that the journey of transforming chemistry into marketable gold has merely unfurled its opening chapters. In the stories of innovators and entrepreneurs, the wisdom of experts, and the confluence of insights, you have glimpsed the alchemical essence that can turn concepts into reality. This is not an endpoint but a gateway—a gateway to a realm where your vision, your passion, and your determination shape a trajectory of unbounded potential.

In the crucible of entrepreneurship, challenges and opportunities stand as twin companions, intertwined in a dance that defines progress. Every challenge is an invitation to innovate, to adapt, and to discover the strength that resides within you. Every opportunity is a canvas where your chemistry-inspired ideas meld with innovation, producing strokes that resonate beyond the confines of commerce.

This journey isn't solitary; it's a legacy you craft—one that reverberates through the industries you touch, the lives you impact, and the innovations you birth. Just as chempreneurs before you have left their marks, your endeavors hold the potential to leave footprints that echo through time.

As you step into this dynamic landscape, remember that you are not alone. The wisdom of the past, the expertise of the present, and the vision of the future are your companions. Armed with stories of transformation, strategies for success, and the insights of experts, you are equipped to navigate the twists and turns that lie ahead.

In the grand tapestry of human progress, your journey from inspiration to implementation is an integral thread—one that weaves the brilliance of chemistry with the audacity of entrepreneurship. The world stands at the cusp of your alchemical touch, eagerly awaiting the innovations that will emerge from your ingenuity. With every challenge you surmount, every idea you manifest, and every product you create, you take a step closer to turning the promise of chemistry into tangible, marketable gold.

So, as you close this chapter and step into the next phase, do so with a heart full of audacity and a mind brimming with possibilities. Embrace the challenges, seize the opportunities, and embark on a journey that has the potential to redefine industries, invigorate economies, and inspire generations. Your alchemical touch is the catalyst that transforms ideas into reality, and the world is poised to witness the magic you bring to life.

Embark on your journey, and may your chemistry create a future that gleams brighter than gold.

17.11. References

[1]   Fracaro, S. G., Chan, P., Gallagher, T., Tehreem, Y., Toyoda, R., Bernaerts, K., ... & Wilk, M. (2021). Towards design guidelines for virtual reality training for the chemical industry. *Education for Chemical Engineers*, *36*, 12-23. https://doi.org/10.1016/j.ece.2021.01.014

[2]   Kanda, W., Geissdoerfer, M., & Hjelm, O. (2021). From circular business models to circular business ecosystems. *Business Strategy and the Environment*, *30*(6), 2814-2829. https://doi.org/10.1002/bse.2895

[3]   Katiyar, N. K., Goel, G., Hawi, S., & Goel, S. (2021). Nature-inspired materials: Emerging trends and prospects. *NPG Asia Materials*, *13*(1), 56. https://www.nature.com/articles/s41427-021-00322-y

[4]   Nainggolan, B., Hutabarat, W., Situmorang, M., & Sitorus, M. (2020). Developing Innovative Chemistry Laboratory Workbook Integrated with Project-Based Learning and Character-Based Chemistry. *International Journal of Instruction*, *13*(3), 895-908. https://eric.ed.gov/?id=EJ1259673

[5]   Prasad, M. M., Dhiyaneswari, J. M., Jamaan, J. R., Mythreyan, S., & Sutharsan, S. M. (2020). A framework for lean manufacturing implementation in Indian textile industry. *Materials today: proceedings*, *33*, 2986-2995. https://doi.org/10.1016/j.matpr.2020.02.979

[6]   Richard, D., Jang, J., Çıtmacı, B., Luo, J., Canuso, V., Korambath, P., ... & Morales-Guio, C. G. (2023). Smart manufacturing inspired approach to research, development, and scale-up of electrified chemical manufacturing systems. *Iscience*, *26*(6). https://www.cell.com/iscience/pdf/S2589-0042(23)01043-X.pdf

[7]   Udugama, I. A., Gargalo, C. L., Yamashita, Y., Taube, M. A., Palazoglu, A., Young, B. R., ... & Bayer, C. (2020). The role of big data in industrial (bio) chemical process operations. *Industrial & Engineering Chemistry Research*, *59*(34), 15283-15297. https://doi.org/10.1021/acs.iecr.0c01872

[8]   Woodley, J. M. (2019). Accelerating the implementation of biocatalysis in industry. *Applied Microbiology and Biotechnology*, *103*(12), 4733-4739. https://doi.org/10.1007/s00253-019-09796-x